D1252488

British Immigrants in Industrial America

1790–1950

British Immigrants in Industrial America

1790–1950

by Rowland Tappan Berthoff

HARVARD UNIVERSITY PRESS · CAMBRIDGE · 1953

Distributed in Great Britain by
Geoffrey Cumberlege, Oxford University Press, London

Library of Congress Catalog Card Number 53–6028
Printed in the United States of America

To Robert Samuel Fletcher

Preface

In embarking on a history of immigrants of a particular nationality, author and reader may well keep a weather eye out for the shoals on which many such books have foundered. All too often their writers, ardent partisans seeking to redress some rankling grievance of their chosen people — native Americans' intolerance or simply historians' neglect — have grossly overstated their cases. Impressed by schoolbook emphasis on discoverers, Constitution signers, and military heroes, they have frequently filled their books with names of such persons who happen to be identifiable with their immigrant group. The "contributions" of the foreigners in question are made to seem the keystone of the country's history.

Even the more discerning accounts of particular foreign nationalities have often inadvertently demonstrated not the unique but the similar experiences which all groups have undergone in the new environment. In fact, the best histories of immigration stress these broader likenesses rather than national peculiarities. Why then single out the British?

First, few historians have noticed the nineteenth-century English, Scottish, and Welsh newcomers to America. The few who have, have been concerned more with Canada than with the United States and with the process of movement than with the adjustment to the new home. But historians have had an excuse for taking the British immigrants for granted; so did the latter's American contemporaries. Apart from bare immigration and census statistics, neither newspaper editors, official commissions, nor other writers of the time mentioned their British neighbors.

Such unconcern, so unlike the recurrent uproar over Irish, Italian, or Slavic newcomers, suggests the most significant reason for investigating the British separately. In some essentials they must have fitted into American life differently than the broad run of immigrants. Generalizations about the latter may not always apply to the British. Indeed, the inference is easy that they merged imperceptibly with the native population.

This book tests this prevailing assumption. Did British immigrants in fact enjoy a place in nineteenth-century America unlike that of other foreigners? The latter, in general, were those peasants from European villages into whose lives, minds, and hearts Oscar Handlin has penetrated in *The Uprooted*. Whether the British were different or much the same, their history is most meaningful when played as counterpoint to the experiences of the great mass of immigrants of the time.

The use of certain terms in this work should be explained. "British-American" here will indicate an immigrant born in Great Britain, that is, in England, Scotland, or Wales. "English-Americans," "Scottish-Americans," and "Welsh-Americans" thus are all British-Americans. Although Ireland was part of the United Kingdom during the nineteenth century, "Irish-Americans" were distinct, as will appear. Though awkward, "Canadian-American" here will be useful to indicate Canadian-born migrants to the United States. Among them, "British Canadian" will distinguish English-speaking persons, generally of English and Scottish descent, from the French Canadians.

In several years' research, ten thousand miles of travel, and scores of interviews and letters I have profited from the willing help of far more people than a preface can mention. To the officers of dozens of British-American societies, many clergymen and trade-union officials, and the staff of the British Information Services I wish to express my warm thanks. I should like to single out at least a few who, being able to supply information from their unique files, have been particularly helpful: Professor Robert Bruce, Mr. George Bundy, Mrs. Willie Culpan, Mr. David Dawson, Mr. Thomas R. P. Gibb, Mr. Andrew J. Keith, Mr. Emrys Lewis, the late Norman D. MacKay, Mr. Bob Owen, Mr. Gordon Peacock, Mr. Owen W. Roberts, and Mr. Edgar L. Ryerson. Miss Charlotte Erickson, Mr.

Edwin Fenton, Professor Elting Morison, and Professor David Williams have generously shared their own discoveries.

Many librarians have assisted me through their relevant holdings, especially at Harvard University, the Boston Public Library, the Massachusetts Historical Society, the Boston Athenaeum, the Massachusetts State Library, the Essex Institute, the American Antiquarian Society, the Fall River Public Library, the New York Historical Society, the New York Public Library, the Historical Society of Pennsylvania, the Presbyterian Historical Society, the University of Pennsylvania, the Johns Hopkins University, the Chicago Historical Society, the Newberry Library, the University of Illinois, the University of Minnesota, the Huntington Library, the Library of Congress, the Manitoba Provincial Library, the British Museum, the Public Record Office, the Bodleian, the London School of Economics, the University of London, the University of Manchester, the University College of North Wales, and the National Library of Wales.

I have deeply appreciated, furthermore, grants from Harvard University and the administrators of the Fulbright Act, for research in the United Kingdom, and assistance from the English-Speaking Union of the United States toward the cost of publication. At different stages the manuscript has profited from the critical suggestions of Mr. Warner B. Berthoff and Mr. Alan A. Conway. My chief debt obviously is to Professor Oscar Handlin, who has been as cheerfully unsparing of his time as he has been inspiring in his whole approach to the subject of immigration. The shortcomings of the book are my own; any merits owe most to him — and to the people whose story it is.

R. T. B.

Aberystwyth
December 1952

Contents

MAPS

CHARTS

TABLES

British Immigrants in Industrial America
1790–1950

1

Great Britain: Immigrants and Emigrants

"This mighty Anglo-Saxon race" — in the common phrase of the nineteenth century — "the English, the British colonists, and the people of the United States" were all one.[1] It was a queer description to apply to Americans, newly drawn from the four corners of the earth. And even at the fountainhead of Anglo-Saxondom, the British likewise were no single, undifferentiated "race."

Though Germanic tribes called Angles and Saxons had indeed spread through most of Britain during the fifth and sixth centuries, the ancestry of nineteenth-century Englishmen was more complex. In the eastern parts of the island, where the Saxon conquerors had absorbed such of the previous Celtic inhabitants as they had not slaughtered or driven west, English culture swallowed up the Celtic strain. New invaders — Danes, Norsemen, and finally Normans — settled in their turn. During the later Middle Ages, Flemings, Walloons, and Germans arrived to carry on the special trades of their homelands in English towns. The Reformation brought thousands of Protestant refugees from the Low Countries and France.[2]

Thus well before the nineteenth century every part of England was more than "Anglo-Saxon." In different corners of the country, furthermore, the varied ethnic and cultural mixtures had produced provincialisms which set Yorkshire tyke apart from Lancashire lad and both from Westcountryman or East Anglian. Finally during the eighteenth and nineteenth centuries, as the agricultural and industrial revolutions set people on the move, Irishmen yearly crossed over to work in England as harvesters and navvies or settled in industrial and commercial districts like Lancashire and London.[3] Many Scots and Welshmen likewise sought their fortunes in English cities. Polish Jews and other continental newcomers planted their little urban enclaves. Not all merged rapidly or easily into the English population, though if they happened later to come to the United States, they were all marked down as Englishmen.[4]

North of the Tweed the simple designation "Scot" also hid essential differences. Lowlanders and Borderers, like northern Englishmen, combined Anglo-Saxon, Celtic, Scandinavian, and Norman blood and culture. To the northwest, above the Highland line, lived another breed of Scot. Although Viking settlers had modified Celtic ways, the Highlanders still spoke the Gaelic. In speech, in fact, Lowlanders with their "broad Scots" dialect were more like Englishmen than like Highlanders. The vernaculars on opposite sides of the Highland line belonged to "two distinct linguistic families, more remote from each other than English or Russian, or English and Sanscrit."[5] Yet some Highland districts shared the Lowlanders' Presbyterianism, while others remained Catholics, though of an austere, quasi-Calvinist variety.[6] Finally during the nineteenth century the growing Lowland industrial towns drew many Highlanders south.[7] Irishmen, too, came to the Lowlands as they did to England. But while Irish and Scottish workingmen might come to blows in Glasgow or Galloway, in the books of Castle Garden and Ellis Island both groups were equally Scotsmen.[8]

As culturally distinct from the English as Highlanders were from Lowlanders, the Welsh carried on the Celtic culture of pre-Saxon Britain in their poor and rugged land. Though conquered by medieval English kings and marcher lords, they maintained their national identity, especially in the mountains of North Wales. The South, always easier terrain for invading armies and better supplied with resources for modern industry, had long been more Anglicized. Medieval English and Flemish settlers had even turned the southwestern peninsulas into a "Little England beyond Wales." During the first half of the nineteenth century, incoming Irish and English laborers made South Wales still less Welsh.[9] Yet much of the new labor force there was recruited from thoroughly Welsh-speaking districts.[10] Though the English language gradually gained ground throughout the Principality, in the 1870's more than 70 per cent of the population still spoke Welsh.[11]

Though Cornwall was officially only an English county, until the eighteenth century its vernacular likewise survived, a Celtic tongue closely akin to Welsh. Even thereafter, the Cornish remained, in their English dialect as in tradition, a distinct people.[12] The Manx, governing themselves in the middle of the Irish Sea, still clung to Gaelic.[13]

Three nations, each with its distinct provinces — despite these ethnic and cultural divisions, the peoples of Great Britain counted themselves equally British. Ireland was a land apart. There, too, race and culture had long divided men. Between the twelfth and the seventeenth centuries Englishmen, Lowland Scots, and Welshmen settled as conquerors among the Gaelic-speaking Irish. Those who arrived after the Reformation were Protestants; most of the indigenous stock remained true to Rome. By the later nineteenth century even Catholic Irishmen in all but the remote western fringes of the island adopted the English speech of their overlords. Yet out of the ethnic and religious division of Ireland sprang up a new conflict, of political loyalties. As Irish nationalism flowered in the south and west, the Protestant sections held ever more devotedly to the United Kingdom. In race, religion, and politics the Protestant Irish stood with the British. Nevertheless, while Anglo-Irishmen and Ulster Scots were not Celtic Catholics, neither were they a mere breed of Englishmen and Scotsmen.[14]

But as the Irish split widened, in industrial Britain all national and provincial differences began to break down. As cities grew and steam made travel easier, Irishmen moved to Lancashire, London, the Clyde, and South Wales; Highlanders came south; Scots and Welshmen went to better their fortunes in England; English skilled workers entered newly created manufacturing areas in South Wales and the North of England, and everywhere countrymen deserted their ancestral villages for the mines, factories, and towns.[15] But cultures and loyalties which had flourished through the centuries succumbed slowly to the pressures of the age. The strong consciousness persisted of being Cornishman or Lancashire lad, Aberdonian or Paisley body, *Northyn* from North Wales rather than *Hwntw* from the South.

Across the sea Canada remained a loyal British outpost despite the obstreperous republic to the south. Canadians had their own ethnic divisions. French Canadians, like the Celtic Catholics of Ireland, were distinctly not British, but most English-speaking Canadians and Newfoundlanders, whether of English, Scottish, or Irish ancestry, felt themselves British. Varying in ethnic inheritance from province to province and township to township, they too reflected their migrant origins.

In Nova Scotia during the 1760's New Englanders and British, German, and Swiss immigrants took the ousted French Acadians' place. Soon the American Revolution drove loyal subjects out of the thirteen former colonies northward into the Maritime Provinces and Lower Canada. For another century Americans and Scots, Englishmen, and Irishmen continued to seek virgin soil in Upper Canada and beyond.[16] Most notable, perhaps, were the Highlanders, both Presbyterians and Catholics, who, uprooted from their native glens by agrarian reorganization early in the nineteenth century, made Gaelic the language of Cape Breton, Prince Edward Island, and parts of Upper Canada and the Red River valley.[17] The census of 1881 estimated that among the English- and Gaelic-speaking population of the Dominion about 30 per cent were English by ancestry, 25 per cent Scottish, less than half of 1 per cent Welsh, and 33 per cent Irish.[18]

When men and women came from all these variegated British lands to the United States during the nineteenth century, they formed the rearguard of a column whose van had settled Jamestown and Plymouth. Most colonial Americans were descendents of Britons: Englishmen who had scattered throughout the colonies; Welshmen who had come to William Penn's province; and Scots and Ulstermen who had pushed the frontier across the Appalachians. In 1790, it has been estimated, about 60 per cent of the white population was of English and Welsh stock, 8 per cent Scottish, and 6 per cent "Scotch-Irish," while less than 4 per cent was Southern Irish.[19] Of course these Americans, having lived a century and a half in the New World, were no longer Englishmen, Welshmen, Scots, or Irishmen like their immigrant ancestors. Furthermore, with immigration blocked by war between 1793 and 1815, the next generation grew up wholeheartedly American.[20] Yet it was a British acorn from which the young oak had sprouted.

Table 1.

Immigration from the United Kingdom to the United States, 1820–1950.*

	England	Wales	Scotland	Ireland	Not Specified
1820–1830	15,837	170	3,180	54,338	8,302
1831–1840	7,611	185	2,667	207,381	65,347
1841–1850	32,092	1,261	3,712	780,719	229,979
1851–1860	247,125	6,319	38,331	914,119	132,199
1861–1870	222,277	4,313	38,769	435,778	341,537
1871–1880	437,706	6,631	87,564	436,871	16,142
1881–1890	644,680	12,640	149,869	655,482	168
1891–1900	216,726	10,557	44,188	388,416	67
1901–1910	388,017	17,464	120,469	339,065	
1911–1920	249,944	13,107	78,357	146,181	
1921–1930	157,420	13,012	159,781	220,591	
1931–1940	21,756	735	6,887	13,167	
1941–1950	112,252	3,209	16,131	26,444	
Total	2,753,443	89,603	749,905	4,618,552	793,741

* U.S. Commissioner-General of Immigration, *Report*, 1930, pp. 202–203; Bureau of the Census, *Statistical Abstract of the United States*, 1951, p. 94.

After 1815 it was the unprecedented immigration of masses of Germans, Catholic Irish, Scandinavians, and, with the approach of the twentieth century, of Italians, Slavs, Jews, and Orientals which aroused American attention. But this was no less the epoch of the largest movement from Great Britain to the United States. The available statistics unfortunately are faulty, particularly before 1870. Between 1820 and 1870, American officials counted some three and a half million immigrants arriving from the United Kingdom (Table 1). The nationality of a fifth of these was not recorded; it would be mere guesswork to say how many were English, Welsh, or Scots, and how many Irish. Of those who were classified, however, nearly two-thirds were Irish, increasingly Celtic Catholics instead of Protestant Ulstermen.[21] Only 14 per cent of the immigrants from the United Kingdom during these fifty-five years were identified as English, another 2.3 per cent as Scots, and but 0.3 per cent as Welsh. British Canadians came too, but mostly unrecorded. On the other hand, no count was made of those immigrants who, after a longer or shorter stay in America, eventually sailed back to Britain.

By 1870 the English, Scots, and Welsh together made up about 14 per cent of the foreign-born in the United States. Fully another 33 per cent were Irish, probably most now Catholics from southern and western Ireland. Among the 9 per cent born in British North America, those who spoke English still far outnumbered the French Canadians. Thus more than 20 per cent of the foreign-born, or between 2 and 3 per cent of the total population, could be called British by birth (Table 2).

During the next half century, when southern and eastern Europeans and Orientals were the "new immigrants" who frightened editors, politicians, and sociologists, there were many British people who were just as new to the United States. It is probable that more Englishmen, Scots, and Welshmen — not to mention their cousins from Ulster and Canada — came to America during these fifty years than had come during the entire preceding two hundred and fifty (Table 1 and Fig. 1).

As governments on both sides of the Atlantic began to supervise the immigrant traffic more closely, statistics of the movement grew more accurate. Yet an exact balance sheet is still unattainable. From 1871 until 1920, American officials marked down nearly two million immigrants from England, nearly half a million from Scotland, and sixty thousand from Wales, as well as two million from Ireland. Before beginning their ocean crossing, they had been counted also in the ports of their own country. The British statistics of emigrants bound for the United States between 1871 and 1920 are far more liberal: three million English and Welsh together, six hundred and

Table 2.

British-born Population of the United States, 1850–1950.*

	Total Population	Total Foreign-born	English	Welsh	Scottish	Irish	British Canadian	French Canadian	Nfdld.	Aust.
1850	23,191,876	2,244,602	278,675	29,868	70,550	961,719	147,711			
1860	31,443,321	4,136,175	431,692	45,763	108,518	1,611,304	249,970			1,419
1870	38,558,371	5,567,229	555,046	74,533	140,835	1,855,827	493,464			3,118
1880	50,155,783	6,679,943	664,160	83,302	170,136	1,854,571	717,157			4,906
1890	62,947,714	9,249,560	909,092	100,079	242,231	1,871,509	678,442	302,496		5,984
1900	75,994,575	10,341,276	840,513	93,586	233,524	1,615,459	784,796	395,126		6,807
1910	91,972,266	13,515,886	877,719	82,488	261,076	1,352,251	819,554	385,083	5,080	8,938
1920	105,710,620	13,920,692	813,853	67,066	254,570	1,037,234	817,139	307,786	13,249	10,801
1930	122,775,046	14,204,149	809,563	60,205	354,323	178,832[a] 744,810[b]	915,537	370,852	23,980	12,816
1940	131,669,275	11,419,138[e]	621,975[e]	35,360[e]	279,321[e]	106,416[a] 572,931[b]	770,753[e]	273,366[e]	21,361[e]	10,998[e]
1950	150,697,361	10,161,168[e]	554,625[ed]	30,060[ed]	244,200[e]	520,359[e]	756,153[e]	238,409[e]		

* *Sixteenth Census of the U.S.* (1940), II, 43; 1950 figures from U.S. Bureau of the Census.

[a] Northern Ireland.

[b] Eire.

[e] White foreign-born only; the difference in number between white and colored British immigrants in 1930, however, was only about one thousand.

[d] Estimate based on 20 per cent sample; actual total English and Welsh, 584,615.

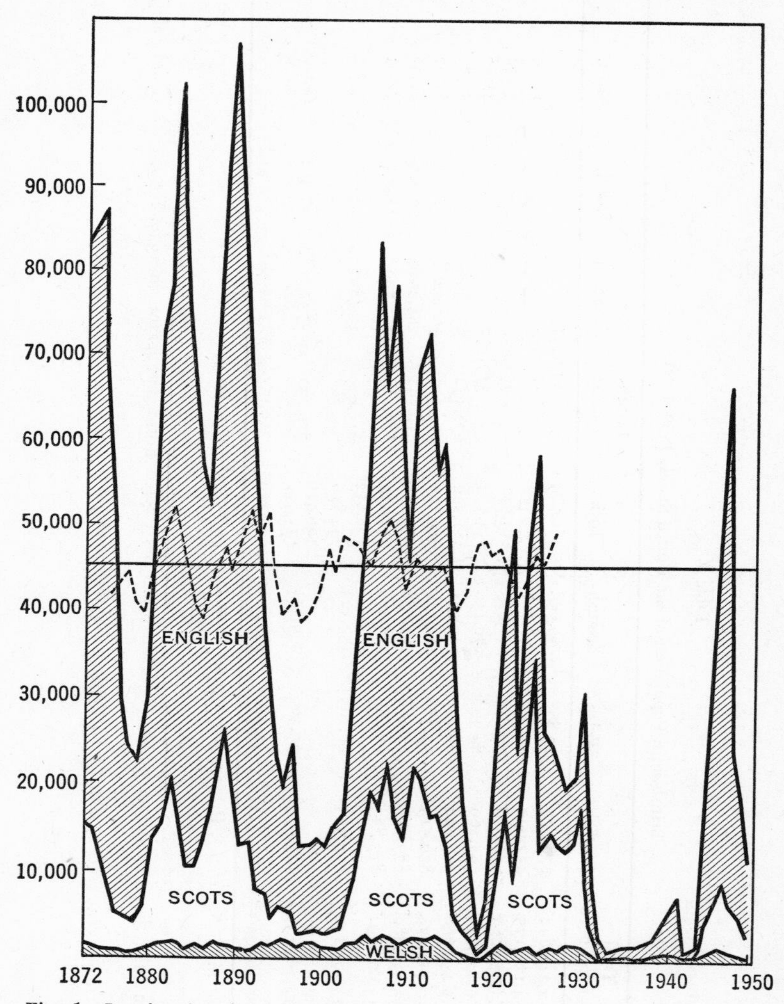

Fig. 1. Immigration from Great Britain to the United States, 1872–1950. The dashed line shows United States business fluctuations, 1875–1925.

fifty thousand Scots, and two million two hundred thousand Irishmen.

The discrepancies between the British and American figures resulted from different definitions of an "immigrant." Until 1904 the United States counted only steerage passengers, though many a British immigrant sailed second or first class. More or less balancing this omission, American authorities did list aliens who were merely passing through the country and, until 1904, immigrants who had already been counted on an earlier entry. The British government, on the other hand, until 1912 lumped together all passengers bound for the States, travelers as well as settlers. Thus the British statistics are inflated; the American, far too low.[22]

How many Irish immigrants were Scottish- or Anglo-Irish Protestants can be no more than roughly estimated. If from each county of Ireland Protestants and Catholics had emigrated in proportionate numbers between 1876 and 1918, about 15 per cent would have been Protestants, twice as many of them Episcopalians as Presbyterians. But actually after the 1830's Catholics were more apt than Protestants to go to the United States, while a large majority of the Irish who went to Scotland and Canada between 1876 and 1918, and in certain years to England, came from predominantly Protestant Ulster. To take another approach, the six northern counties at present attached to Great Britain contributed 13.5 per cent of the Irish emigrants to the United States during this period. At all events, it is unlikely that those Irish newcomers whose religion and politics allied them with the British much exceeded two hundred thousand.[23]

Still more conjectural is the number of emigrants who were natives or residents of England, Wales, and Scotland but whose parentage, religion, and way of life identified them with Catholic Ireland. Many persons who appear in the American immigration and census reports as Englishmen, Welshmen, or Scots would better have been called Irish.

These imponderables considered, a rough reckoning from 1870 to 1920 yields between two and a half and three million English immigrants to the United States, well over half a million Scots, and fewer than one hundred thousand Welsh: a total of three to three and a half million British. From these should be subtracted an unknown number of persons who were properly Irish, and to them may be added perhaps two hundred thousand Irish Protestants who were British in some respects.

But by no means all these immigrants remained in America for the rest of their lives or even for more than a season. Unfortunately, the United Kingdom until 1895 did not distinguish the nationality of persons sailing back eastward; only after 1908 did the United States record them. According to the British figures between 1895 and 1918, 55 per cent as many Englishmen and Welshmen, taken as one group, came back as left for the United States; among the Scots the proportion was 46 per cent, and among the Irish, 42 per cent. The American record of remigration from 1908 to 1918 is much lower: for England 16 per cent, Wales 7 per cent, Scotland 14 per cent, and Ireland 10 per cent. The discrepancies may be due to American omission until 1918 of naturalized citizens and the British government's indiscriminate listing until 1912 of all departing and arriving travelers as well as actual migrants. At any rate, a strong return current before as well as after 1895 evidently reduced the British-born population of the country.[24]

As in earlier periods, the United States between 1870 and 1920 attracted the lion's share of all those who left the United Kingdom. But at the same time many British (though few Irish) emigrants sought new homes under the Union Jack rather than the Stars and Stripes. Only 45 per cent of the English and Welsh emigrants and 53 per cent of the Scots went to the United States. Canada drew more of the balance than did any other part of the Empire.[25]

Canadians in turn came to the United States. Adequate records of movement across the northern border were not kept until 1908; even thereafter the partial figures may not be trusted since they included Europeans entering the United States by way of Canadian ports. Between 1866 and 1885, however, officials did count 895,520 persons coming from British North America.[26] Then from 1908 through 1918 Canada and Newfoundland sent 741,384 persons. The proportion of British Canadians among them, though indeterminable, was always high; after 1900 it increased as French Canadian migration slackened.[27]

After these statistical vagaries of the immigration officials, it is pleasant to find that the census takers have been more precise in counting the British-born persons in the United States from decade to decade since 1850. The number of British Canadians and of Protestant Irish is still conjectural, but the total number of British immigrants living in the country was some six hundred thousand in 1850 and over two million in 1890. Over these forty years their rate of increase kept pace with that both of the foreign-born in general and of the total population. But after the peak of 1890 they declined fairly steadily in absolute numbers and precipitously in relation to the other elements in the American population (Table 2). For some reason America no longer attracted the British as it once had; the long-flowing stream of migrants was drying up.

Part I. The Economic Adjustment

2

"Pies and Puddings"

Since 1607 many diverse forces have led men and women to abandon the Old World for the New. From time to time political or religious oppression has driven true believers to seek a land more tolerant, at least of their particular heresies. Others have been forcibly transported to America as convicts or slaves; taxpayers have cheaply disposed of paupers by paying their ocean passage. And of course there have been nearly as many personal motives for emigration as there have been emigrants. Throughout three centuries, however, humdrum economic forces have probably moved most of the venturers.

Among no group of migrants did material ambition bulk larger than among the nineteenth- and early twentieth-century British. Yet other circumstances did account for some. The very name of America conjured up for Europeans a bright if hazy vision of a promised land. "There is a charm connected with the word 'America' which silences the most ordinary dictates of caution," a British consul stationed there remarked in 1881. A sober man would cross the Atlantic "with less inquiry as to his prospects in general and as to the particular place in which it may be best for him to settle than he would make if the contemplated removal were, say, from Kent to Yorkshire."[1] Yet after two hundred years of emigration the Kentishman might well have more friends and relatives in America than in Yorkshire to post him on current conditions. Few British towns or villages did not know the States through the letters of their Yankee sons and daughters. Few of the stay-at-homes had not themselves thought of shaking the old-country dust from their heels.

Religious and political freedom partly accounted for America's good fame. In the 1850's that country's equalitarianism still inspired obscure British radicals to cross the Atlantic. One Welsh-American long afterward recalled that reading Francis Lieber's *On Civil Liberty and Self-Government* had turned his heart and steps westward. "The book had more inspiration in it than any book of its kind I ever read . . . It painted American institutions and the principles of American civil liberty in the most glowing colors." [2] But during the nineteenth century such attractions lost significance. As the British constitution grew more democratic, emigrant ships no longer bore political exiles to the western republic. After the widening of the suffrage in 1867 and 1884, men on all levels of British society could hope to reform abuses rather than to have to flee them. Likewise, while thousands of Mormon converts and at least a few Welsh Nonconformists left Britain for religious reasons, toleration grew substantially as broad at home as in America.[3]

Political reform made emigration unnecessary for some, but improving means of ocean travel made it much easier for all. As sail gave way to steam on the North Atlantic between 1840 and 1870, the length, discomfort, and danger of the voyage ceased to deter emigrants. Governmental regulation made the crossing relatively safe and comfortable even for steerage passengers. No more the weeks of beating against the westerlies or lying hove-to in a gale, with water and provisions running low, "ship fever" decimating the company, and profit-hungry captains tyrannizing over the crowded steerage: now the bored emigrants merely idled away ten or fourteen uneventful days.[4]

Nevertheless, to landsmen cooped up in even a liner's hold two weeks on the North Atlantic was unsettling and irksome enough. The food, said a young Scot who crossed to Quebec on the Allan Line's *Corinthian* in 1871, was

> absolutely disgusting, unfit to be set before human beings or even pigs . . . There was one meal a day, oatmeal, which they could not spoil, but all the rest — the odor of them was enough. The quarters where we slept were simply scandalous. On my side of the ship there were five

beds below, over there another tier of five, and then an upper tier, and in each bed there was about fifteen inches of canvas to sleep on.

And all the while the ship "jumped on the sea like a catboat." [5]

Thirty-two years later, when a British machinist sailed from Liverpool to New York on "one of the best" liners, conditions seemed no better, and the "Jews, Hungarians, Poles, Finns, [and] Norwegians" among his fellow passengers added to his malaise. Under the battened steerage hatches during a storm,

the stench of so many human beings cooped up without ventilation became awful, and sickness prevalent. Our meals were unbearable, even for healthy folk. The only food one cared for was oatmeal. We were treated more like cattle than human beings . . . I really should say to anyone coming West — book second and thus escape all the horrors of steerage.[6]

Many British emigrants, even of the working classes, in fact did travel second class.[7]

Crossing to the States in 1879, Robert Louis Stevenson belittled the steerage passengers' outcries against rations "not food for human beings" and "only fit for pigs." "Many of them," he observed, "lived almost entirely upon biscuit, others on their own private supplies, and some paid extra for better rations from the ship." But all was not grumbling. From the steerage appeared fiddlers, and a Welshman improvised a choir. Hornpipes and reels helped the sober Scottish and English workingmen to while away the time.[8] If the ocean crossing was not yet pleasant, at least the steamship made it so commonplace that some British artisans were able to undertake an annual round trip for a summer's work in the United States.[9] Thus the immigrant traffic grew.

State and private aid sent various classes of poor emigrants from the United Kingdom, but few came to the United States. The British government, even before its revival of interest in the Empire in the 1870's, encouraged its subjects to move only to the colonies. And sparsely populated colonies from time to time brought immigrants out from the mother country.[10]

After the Civil War, private philanthropists likewise directed slum dwellers or destitute Highland crofters to Canada, Australia, and New Zealand but only very occasionally to the United States.[11] In 1870 a London charitable society sent a few families to West Virginia.[12] Descendants of the pre-Revolutionary Highland settlers of North Carolina, their towns still known in 1884 as the "Scotch Settlements," welcomed three hundred poor crofters whom a wealthy benefactress sent from Skye.[13]

These few assisted paupers from Great Britain, together with larger numbers from Ireland, seemed to Americans like a menacing horde. Consequently a federal act of 1882 excluded persons likely to become public charges.[14] Under this law a party of unemployed English men and women whom the Duke of Buckingham sent in 1888 were promptly deported.[15] Most of the pauper immigrants of whom the American government complained in 1887 and 1888, however, were Irish crofters. The American consuls in Great Britain could discover very few recent cases of assisted emigration to the United States, and to avoid further protests the British Local Government Board discouraged all such expenditures.[16] In 1891 Congress tightened the legal restriction.[17]

Long ago British authorities had sent many a convict to the American colonies, but in the independent United States "ticket-of-leave men" met no welcome. During the later nineteenth century these paroled prisoners were customarily supervised by a local aid society. If a prisoner could be persuaded to emigrate, government and the society together paid his passage. In 1875, however, Congress excluded alien convicts.[18] Although British authorities averred that such men were being shipped to Canada, American officials suspected that many soon crossed the border or were even sent directly to the nearest American port, usually Boston. These clandestine immigrants, like the assisted paupers, were probably not numerous.[19]

Upon one class of assisted immigrants American law never frowned. Many a poor man or family made the voyage on a few sovereigns or prepaid tickets which some successful relative or friend sent from America. Young Scotswomen, sometimes in groups of as many as thirty-five, sailed together as soon as their emigrant sweethearts with whom they had "broken saxpences" could save enough for their cabin passage.[20] The Irish, however, were more dependent upon such means than were the English and Scots.[21]

Advertising also stimulated British emigration. Steamship and railroad companies, Western states, and others with tickets or land to sell sent agents wherever in Europe immigrants might be recruited. The American Emigrant Aid Society of London in 1869 even conducted a lottery which held out the hope of passage to San Francisco.[22] Other short-lived but more plausible promoters frequently solicited migrants in British newspapers.[23] Speculators rose and fell, but in so far as advertising could stimulate emigration, the shipping lines and railroads kept Britons moving westward.[24]

But all these factors — the fabled charm of the New World, letters from successful immigrants, better means of travel, charitable or friendly aid in raising passage money, and advertising — accounted for only the minor part of British emigration to America. The essential forces behind the movement were economic. Although during the nineteenth century few fled outright starvation at home, most did hope to improve their fortunes abroad. America offered myriad jobs at wages unmatched by the crowded labor market of Britain. Thus many a man with a good British job hoped to earn a fatter pay packet and to rise farther and faster than would ever be likely at home. And rise or not, a man could give his family a fuller table. "In America," gloated an English workingman in mid-Atlantic in 1879, "you get pies and puddings."[25]

Thus the tide of migration between Great Britain and the United States flowed and ebbed with the cycle of prosperity and depression. Of course, since these commercial and industrial nations were economically interdependent, the British and American business cycles roughly coincided. Just when jobs were most plentiful at home, therefore, British workingmen left in the greatest numbers to enjoy high American wages. Conversely, when lean years made their homeland least bearable, dull prospects across the sea discouraged intending emigrants and even drove others back home from the States. The economic forces which moved these millions, then, were more American than British. During most years the cycle of British migration to America closely followed the American business cycle [26] (Fig. 1).

Since the patterns of economic expansion and contraction on opposite sides of the Atlantic seldom exactly coincided, however, British conditions did modify the yearly movement. A relatively good year in Britain, such as 1870, could accentuate the effect of a brief slump in America. During the long depression of 1873–1879, when unemployment was severe in the United States, the British worker was better off at home than if he were abroad. Real wages in Britain slowly rose, working hours were shortened, and unemployment was not acute.[27] Many British emigrants returned home, where, employed or not, they could live more cheaply than in America. Yankee laborers even went to the United Kingdom to work.[28] Canada provided an uncertain refuge for other American, British, and of course Canadian workingmen who had been in the States.[29] Several hundred men sailed from New York in 1876 and 1877 for Australia.[30] Then in 1879 good times suddenly returned to America just when the British economy touched bottom; at once the westward ships were crowded again.[31]

Although during the 1880's British emigration continued to follow the swings of the American economic pendulum, after 1888 the coincidence became less exact. Between 1888 and 1892, though America prospered and, beginning in 1891, the United Kingdom was depressed, the number of British immigrants annually declined. Then from 1893 to 1895 depression in both countries choked off migration even more than had the slump of the 1870's. Since in 1896 and 1897 conditions improved more rapidly in Britain than in America, the movement remained small. After 1900 American prosperity and British depression released a new flood of migrants which, despite setbacks in 1904 and 1907–08, reached the highest level in twenty years. America's economic health being poorer than Britain's from 1910 to 1913, migration again slackened. The war brought it to a virtual stop.

The American economy had not ceased to expand from decade to decade, and it could draw immigrants from a still rising British population. Yet after 1900 British migration to the United States did not match that of a few decades before. Englishmen and Scots, though leaving the homeland in unprecedented numbers, now went increasingly to the Dominions rather than to the States. Canada in particular, with its new industries as well as its western lands, attracted many who formerly would have gone south of the boundary. By 1905 more Englishmen and by 1907 more Scots were going to British North America than to the United States[32] (Figs. 2 and 3).

To some degree this shift of direction was due to the exhaustion of cheap new land in America for the immigrant farmer. But a more important factor was a certain economic peculiarity of the nineteenth-century British immigrants to the United States. As the superintendent of the American census observed in 1874:

> In respect of their industrial occupations, the foreigners among us may be divided as those who are where they are because they are doing what they are doing; and those who are doing what they are doing because they are where they are. In the former case, occupation has determined location; in the latter, location has determined occupation.[33]

The second category included the bulk of the Irish and continental European immigrants, peasants who had no labor skills of value in America and so did the rough work of the ports and industrial cities where their wanderings happened to end. The British, too, included many such men. But a large proportion of the British, on the other hand, arrived as experienced craftsmen from the nation which had pioneered the Industrial Revolution. Their training was directly usable by the new American industries. It was not at all accidental that they came to the United States in this epoch and immediately went to work in particular manufacturing cities and mining camps.

Of more than one and a quarter million British working people who disembarked in American ports between 1873 and 1918, over 40 per cent declared that they had been in skilled trades, while only

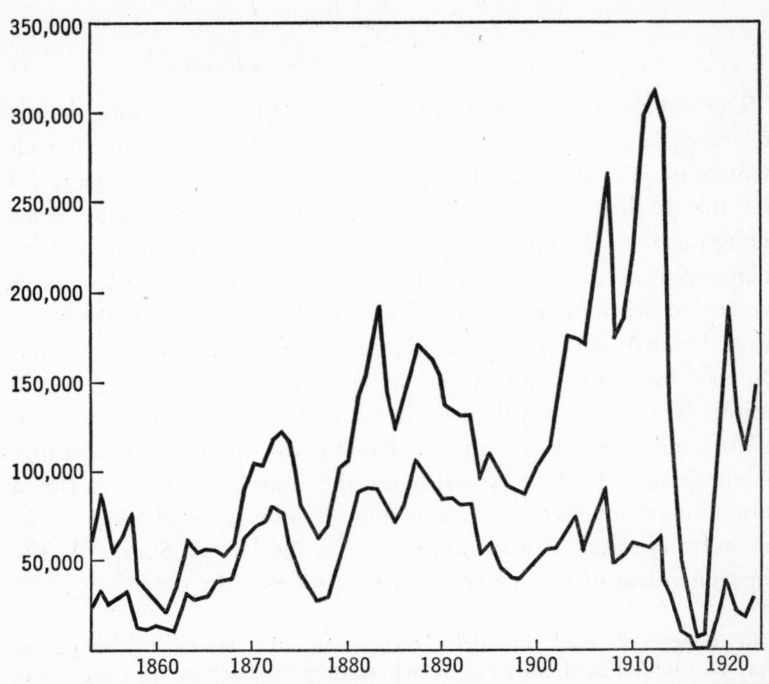

Fig. 2. English and Welsh emigration from the United Kingdom, 1853–1923. The upper line represents total emigration; the lower line represents emigration to the United States.

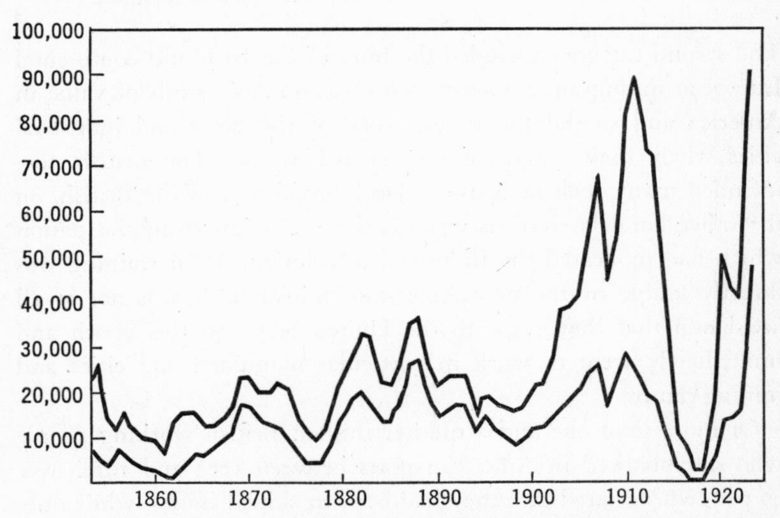

Fig. 3. Scottish emigration from the United Kingdom, 1853–1923. The upper line represents total emigration; the lower line represents emigration to the United States.

25 per cent had been unskilled laborers at home.[34] Furthermore, among English, Welsh, and Scottish immigrant workers listed by the American census of 1890, fully 48 per cent of the men and 42 per cent of the women were in industrial occupations. The comparable proportion of all other gainfully employed foreign-born men was only 34 per cent, and of women, 27 per cent.[35]

Some other immigrants, for example the French Canadians, in 1890 had a higher proportion of their workingmen and women in mining and manufacturing than had the British. But few of them were as skilled. Among the thousands of industrial employees investigated by the federal Immigration Commission of 1907–1910, a far greater proportion of the British than of any other nationality had resumed their old trade upon coming to the new country. In the Commission's list of bituminous-coal miners, 88 per cent of the Scots and of the Welsh and 83 per cent of the English had been miners before immigrating, but only 59 per cent of the Irish and 55 per cent of the Germans. In copper mining and smelting the English had the highest proportion of former miners — 60 per cent — followed by the Swedes with a mere 18 per cent and the Germans with 13 per cent. As iron miners the English with 54 per cent led the North Italians' 15 per cent and the Swedes' 10 per cent. Among iron and steel workers who had been in the same industry at home were 72 per cent of the Welsh, 48 per cent of the English, 43 per cent of the Scots, and only 21 per cent of the Swedes and 17 per cent of the Germans.[36]

In the textile industries more than half of the British whom the Commission sampled had had similar jobs before immigrating. Among male cotton operatives the English had the highest proportion, 70 per cent; the French and Germans followed; the Scots had 39 per cent; the Irish, 21 per cent; and the French Canadians, only 6 per cent. In American woolen mills a greater proportion of the French and Germans had likewise worked in such mills at home, but the English had a good 56 per cent, the Scots 45 per cent, and the Irish and French Canadians only 14 and 9 per cent. In silk, though Russian Jews, North Italians, and Germans stood higher, a

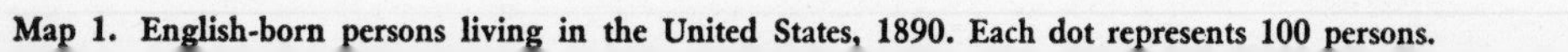

Map 1. English-born persons living in the United States, 1890. Each dot represents 100 persons.

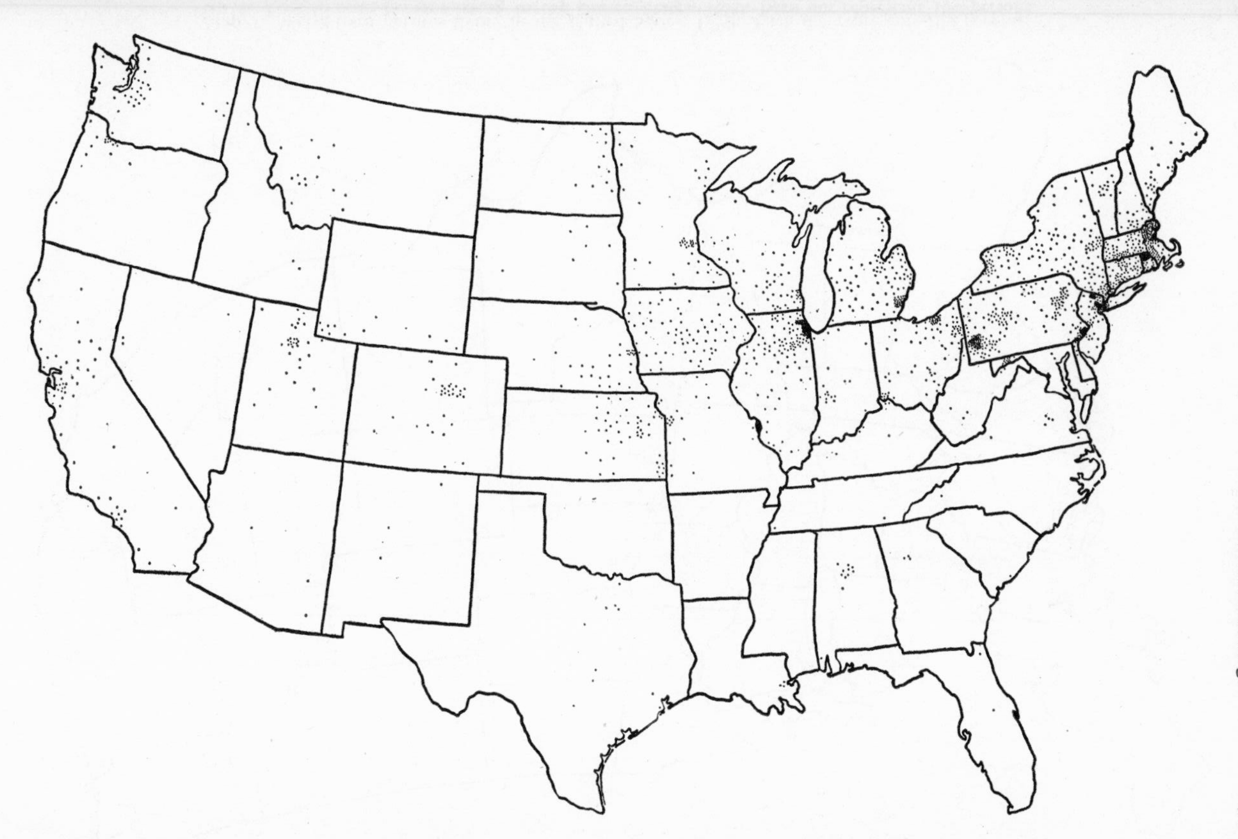

Map 2. Scottish-born persons living in the United States, 1890. Each dot represents 100 persons.

Map 3. Welsh-born persons living in the United States, 1890. Each dot represents 100 persons.

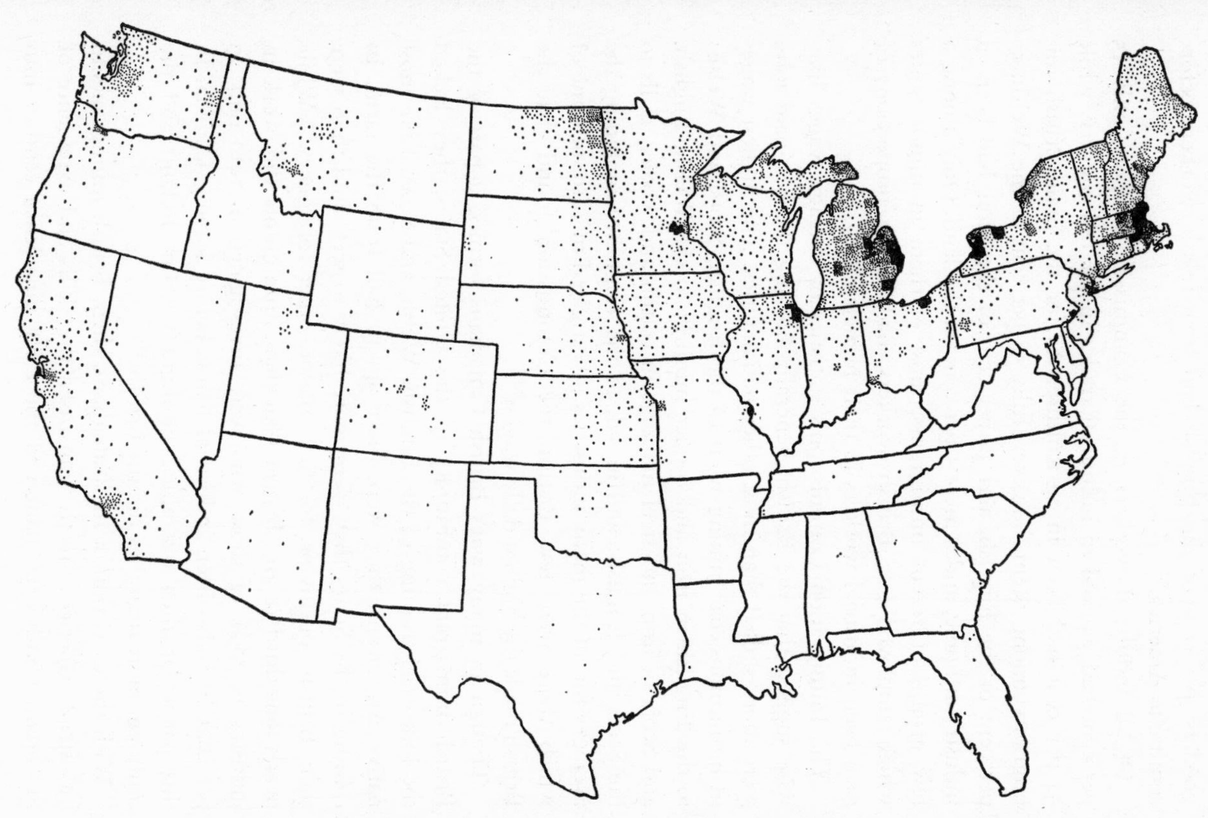

Map 4. British-Canadian-born (English-speaking) persons in the United States, 1900. Each dot represents 100 persons.

good 68 per cent of the English had been textile workers before coming to America.[37]

Of all industrial workers in the Commission's report, only 15 per cent had worked in industrial trades in the old country, while 54 per cent had been in agriculture. As for the male British immigrants among them, however, fully 58 per cent of the Welsh, 50 per cent of the English, and 36 per cent of the Scots had been in industry at home, and a mere 5 per cent on the land. Only among a few groups of recent immigrants, most of them in minor trades which employed few British workers, had higher proportions of men been industrial workers in their homelands.[38]

The Immigration Commission's statistics of average wages likewise suggest that the British, generally holding the best-paid jobs, were more skilled than most other nationalities. The highest wages in bituminous-coal mining went to the English, Scots, and Welsh; to the English in iron and copper mining; to the Welsh, English, and Scots in iron and steel making; in cotton and woolen mills to the Scots and English; and in silk to the English. Combining the averages for all the many industries investigated in 1910, in some of which there were few British, the Commission found that the British made the highest daily wages.[39]

Though in many ways British Canadians formed a part of the British immigrant community in the United States, they lacked the industrial training of the English, Welsh, and Scots. Like most native Americans, they were more apt to hail from the farm. In coming to the States they were more likely to seek land than were their British cousins or, for that matter, other foreigners.[40] While nearly one-third of the British Canadian immigrants did work in industry in 1890, of those who were investigated in 1910 only 27 per cent had also been industrial hands before leaving Canada. In this particular they resembled immigrants from Ireland and the continent more than they did the British.[41]

With the exception of the Canadians, then, British immigrants to industrial America directly transfused the skills and experience of the premier industrial nation of the early nineteenth century into the veins of the rising giant of the twentieth. Unlike unskilled peasants, the English, Welsh, and Scottish workingmen did not come merely hoping for work. They moved instead from specific British industries to the comparable American mines or mills. American contemporaries with their eyes on this or that industry failed to notice this broad pattern; only during the acute labor shortage of the Civil War was it strikingly evident. Thus in a single ship which an emigration agent dispatched to Northern employers in 1864 there were British "iron puddlers and their helpers, roughers, rollers, finishers, and blast-furnacemen; engineers, comprising iron turners, fitters, planers, brass turners and brass finishers . . . flax-dressers, woollen-cloth weavers, carders, scourers, dyers, bleachers, colour-makers, calico-printers, calenderers, shepherds, farmers, and domestic servants." Worsted spinners and fishcurers were to follow.[42]

Foreigners who sailed with such specific jobs in mind reflected more complex economic forces than the simple alternation of booms and slumps which governed most year-by-year migration. However large and rapidly expanding the American economy as a whole might be, a British workingman was not likely to cross the ocean unless he expected to find work in his proper trade. If such a job awaited him in the United States, neither government propaganda nor trade-union subsidy could persuade him to settle instead on a farm within the Empire.[43] Thus nineteenth-century British migration to the United States ran not in a broad, undifferentiated stream but rather in many parallel channels. Textile operative, miner, machinist, potter, and stonecutter, though passengers aboard the same emigrant ship, followed each his own course. The economic forces which brought the British to America in the nineteenth century are to be discovered mainly in the histories of certain industries on both sides of the Atlantic.

3

Spindle and Shuttle

"The manufactures of America are yet in their infancy," an English resident of that country in 1823 warned British "weavers, cotton-spinners, and working manufacturers." Such men, when they could get work, received good wages, but many tramped up and down the country without finding any call for their special skills.[1] Yet the time when they could be sure of employment only during the harvest season was fast ending. Factories were already springing up to rival Lancashire; within another decade the American industrial revolution would be turning under a full head of steam. Soon from nearly all those trades which together had made Britain the world's workshop a hundred kinds of skilled hands would cross the ocean.

In Great Britain textile manufacturing—of cotton in particular—had heralded the new factory age. As weaving, spinning, and carding successively became mechanized and powered by water or steam during the late eighteenth and early nineteenth centuries, workingmen and their wives and children left household wheels and looms and worked within factory walls. By 1850 cotton hand-loom weaving practically disappeared. The new industrial age concentrated most of the half million cotton operatives in the towns of Lancashire, Cheshire, and the valley of the Clyde.[2]

When New England merchants in the 1790's began to invest in cotton mills, Great Britain determined to maintain her lead by forbidding both the export of textile machinery and the emigration of skilled artisans. But British workingmen would not be held back when America offered fortune and fame. Samuel Slater, superintendent of an early Lancashire mill, memorized the plans of the new machinery, slipped out of England, and set up mills in Rhode Island

and Massachusetts; ultimately he became one of America's leading manufacturers.[3] During the following decades Lancashire specialists likewise introduced calico printing and other processes new to the United States.[4] In 1825, when Parliament repealed the ban on the departure of artisans, a Lowell cotton-mill owner, by offering a salary nearly twice his own, secured a Manchester expert to supervise his new print works. Lancashire calico printers soon filled "English Row" in Lowell. Other new print works there and in Lawrence, Fall River, and New York state also relied on English or Scottish superintendents and craftsmen.[5] During the late 1820's and the 1830's American employers paid many calico printers' passage from Liverpool and were said to be encouraging operatives to bring British machinery with them.[6]

British immigrants also appeared among the ranks of ordinary American mill hands during the 1820's. The original New England operatives were the sons, and more often the daughters, of Yankee farmers.[7] But as handloom weavers in England lost their livelihood to the new power looms, they hastened by the shipload to leave for America before being completely immobilized as their savings dwindled. In these years English and northern Irish handloom weavers, attracted by wages three or four times those at home, established the fine cotton-goods trade of Philadelphia.[8]

Although during the 1830's English, Scottish, and Irish operatives began to supplant the famous American mill girls of Lowell, not until the 1840's did immigrant labor dominate New England factories. Then it was Irish refugees from an overpopulated and famine-scourged island who, though they lacked industrial experience, tried their hands as mill laborers. English and Scottish hands also immigrated during the later 1840's and the 1850's; less numerous but more experienced than the Irish, they were welcome to take the better jobs.[9] When the Wamsutta Mill, New Bedford's first, opened in 1846, many employees were English.[10] A few years later mills in Holyoke imported two or three hundred Scotswomen with training as weavers.[11]

During the Lancashire "cotton famine" brought on by the American Civil War blockade, unemployed English operatives clamored for assistance to emigrate, while the American labor shortage led Northern manufacturers to recruit hands in Scotland and England.[12] After the war American cotton workers returning from the army often found skilled foreigners in their old jobs. One Yankee mule spinner complained that, in consequence, many of his sort had become tramps: "They cannot get work; English help are preferred."[13]

With unemployment, wage cuts, and strikes throughout Lancashire in 1869, trade unions helped hundreds of their members to emigrate, and thousands more pressed to follow.[14] This slump was soon over, but New England's need for trained hands permitted no slackening of migration. Especially notable was the rush of mill building about Fall River in the 1860's and 1870's and in New Bedford in the 1880's; consequently southern Massachusetts drew the incoming Englishmen. While foreigners also manned the more slowly expanding cotton mills of Rhode Island, the Merrimack valley, and Maine, they were usually either Irishmen joining their countrymen already there or French Canadians from neighboring Quebec. Irish and French came also to Fall River and New Bedford, but the English influx made those cities a second Lancashire.[15]

The name of Fall River soon became synonymous with "America" among the spindles and shuttles of Preston and Oldham. Emigrant operatives encouraged friends at home to follow them. Ben Brierley, the Lancashire dialect writer, saw many of the latter on a voyage from Liverpool in 1885:

> I looked down among the steerage passengers . . . an' seed three or four faces ut looked like gradely uns.
> 'Wheere dun yo' come fro'?' I axt 'em.
> 'Owdham an' Mossley,' they said.
> 'Wheere are yo' goin' to?'
> 'To Fall River.'
> 'Han yo' shops to go to?'
> 'Nawe, but we'n friends theere.'[16]

"When they reach Newfoundland or about there," an old hand observed in 1884, "the first question they ask is, 'Where is Fall River?" The nightly boat from New York made Fall River the easiest cotton-mill town for most English newcomers to reach; "picked help" who landed at Boston also were soon there.[17] In Fall River Brierley saw so many Lancashire lads that he wrote, "I soon forgeet wheere I wur, an' fancied I're i' England, an' wur th' only Yankee i' th' company. I towd 'em I wouldno' forget 'em when I geet back to Ameriky."[18]

Some of these Lancashire people in Fall River were more Irish than English. Since the 1820's Irish laborers had been crossing over into the Lancashire mill towns. Though unskilled peasants when they arrived there, they or their children often had become mill operatives. While those who subsequently came to America generally remained Irish in religion and sentiment, at least their economic role in Fall River, derived from Lancashire rather than Mayo, rested on an English foundation.[19]

Good years and bad, the English kept coming during the 1880's and 1890's. Some old-country unions regularly helped unemployed members to emigrate, despite the protests of Fall River union officials.[20] The British Cotton Spinners' Society gave an emigration benefit to "members who have become marked men, or 'victims,' for taking an active part in the society's business, or who have been prominent in any trade dispute."[21] British machine manufacturers forwarded lists of prospective emigrants to American employers along with consignments of new looms or mules; they sometimes paid operatives' passage to America if they would install such equipment there.[22] In such ways, until federal law in 1885 forbade importation of alien workers under contract, American mill owners continued to secure British operatives.[23]

Besides filling southern Massachusetts' sudden demand for new hands, the English specialized in spinning and weaving the finer counts in which American mills were striving to match Great Britain.[24] In 1869 the Amoskeag Mill of Manchester, New Hampshire, imported about fifty Scottish girls skilled at weaving fancy ginghams.[25] Scots in a new Fall River mill fourteen years later turned out "the first high quality gingham ever produced in this country." [26] Though long established in America, calico printers also welcomed British and likewise French printers, pattern designers, sketch makers, and engravers.[27]

Whatever a man's craft — carding, spinning, weaving, dyeing, printing, loom fixing — he was sure, when seeking a new job, perhaps as overseer or superintendent, to mention his years in the mills of England, Scotland, or Ulster.[28] Throughout the cotton industry men from Lancashire and the vicinity of Glasgow were in charge of many departments and even of entire mills. In New Bedford, "the Bolton of America," and in Fall River about 1900 the heads of the textile trade schools were English experts.[29] Such men helped the American industry to emulate and eventually to surpass the technology of Great Britain; most famous was James Northrop, inventor of the automatic loom which bore his name.[30]

Working under their countrymen, however, did not reconcile the ordinary English operatives of Fall River to some things for which they had not bargained when seeking high American wages. Some held that English overseers, accustomed to steady production in their own country and anxious to please their American employers, did not allow for the frequent stoppages caused by the poor grade of raw cotton used by American mills.[31] The resulting "drive," furthermore, stretched on through long hours. At home, Parliament in 1874 reduced the textile mills' sixty-hour week by three and a half hours, but in Massachusetts, except for a temporary concession of an hour a day in 1869, mills ran eleven hours a day, six days a week, until the ten-hour act of 1874. In 1901 the working week was still fifty-eight hours.[32]

English spinners in America disliked having only one assistant, or "piecer," since in Lancashire they had had two, and they resented the unaccustomed speed of the mules. Weavers objected to having to tend as many as eight looms, the English limit being four, and to an uncompensated lengthening of the standard "cut" from thirty-six yards in 1858 to as much as forty-five by 1875.[33] In 1910 they and other operatives — picker tenders, card tenders, spoolers, warpers, and sizers — still had to manage more machines than was customary in England.[34]

The mills of free America seemed tyrannous as well as exhausting to the British. In Fall River spinning rooms the operatives were spurred on to outproduce each other by slates chalked with each man's record for all to see; English mills, on the contrary, kept a private book for each operative's stint.[35] "I always thought they were tyrants at home," said one spinner, "but found out differently when I came here. We could always make a complaint of any grievance there; but here . . . we are told that if we don't like it we can get out." [36] Many a Lancashire man grumbled, "What, call this a free land and ask a mon to slave in such a fashion! Here's back t'owd England." [37]

Nevertheless, most of the immigrants held on for the sake of the high wages which had tempted them to cross the sea. While the weaver got only three-fourths the English rate per cut, by tending twice as many looms under a "driving" overseer he made nearly twice as much as at home.[38] Such pay more than balanced the high cost of living in the States. Actually one *could* live nearly as cheaply in America as at home. A British visitor to Fall River in 1902 spoke to a Darwen weaver who by three years of frugal living had saved $200 from his weekly $11 or $12. His mates, however, were apt to "fling money about." [39] But if most English operatives saved no more in the new country than in the old, it was because their standard of living had risen to "lower middle class," and to achieve that, after all, was why they had come.[40] What wonder that American union officials found it impossible to dissuade English cotton operatives from immigrating even during spells of unemployment in America? Said a Fall River labor leader in 1885, "I have written hundreds of letters to secretaries of operative associations in England and have told them that England is better than Fall River; but they have said in answer that it is no use telling the operatives; they will insist on coming to see for themselves." [41]

But during prolonged depressions or strikes in the United States, when British cotton workers could live more comfortably at home than unemployed in America, few new hands arrived in Fall River, and many old ones returned to Lancashire.[42] The 1904 lockout in Fall River luckily coincided with a rate-cutting war between the transatlantic lines. With steerage fare down to $15 and with a boom in the old-country mills, many took ship for England.[43]

Although in 1904 some English-Americans went no farther from Fall River than the Rhode Island mills, the Lancashire epoch was closing in New England and Middle Atlantic cotton towns. As superior skill in operating the original British machinery had made the immigrants desirable hands, so the advance of American technology undermined their favored position. Ring frames for spinning, the Northrop loom, and other new automatic machinery enabled employers to dispense with the British. When mule spinners at one Fall River mill in the 1890's demanded higher pay, they were easily replaced. "On Saturday afternoon after they had gone home," the superintendent chuckled, "we started right in and smashed up a room-full of mules with sledge hammers . . . On Monday morning they were astonished to find that there was no work for them. That room is now full of ring frames run by girls." [44]

Since inexperienced laborers could learn to operate the new machines in most of the cotton crafts, the nationality of the bulk of the mill labor began to change during the 1890's. Not only the English and Scots but also Irish and French Canadian operatives, who had learned the trade in the United States, gradually lost place to unskilled Mediterranean, Slavic, and Portuguese immigrants.[45] Although British operatives continued to arrive whenever the prospect was good, especially for the most highly skilled crafts or for supervisory jobs, their country's mark on American cotton manufacturing had already been made.[46]

In textiles with more high-grade and fewer automatic-machine-made fabrics than in cotton, old British skills were more secure. The foremost such trade was woolen. This ancient industry, an English specialty for centuries, adopted power-driven machinery and factory organization more slowly than did the upstart cotton. But although handlooms wove a considerable portion of British woolens until after the mid-nineteenth century, the new conditions which had centered cotton about Manchester and Glasgow similarly made the West Riding of Yorkshire dominant over the old Westcountry and East Anglian woolen and worsted towns.[47]

As in cotton, the foundations of the American woolen industry were laid largely on English experience. Arriving from Yorkshire in 1793, John and Arthur Scholfield built machinery from memory and started a mill at Byfield for Massachusetts capitalists. Later they and their families operated mills in several New England towns. Both before and after their advent much American woolen machinery was of British design and make. Americans, however, soon worked out their own improvements. But although the technical advances of either country were quickly adopted in the other, in each the relatively late predominance of power-driven, automatic machinery left an open field for skilled craftsmen.[48]

There were Englishmen, therefore, wherever woolen was woven in the United States during the 1820's and 1830's. As the industry declined in the West of England, artisans often preferred to sail overseas from Bristol rather than trudge two hundred miles to the new Yorkshire factories.[49] Philadelphia thereby became a center of British — together with some Flemish — handloom weavers, who, as in the old country, were able to forestall the complete shift to water power and steam until the 1880's.[50] In 1837 the agent of a Lowell mill, finding sixty persons about to emigrate from the old Gloucestershire broadcloth town of Uley, persuaded half of them to come to his mill. Other Westcountry woolen workers followed them to Lowell during the next few years.[51] Before 1860 most woolen operatives were native Americans, but, as in the cotton mills, English immigrants worked in the more intricate crafts, such as weaving and jackspinning, and often became foremen.[52]

Though between the Civil War and the first World War New England won the lion's share of the American woolen industry, the Yankees enjoyed no such predominance as in cotton.[53] Nor were there any hives of English woolen operatives to match Fall River and New Bedford. Nevertheless, woolen workers continued to immigrate. Such Westcountry towns as Trowbridge still supplied a few each year during the 1880's.[54] In at least one woolen mill, in western Massachusetts, Welsh operatives outnumbered any other nationality.[55]

When during the 1880's the trade was prosperous in America but depressed in Yorkshire, emigration was brisk. Operatives left Bradford at the rate of fifty a week, almost all for the States; one organized group of 750 sailed together.[56] Bradford emigrants, said the American consul there, were "almost wholly of the high artisan class . . . expert wool-sorters . . . machinists, foremen, managers, and supervisors . . . whom the mills here are as loth to lose as we are pleased to gain." [57] From Huddersfield, Leeds, Morley, and other West Riding towns came men of the same caliber.[58]

As in cotton, however, American woolen manufacturers were anxious to dispense with skilled handworkers, especially the English hand-jack spinners. During the 1870's most mills introduced woolen mules, already in use in England, which allowed unskilled men or even boys to supplant the old spinners. Yet other techniques changed slowly; the Northrop loom was not adapted to wool until 1905, eleven years after its introduction in cotton weaving. Such delays probably account for the fact that in 1890 only one-fifth of the country's foreign-born cotton operatives but fully one-third of those in woolen were British. Although between 1890 and 1910 green European hands gradually took over all the simpler processes, experienced British newcomers, with some Germans and French, still found niches as expert operatives and as overseers.[59]

When the worsted section of the woolen trade suddenly began to expand in the 1860's, employers relied on standard British equipment operated by Yorkshire tykes.[60] Thus Lawrence, the rising worsted center, attracted many Englishmen and Scotsmen too.[61] A Yorkshireman visiting this "Bradford of America" in 1880 found the mills full of Bradford workmen, managers, and machinery; Bradford men even ran saloons and stores. Although travelers from the West Riding doubted whether American living costs left their countrymen of Lawrence much better off than at home, the immigrants seemed content.[62] New worsted mills in Philadelphia likewise depended on newly arrived English overseers about 1880.[63]

The American mills, some of which were established by British manufacturers, imported English hands until Congress in 1885 forbade labor contracts; even thereafter their agents advertised for men in Yorkshire newspapers and came to tacit wage agreements, unenforceable and often unhonored, with emigrating operatives. But manufacturers complained that the legal restriction hampered them in opening new mills; prospective emigrants disliked risking the voyage without a prior understanding on wages. Thus even in the section of the woolen industry which still needed skilled foreigners the immigration of British operatives declined as the century closed.[64]

In carpet weaving, a still more intricate process, Kilmarnock in Ayrshire divided the nineteenth-century British trade with Kidderminster in Worcestershire. In the carpet works of New England and the Middle Atlantic states, therefore, Scots were as prominent as Englishmen. After the first American manufacturer of Brussels or Wilton carpets hired Kidderminster weavers for his Philadelphia mill about 1815, English, Scottish, and northern Irish artisans made the Kensington section the city's carpet center.[65] In Lowell weavers and overseers from Paisley established the ingrain carpet industry in 1829.[66] The Connecticut carpet village of Thompsonville, to which Kilmarnock operatives flocked in 1828, became virtually a Scottish town.[67]

Like woolen and cotton manufacturers, the American carpet industry developed efficient power looms, such as Bigelow's ingrain machine of the 1840's, to eliminate costly British hand skills.[68] Yet while technical improvements permitted female loom tenders and unskilled newcomers of various nationalities to enter the industry, until the 1880's weaving remained largely a heavy hand trade requiring great skill as well as strength. In Philadelphia in 1876 there were 3,517 handlooms at work on carpets and only 592 power looms.[69]

Four years later a trade journal found six thousand Englishmen in Philadelphia carpet works both large and small.[70] During the next decade English and Scottish carpet towns supplied the American industry with still more machinery and weavers, designers, and superintendents.[71] In 1890 more than a quarter of the immigrants, or one tenth of all workers, in the trade were British-born.[72]

In 1903 an English visitor discovered a large Philadelphia carpet mill full of Kidderminster weavers and Lancashire machines.[73] As late as 1907 a New Jersey factory commenced with men hired in Kidderminster.[74] When Philadelphia added tapestry carpet weaving to its textile trades after 1900, most of the weavers were of English or Scottish origin.[75]

Another Philadelphia fine textile trade, upholstery and drapery fabrics, in the 1870's brought its first weavers, adept in a variety of cloths, from Yorkshire and Scotland. Later some skilled newcomers were Belgian, German, and French. In 1906 about a quarter of the industry's employees were English and Scottish; as late as the 1920's the trade relied on British weavers.[76]

Hosiery, despite the early start which the sixteenth-century stocking frame gave to machine knitting, became a factory industry decades after most other textiles. But by 1840 the heyday of framework knitting by Midland cottagers was long past; power-driven machinery gradually substituted factory operatives for the stockingers of old.[77] As English handframe knitting declined, emigrants took the old skill to America. In the 1830's Nottingham and Leicester knitters came to Philadelphia, where Germans had already introduced the trade. As in England, manufacturing in the workers' homes persisted to some extent throughout the century in Kensington and Germantown. Small mills gradually took over the bulk of the trade, but in 1880 they too depended on English, and some German and French, machines, workmen, and even mill proprietors.[78]

During the 1850's English manufacturers and knitters also established knitting mills at Needham, Massachusetts; twenty years later most of the knitters there and elsewhere in the state were Englishmen.[79] A Nottingham manufacturer, complaining of German competition for his American market, in 1884 came with more than one hundred employees to carry on the struggle at his new mill at Thornton, Rhode Island.[80] Other mill owners advertised for knitters in Nottingham newspapers.[81] Throughout the industry in 1890 more than a third of the foreign-born male operatives were British immigrants.[82] As with other British-American textile workers, however, the knitters' day was ending.[83]

Nearly the whole English silk industry migrated to America after the Civil War. Introduced into London by Huguenot refugees in the seventeenth century, silk was always a tariff-protected exotic in England, although the first textile trade to adopt power and factory organization. Lacking the natural economic advantages enjoyed by other British textile manufacturers, the industry, by then centered at Macclesfield, dwindled after the Cobden treaty of 1860 opened the door to French silks. Some unemployed operatives shifted into other British textiles, but many emigrated to new mills in the United States.[84]

Although in 1860 a few factories constituted the entire American industry, they had already used immigrant skill — English, French, and German. A new company at Mansfield, Connecticut, in 1827 constructed its machinery from plans drawn by an English throwster. But ultimately the American trade clustered at Paterson, New Jersey, where a Macclesfield weaver in 1840 established the first successful mill. During the next twenty years several other Englishmen started factories at Paterson and elsewhere.[85]

Free-trade dogma wrecked silk in Great Britain just when the United States switched to a protective tariff; during the Civil War the duties on silk more than doubled.[86] As the favored industry prospered after 1865, operatives swarmed in from Macclesfield, Coventry, and lesser silk towns of England and Scotland. Owners of British factories crated their machinery and left for New Jersey with their workmen.[87] Some returned home temporarily when the British industry briefly revived during the Franco-Prussian War.[88]

In the late 1870's many English master weavers arrived in Paterson, set up their archaic looms in their own houses, hired journeymen, and attempted to carry on the old household manufacture.[89] Hand-looms and the "family shop" long characterized the Paterson silk industry.[90]

But the future really lay with the factories, where a thousand Englishmen worked by 1879; thousands of new "sparrows," attracted by advertisements in British newspapers, flocked in.[91] Early comers assisted friends at home to join them, while the Macclesfield unions sent others. Their belongings filled the Paterson depot: "the large, square boxes with ropes tied about them, the packages done up in coarse homespun canvas and the strings of tins and kitchen utensils." [92] In 1882, as an English traveler observed, "a well-skilled artizan," such as one he met on shipboard, who "by a thoroughly experienced knowledge made himself invaluable to his firm, especially in the dyeing of the blended shades which have been so fashionable," could command handsome wages along the Passaic.[93] Even though American techniques changed during the 1880's, the mills welcomed experienced English, Scottish, German, and French weavers and paid them to learn the new methods.[94]

It has been estimated that between 1870 and 1893 about fifteen thousand Macclesfielders, as well as many Frenchmen, emigrated to Paterson.[95] "Here," Brierley wrote, "I could listen to my native dialect in its almost pure state, and stumble upon faces that I had missed without knowing to what 'bourne' they had gone." As for the Paterson mill girls, "They'n some bant about 'em, thoose han, an' fit to be th' mothers of a young nation. Besides, they'n lost noane o' their English prattiness, an' they are no feart o' wark." [96] Standing over their looms, Paterson ribbon weavers sang Methodist hymns together as they once had done in Coventry.[97] In Macclesfield, men spoke of Paterson as familiarly "as if it were only a run of half an hour by train." [98] They shuttled easily between America and the homeland as wages rose and fell.[99] Of course, the English were not the only skilled hands in Paterson; it was "Pfingsten Monday" rather than Whitsuntide when the mills took an annual holiday.[100]

In 1890 higher American protection for plush and velvet brought more silk manufacturers and operatives to the States.[101] But the law of 1885 against alien labor contracts, even though it exempted men with novel skills, obstructed the velvet weavers' coming.[102] And like the cotton operatives, silk workers were discouraged by Paterson's high rents and food prices and by "the tyranny and oppression of the moneyed autocrats."[103] Furthermore, during the late 1880's and the 1890's improved throwing and weaving machines permitted manufacturers to leave Paterson and turn to women and other untrained hands in place of the Macclesfield and Coventry men.[104] In 1890 a fourth of the foreign-born silk workers in America were British, but thereafter Italians and other foreigners, first appearing as strikebreakers, gradually replaced them.[105] By 1910 few British silk workers were coming to the United States.[106]

The machine-made lace and lace-curtain industry of America also grew up on a blend of tariff protection and immigrant skill and capital. In Britain, lace was a Nottingham specialty, though by the 1870's it had spread to Ayrshire as well.[107] In 1883 a small Brooklyn plant hired eight Nottingham men to operate its new machines, but the American industry was puny until the McKinley tariff of 1890.[108] Since the British industry could not prevent tariff-supported American wages from luring its men, English and Scottish firms themselves soon established mills in Pennsylvania and Connecticut. There were also new plants in New York state.[109]

New to America, the lace mills could legally import skilled men from abroad even after 1885. By the end of the century most of the experts were Nottingham men, and for many years thereafter weavers, designers, and draftsmen were usually English, Scottish, or French.[110] At the largest Philadelphia lace works in 1903 nearly all the weavers were English, some brought over by the company and some by friends who had preceded them.[111] The Kensington section, which had seen two generations of British textile workers, welcomed more Englishmen and Newmilns Scots.[112]

While British skills were necessary to launch this like many another American textile trade, mill owners as usual hastened to train less expensive laborers. They situated new mills in northeastern Pennsylvania to exploit the unoccupied women of the coal towns.[113] But although many British lacemakers returned home whenever depression hit the American trade after 1905, as late as the 1920's their countrymen still filled the best jobs.[114]

American thread making was a particularly exclusive province of British capital and labor. Scottish and Ulster companies set up American branches and recruited operatives from their home mills. The Clark company of Paisley introduced machine making of cotton thread to Newark, New Jersey, during the 1850's.[115] Barbour's linen thread works at Lisburn in Ulster established a Paterson branch in 1864 to get within the new tariff wall.[116] Most of Clark's employees during the rest of the century hailed from Paisley, and Barbour's, including many girls, from the North of Ireland.[117] During the 1880's a Glasgow linen-thread firm filled its mill at Grafton, Massachusetts, with Scots; J. & P. Coats of Paisley operated a large Pawtucket mill; and the 1890 tariff prompted the Kerr Thread Company to move its Paisley plant to Fall River.[118] Wages at Clark's and Coats's American factories were nearly double those paid in Scotland.[119] When companies controlling over four-fifths of American thread production combined in 1898 as the American Thread Company, this was called "a British-American affair."[120]

Linen-thread spinning thrived better than did linen-cloth weaving in the United States. During the nineteenth century Irish linen production had far outstripped that of the English and even the Scottish mills.[121] In America linen had never outgrown the household manufacturing of colonial days. The few nineteenth-century mills relied largely on Scottish or Northern Irish skill.[122] Two Forfarshire men in the 1870's made Andover, Massachusetts, "a second Brechin"; thirty years later Brechin, Arbroath, and Dundee people were still coming to their linen works.[123] As for jute, Dundee capitalists and superintendents in 1844 started a Paterson mill which for many years was practically the entire American industry, and

Dundee operatives arrived in California in 1868 to make jute bags.[124] But although American thread manufacturers recruited young women spinners from around Belfast, there was little chance for other linen workers to ply their trades in America.[125]

Besides the British thread, lace, and silk manufacturers who set up branch mills in America, foreign textile operatives often rose through the ranks of overseers and superintendents eventually to establish their own factories. Many woolen, carpet, and hosiery manufacturers in Philadelphia had begun as English and Scottish immigrant weavers or knitters. Paterson silk was the special bailiwick of English, French, Swiss, and German mill owners. Though few English or Scottish operatives worked in the Hudson and Mohawk valleys, several ultimately acquired knitting mills there. New England likewise had its British-born knitwear manufacturers. In the management of the much greater woolen and worsted trade the British predominated as in the weaving rooms. Several dyeing and printing works in the Northeast were also in the hands of men who had learned their chemistry in England.

In the Fall River and New Bedford area, however, where Lancashire cotton operatives abounded as nowhere else, old Yankee families kept control throughout the century. Many Lancashire lads bossed departments, but very few became superintendents, agents, and treasurers. Though elsewhere in New England there were far more Irish and French Canadian than English cotton workers, many of the latter did rise to the top. Of the entire American textile industry, Englishmen and Scots owned and managed a greater share than all other foreigners together.[126]

Despite differences in time and rate of development between various branches of the textile trade in the United States, the immigration of their British operatives followed a general cyclic pattern. Coming in the early years of American manufacture of cottons or woolens, silks or hosiery, they were well rewarded for their old-country skills. Eventually, as American mills perfected new machinery, British training lost its value to Fall River, Lawrence, Paterson, or Philadelphia employers, who hired Italian, Slavic, or native American laborers. In a branch of the industry like cotton, with a high proportion of cheap, coarse fabrics adaptable to simple machine production, this change came earlier than in finer goods. And in the coarser grades high speed made working conditions uninviting to British artisans. But though displaced as operatives, in every textile trade English and Scottish spinners and weavers climbed into managerial jobs and even to proprietorship. All together, as mill owners, superintendents, overseers, carders, spinners or throwsters, weavers or knitters, dyers or printers, British immigrants formed the strong warp threads of the rising American textile industry.

4

Pick and Powder Charge

Coal and ore miners were workingmen as skilled as any of the British immigrants who helped establish American industries. Labor underground and life in isolated mining villages set them apart from other men. Even if not born into the calling, one usually entered it as a boy and, having learned to work and survive in the depths, was unlikely to leave for the lower pay of some unskilled job.[1] Only news of more promising mines abroad led a miner to emigrate. Since coal-hewers and ore-diggers had unlike skills, each group went to its own kind of pit in America. And, like the textile operatives, miners immigrated only when their own skills were in demand.

On both sides of the Atlantic, coal fed the fires of nineteenth-century industry and commerce. Blast furnaces, factories, railways, and steamships — first in Great Britain but soon in America — burned an ever-mounting tonnage. In Britain the mining industry boomed in the old coal regions near the coasts and up the river valleys of Durham, Northumberland, Cumberland, the Lowlands, and South Wales and spread inland by canal and railway into Lancashire, Yorkshire, and the Midlands. During the four post-Napoleonic decades the annual British output doubled and redoubled; by 1914 it had quadrupled yet again. During the 1860's there were over three hundred thousand men in the pits; thirty years later, more than five hundred thousand.[2]

From this ever-growing labor force British collieries had miners to spare for the United States. American forests provided plenty of charcoal for iron smelting long after England perforce had resorted to anthracite or coke, but after 1830 the American iron industry as well as the new railroads and factories called for coal.[3] Hastening after Yankee dollars, English, Scottish, and Welsh miners kept the new American pits' output abreast of the sudden demand.

"We have been bungling, making shift, and skimming the surface of our coal field long enough," complained the Pottsville *Miners' Journal* in 1827; the first sixteen English miners whom local operators imported were expected to inaugurate "something like a methodical system." [4] For coal-hewing was an exacting trade. Then and during most of the nineteenth century miners won the coal mainly with the pick. Crouching or lying on his side, the collier carefully undercut the seam until a driven wedge or a light powder charge could bring it crashing.[5] Unexcelled at working thin veins in the homeland, immigrant British miners could "use the pick in the narrowest space, right and left, and in all positions . . . Holding it in front and making short, quick strokes, the pick is . . . effective in their hands in a space of three or four feet (or even less)." [6] In order to survive they had also to know the art of shoring up mine ceilings with timbers and to recognize the deadly fumes of "black damp" and "white damp."

Crowds of English miners arrived in the eastern Pennsylvania coal fields during the late 1820's. But all along the upper Schuylkill and Susquehanna valleys from Pottsville to Carbondale they yielded first place to the Welsh. The British anthracite and "steam coal" fields lie in South Wales; the American anthracite, in this corner of Pennsylvania. Since until 1869 most coal raised in America was anthracite, the immigrant miners were apt to hail from the valleys of Glamorgan, Carmarthenshire, and Monmouthshire. Already for thirty years Welsh immigrants had been settling in central New York state, western Pennsylvania, and Ohio. Though some had been miners in Wales, they had no choice but to learn American farming.[7] From 1830, however, Welsh colliers were in demand for their own skill. Soon after twenty families arrived at Carbondale in that year, mine owners dispatched two Welsh preachers home to recruit more miners; the first comers also encouraged their friends and kinsmen to follow them.[8] During the following decades ambitious Welsh pick wielders made for Scranton and Wilkes Barre rather than for bituminous mining towns in nearby England and Scotland or in America.[9] Every collier with whom one traveler through South Wales talked in 1857 had "either a father, brother, son, uncle, nephew, cousin, or at least some near friend in America — and had . . . been cogitating about going himself."[10] Perhaps some English miners in eastern Pennsylvania had likewise worked in South Wales.[11] Others were Durham pitmen.[12] Scots were few, though a Wanlockhead colony grew up in Pittston.[13]

During the depressed years of the late 1830's and 1840's wretched working conditions in British mines shocked Parliament into regulating mine hazards and outlawing female and child labor underground.[14] In Pennsylvania, where the first safety legislation was not passed until 1869, conditions were worse in mining than in most other American industries. But since feeble ventilation and flimsy pit props were less perilous there than in the much deeper British mines, immigrant colliers braved the risks for the sake of the good wages.[15] By 1848 a close observer of the American anthracite industry could say, "The mining population of our Coal regions is almost exclusively composed of foreigners — principally from England and Wales, with a few Irish and Scotchmen."[16]

From the wartime boom of the 1860's until the panic of 1873 more thousands of Welsh and English and a few Scottish miners came to dig Pennsylvania anthracite. When some new mine was opened, the native Pennsylvania Dutch were frequently the first hired, but British immigrants soon trooped in from the older pits, others straight from the steerage not far behind.[17] By 1888 the 3,755 underground workers of one coal company were 29 per cent Welsh, 12 per cent English, and less than 1 per cent Scots (Table 3). When the Civil War profits in Nova Scotian coal collapsed in the late 1860's, Canadian miners also moved to the States.[18]

While the Welsh led in anthracite, there were also bituminous miners among them to exploit the fields of western Pennsylvania, Maryland, West Virginia, Ohio, Illinois, Iowa, Kansas, and the Far West. In the Mahoning and Hocking valleys of Ohio and the

Table 3.

Employees of the Wyoming Division, Lehigh & Wilkes-Barre Coal Company, 1888.*

Nationality	Inside workers	Outside workers
English	439	88
Welsh	1,099	69
Scots	23	15
Irish	744	372
German	94	176
Scandinavian	42	4
French		1
"New immigrants"	989	993
Native American	324	500
Total	3,754	2,218

* Pennsylvania Inspectors of Mines of the Anthracite and Bituminous Coal Regions, *Reports*, 1888, p. 99.

George's Creek field of western Maryland many a Welshman hewed coal.[19] But since it was English and Scottish miners who best knew a bituminous face, in most mines west of the Alleghenies both outnumbered the Welsh. During the 1860's thousands of colliers arrived from Staffordshire, Durham, and Scotland.[20] Of Irwin, Pennsylvania, at that time an English miner later recalled: "The work, locality, and people were all we could desire. There were a number of Durham people and some from other parts of the country. In fact, no matter in what part one might be some English dialect fell on your ears." [21] When Alexander Macdonald, the British miners' union leader, visited coal towns from Maryland to Illinois, he regularly attracted crowds of his brother Scots.[22]

In Illinois, Braidwood was Scottish, and several other pithead towns had large English and Scottish populations.[23] Welsh miners moved from the East to Bevier and Huntsville, Missouri.[24] Such Iowa towns as What Cheer — its name echoing the cry of the Scot who discovered coal there — and Hiteman, where the Welsh worked after 1889, also attracted the British.[25] Between the 1860's and 1890's others went to the new fields of Kansas, Oklahoma, Wyoming, Colorado, Utah, California, and Washington.[26] As late as 1911 there were two hundred Welshmen at the coal camp of Carbonado, Washington.[27] Although in southern Illinois and most coal fields farther south native American labor, white or black, predominated, a few Welshmen moved down from Pennsylvania to Kentucky and Tennessee, and British miners were among the first in the Alabama pits around Birmingham after the Civil War.[28]

Of course the British were not the only immigrants nor even the only skilled miners in American collieries. At many mines during the 1850's and 1860's Irishmen and Germans outnumbered them, and there were other Europeans. Some of the Irish, too, had become skilled in the coal shafts of Scotland, the North of England, and South Wales.[29] But their countrymen who came straight from coalless Ireland, "totally ignorant of any branch of skilled labor," necessarily served first as laborers, above ground or below, leaving to experienced hands the better-paid task of getting the coal.[30] In time they too might join the underground aristocracy. Of men who happened to be involved in mine accidents in 1885 in three Pennsylvania anthracite districts, half the Irish were classed as miners, as high a proportion as among the English and Welsh.[31]

Unlike Ireland, Germany had coal, but strong labor organizations and government-regulated benefit funds kept her skilled miners at home. "Thousands of Germans work in the coal mines of the United States," the Ohio mine inspector noted in 1880, "but question them and you will find that they, with rare exceptions, never saw a coal mine in fatherland." [32] While men of many nations might become expert miners in America, the British most easily proceeded directly from steerage to coal face.[33]

Hard times in Great Britain intermittently spurred the colliers' exodus. During Scottish depressions in the 1860's, Macdonald said a few years later, "thousands of our men left the country." On his travels after the Civil War he had found seven thousand of them in Maryland, three thousand in Pennsylvania, two thousand in Illinois, and "large colonies" in Ohio.[34] The high wages which Macdonald noted there encouraged his followers to emigrate.[35] In 1879 the North Wales Miners' Association offered seven pounds to any member who would go to America.[36] A little later, when good times had returned to the United States but not to Britain, a conference of miners' representatives at Manchester agreed to establish a national emigration fund.[37] The Durham Miners' Association during the 1870's also urged unemployed members to leave the country.[38]

Sending excess miners to America was apt to prove impractical, however. A prolonged shutdown of American mines might bring them back home, perhaps to leave again with better times. They preferred traveling back and forth in steerage to abandoning the mines for some new occupation, as native Americans were wont to do.[39] Thus many left for home during the mid-1870's. In fact, early in 1873, even before depression overtook the American mines, rising wages in Britain drew back hundreds of recent emigrants. Nevertheless, Macdonald told a Parliamentary committee, "many of them have their return passage tickets, and whenever the wages come to 4s. or 5s. or 6s. a day again, they will not be found here but will be off" to America.[40]

News of American prosperity, therefore, usually started British miners streaming toward the docks of Liverpool and Glasgow. In South Wales they kept an eye on the state of trade in America; "good times" at home merely gave them the means to make the voyage.[41] But not all those who were attracted by high wages intended to remain in America, even should that country's prosperity last forever. Macdonald observed in 1873 that "hundreds of youths in Scotland . . . go out for the run in the summer season in the United States." With steerage passage and railroad fare on the "emigrant cars" costing only ten or twelve pounds, they could earn as much as twenty pounds a month during the summer. Returning in October, some resumed work in Scottish pits, and others loafed until the next spring's sailing.[42]

During the 1880's many also went out, as the American consul at Dunfermline reported, "with the purpose of remaining a year or two, or possibly longer, and earning and saving a nice little sum with which to return to Scotland to live in comparative comfort." Miners appeared at the consulate to exchange gold eagles for sovereigns; one "created a sensation by returning to his native village, near Dunfermline, wearing a full suit of broadcloth clothes. He had been absent seven years . . . seemed to have plenty of money, and had no intention of returning to the States." [43] Men who decided to remain in America also made known their success. As early as 1848 the British miners of Pennsylvania were said to be sending home thousands of dollars annually or using their savings to bring their families to join them.[44]

Yet British miners, when asked to compare their condition in America with what it had been at home, bitterly complained of long hours and irregular working days, lack of legislation to enforce safety precautions on mine operators, company stores which fleeced them out of their high wages, and a dearth of reading rooms or other provision for their little leisure time.[45] As for company houses, Macdonald testified that through their roofs the miners "had the benefit of seeing both the sun and the moon." [46] When one collier, who in South Wales had worked a fifty-four hour week for 6s. 7½d. ($1.65) a day, arrived in Pennsylvania "in the flourishing times of 1872," he found soft-coal miners working sixty to a hundred hours a week. Despite their extra dollar a day, he "could not see that their condition was any better than the British miner." "Those who had large families needed all they could get, and they are in need of it yet, God knows." [47]

Macdonald estimated that the American cost of living reduced the real wage advantage there to only two shillings (fifty cents) a day; furthermore, "there is in America at least one shilling's worth less comfort." [48] An Englishman who at home had earned $1.40 for a six-hour day, about two hundred and fifty days in the year, with merely nominal rent and cheap medical care, complained that in Pennsylvania "a miner only gets an opportunity to work a few months in the year and consequently has to work all the hours God sends — in fact, make a beast of himself or else starve." [49] Another immigrant of twenty years' experience in the pits of Scotland held that although miners there had lower wages, coarser food, and fewer luxuries than in Pennsylvania, constant work made them more contented than their countrymen in America.[50] Some Welsh-Americans felt that "many of the workmen of America, especially the miners of Pennsylvania, are in a condition of serfdom as compared with Welsh miners." [51]

Depression could wipe out what wage advantage America did offer. After two slack years in Pennsylvania a Durham bituminous collier complained in 1885 that in spite of working thirteen hours a day he had sunk two hundred dollars in debt.[52] Even Durham pitmen who emigrated during a British slump in 1881, when American mining was thriving, soon warned their friends at home about the adverse American conditions, and many returned as soon as possible.[53]

But at least the experienced British colliers might rise from the ranks to become foremen and superintendents. In Illinois it was a Scottish pit boss, James Braidwood, who introduced "long wall" mining in place of the "room and pillar" method under the town which later bore his name.[54] Looking back to the years just after the Civil War, an old Irish miner of Schuylkill County recalled that "the mine bosses of that day were all either English, Welsh, or Scotch. There was not a single Irishman or German amongst them." [55] During the next thirty years the latter likewise began to rise. Since, unlike most American workers, miners trained their sons to succeed them, toward the end of the century the older immigrant nationalities still retained the best jobs.[56]

After Pennsylvania in 1885 required mine foremen to pass an examination for certificates of competency, the state's anthracite examiners and most of the successful candidates had Welsh, Irish, or English names, and some others, Scottish and German.[57] Scotsmen managed nine large bituminous mines in western Maryland.[58] The names of many Ohio superintendents and foremen were Welsh.[59] Welsh immigrants ran half the collieries of Washington state in 1894.[60] In several states the mine inspectors, appointed to enforce the new safety codes of the 1870's, were onetime immigrant British miners.[61] In 1903, in fact, the seven Illinois inspectorships were divided among five Englishmen, a Scot, and a Welshman, all with lifelong experience in the mines, while the head of the state mining board was an erstwhile Lancashire collier who had become the leading coal operator of the Peoria district.[62] Although it was difficult to become an owner and employer, at least one Welsh miner, James Jones, made a million shipping coal.[63]

But while the British and Irish and their sons bossed the mines, the proportion of their countrymen in the working force steadily declined. As elsewhere, American methods eventually rendered British training obsolete. It was cheaper to blast the coal "from the solid" than to undercut the vein with the pick. For necessary undercutting the American industry also rapidly developed mining machinery.[64] In Illinois, for example, in 1891 only thirty-four mines used undercutting machines; by 1900 thirty-eight depended exclusively and twenty-nine partially on such equipment; seventeen years later ninety-eight mines used only machines, and fifty-three both machinery and pick-swinging men. The number of cutting machines in Illinois increased from 241 in 1891 to 1,920 in 1917. From 1888 to 1909 the amount of blasting powder annually used increased eightfold.[65]

These technological advances heralded the advent of Italian and Slavic laborers among the mineworkers, beginning in the mid-1870's.[66] Clumsy they might be, but with explosives and machines they could send more coal to the breakers and yet work for less than the old pickmen. "Stripping," or surface quarrying of shallow seams, could be done entirely by Hungarians.[67] British miners, already disgruntled with American conditions, began to leave the industry. Down to the Scranton depot on their way back home trooped scores of Welshmen in 1890, their American citizenship forgotten.[68] And while most British-American colliers stayed in the United States, new arrivals no longer kept their ranks full. Many a skilled man landing in America after 1885 was suspected of having broken the law against prior contracts; deportation of a vociferous few further dissuaded others from coming.[69]

The steady change in nationality among Pennsylvania mineworkers went on during the 1890's (Table 4). Between 1892 and

Table 4.

Reading Coal & Iron Company Employees, 1890–1896.*

Nationality and parentage	1890		1895		1896	
	Number	Per cent	Number	Per cent	Number	Per cent
English	2,088	8.4	1,960	7.0	1,799	6.3
Welsh	1,282	5.2	1,112	4.0	1,037	3.7
Scots	210	0.9	223	0.8	168	0.6
Irish	6,887	27.8	6,450	23.0	6,025	21.3
German	3,709	15.0	3,471	12.4	3,207	11.3
"New immigrants"	5,819	23.6	9,000	32.2	10,286	36.2
Native American	4,719	19.1	5,765	20.6	5,838	20.6
Total	24,714	100.0	27,981	100.0	28,360	100.0

* G. O. Virtue, "The Anthracite Mine Laborer," *Bulletin of the Department of Labor*, no. 13 (November 1897), 751.

1918 fewer and fewer British and more and more "new immigrants" were involved in mine accidents in both hard and soft coal mines of the state.[70] Starting as laborers, many Slavic and Mediterranean immigrants ultimately rose to better jobs. Of 543 "new immigrant" mineworkers killed or injured in 1900 in seven of the eight Pennsylvania anthracite districts, 245 were miners.[71]

A British traveler visiting a Scranton mine about 1913 discovered most of the miners to be Poles, Ruthenians, and Russians.[72] At another anthracite shaft, which Welshmen had first worked in 1868, the force in 1910 consisted of: "managers and superintendents, Welsh; foremen and bosses, Irish; contract miners, Poles and Lithuanians; and outside laborers, Slovaks, Ruthenians, and Italians." [73] Throughout the Pennsylvania hard-coal region in 1914 only 5 per cent of the underground workers and 4 per cent of those outside were British-born; "new immigrants" comprised 65 and 40 per cent of these groups (Table 5). As for bituminous miners, though as late as 1897 at a new western Pennsylvania pit four-fifths of the 1,500 workers were skilled Englishmen, within two years they began to give place to Hungarians, Slavs, and Italians.[74] In the soft-coal industry of the state in 1919 a mere 3 per cent of the inside and 2 per cent

Table 5.

Pennsylvania Anthracite Mineworkers, 1914.*

Nationality	Inside	Outside
English	3,240	894
Welsh	3,980	682
Scots	415	180
Irish	4,177	1,362
Canadian	12	11
German	2,065	877
Scandinavian	187	43
French and Belgian	45	12
"New immigrants"	87,203	19,020
Native American	33,496	24,920
Total	134,820	48,001

* Pennsylvania Department of Mines, *Report*, 1914, I, 55–56.

Table 6.

Pennsylvania Bituminous Mineworkers, 1919.*

Nationality	Inside	Outside
English	2,346	414
Welsh	586	140
Scots	1,350	271
Irish	1,253	308
Canadian	29	5
German	1,936	319
Scandinavian	1,098	177
French and Belgian	1,271	126
"New immigrants"	86,859	13,760
Native American	47,592	20,991
Total	144,320	36,511

* Pennsylvania Department of Mines, *Report*, 1919–1920, II, 29.

of the outside employees were British; the "new" nationalities supplied 60 and 38 per cent (Table 6).

Some of the British left Pennsylvania for mines farther west, but the change overtook them there too. In 1890 a fifth of the Illinois skilled miners were British-born; nine years later only 15 per cent of mineworkers of all grades were British, while the "new immigrant" miners had more than doubled in number.[75] In 1904 a tenth of the colliers were British, only half as many as the "new" groups.[76] In one Illinois mine the loaders and many miners were Bulgarians and Greeks, though Scots, Englishmen, and Americans held the responsible positions.[77]

Thus passed the British epoch in American coal. By 1910 at many an old Pennsylvania Welsh-American mining center visitors found that "the Welsh population there had become almost nil . . . In Blossburg, Morris Run, Antrim, and Arnot, Polanders and Hungarians have taken their place." [78] At Lansford and Summit Hill forty or fifty years before, the Welsh "had the control of the mines, outside and inside; and they were also foremost in social and religious spheres." Now the surviving old-timers complained of "being forced out by degrees by the foreign element which crowd our country." [79] In 1913 one observed:

> Enough Welshmen could not be found in the Pennsylvania bituminous mines to organize a prayer meeting. While we have enough Welshmen still left in the anthracite mines to make up a big Eisteddfod . . . fully 75 per cent of those working in the mines here are foreigners . . . Sons of Welshmen never work in the mines unless it is a case of failure everywhere else.

Mining having fallen so low, Welsh-Americans could philosophically rejoice at this "healthy condition of affairs compared to the days when almost every Welshman sought work in the mines." [80]

British ore miners also had their day in America. But unlike colliers, who came from all the coal fields of Britain, most of those who dug lead, copper, and iron in America had learned their trade in the single county of Cornwall. Famous since antiquity for its tin mines, Cornwall during the first half of the nineteenth century produced most of the world's copper.[81] Yet Cornish copper and tin diggings sent more men to the American iron mines than did the great iron districts of Midland and Northern England, Scotland, and Wales. There was work enough in the homeland for iron miners; British ore production could not keep pace with the needs of the British iron and steel works.[82] But copper miners fell on hard times after 1860 as cheap new Spanish and American metal closed deep Cornish workings and drove Cornishmen to seek work in England, the colonies, and South and North America.[83] They hammered their drills into American lead, iron, silver, and gold as well as copper. "If you want to see our Cornish miners," a visitor to the home county was told in 1881, "you must go to Pennsylvania, to Lake Superior, to Nevada; you'll find very few of them in Cornwall."[84]

For a century and a half miners from Britain had been working American ore. In 1737 the son of a Cornish immigrant acquired and named the great Cornwall iron deposit of Pennsylvania.[85] In the 1820's Cornishmen were the first foreigners in the Wisconsin and Illinois lead region, which they, along with Northumbrian, Welsh, and Manx newcomers, dominated during the next twenty years.[86] Later in the century Cornishmen raised iron and copper in New Jersey, emery in Massachusetts, and nickel in Pennsylvania.[87] Welshmen and Scots also knew ore when they saw it. After a Welsh collier in the Mahoning valley in 1854 informed the operators that their refuse coal was really blackband ore, it became the basis of an "American-Scotch" foundry-iron industry. During the late 1870's a Scottish company attempted to work the Tuscarawas County blackband in Ohio.[88]

In the 1850's Cornishmen and Welshmen, as well as many Britons who had never touched a pick, flocked to Leadville, Central City, and other mining camps of the Far West.[89] Nova Scotians, bigger men but less skillful, also appeared in the Colorado mines during the 1880's.[90] English and Scottish capitalists who invested in Colorado and Arizona mining lands sent out managers and miners from home.[91] In southern California in 1891 one such group bought the unique American tin workings; among their miners were seven Cornishmen, digging the ore which had made their ancestors famous for two thousand years.[92]

But the Cornish had their American heyday in the upper peninsula of Michigan, whence between 1845 and 1890 came most of the country's copper and iron ore. No sooner did picks scratch the first Keeweenaw copper and Marquette iron in 1844 than they were on hand. "Sipping beer and talking and singing in the Cornish dialect" aboard lake steamers, they sailed to the north country during the 1850's.[93] The Michigan mines speeded their exodus from the old low-grade copper workings of the homeland, which after 1865 could not hope to compete; immigrant skill redoubled America's advantage. As one new iron range after another was opened in Michigan, Wisconsin, and Minnesota — the Menominee in the 1870's and the Gogebic and the Vermillion in the 1880's — Cornishmen moved in from older American mines and from the home county.[94]

Irishmen, Germans, Swedes, Norwegians, and Finns also came early to upper Michigan, but no more than in the coal fields could they match British skill. The Cornishmen brought their mining techniques and equipment, their contract-labor system, and the lingo of the old "wheals." During the 1880's most mine bosses, or "bal cap'ns," were Cornishmen. Their countrymen, able to contract for the richest stopes, made the highest wages. "If there is a difficult shaft to be sunk or a tunnel to be driven in hard or dangerous ground," a state official reported, "as a general thing it is Cornish miners who are the men to do it." [95]

In the days before mining became an engineering science, empirical Cornish methods were the best. Mine captains sneered at a formally trained expert as "a man who wears eyeglasses, parts his hair in the middle, has graduated at Freiburg, and speaks abominably bad English." [96] If they were overly fond of the way in which ore had long been dug in Cornwall, for a time success justified them. Yet they also perfected new mining machinery and techniques, and in the 1880's their sons were among the first graduates from the new Michigan College of Mines.[97] Old-country skill at rock tunneling had many uses. Most of the men who between the 1850's and 1870's drove the Hoosac railroad tunnel through the Berkshires were Cornish; in 1869 English miners opened a passage under Broadway in New York City.[98]

As in coal mining and other industries, however, simplified processes and cheaper labor eventually took the place of British methods. Ore in the last great iron range, the Mesabi of Minnesota, lay close enough to the surface for open-pit digging. Since skill acquired in the bowels of Cornwall was of little use, few Cornishmen, except for some of the early captains and shift bosses, came to the Mesabi.[99] Copper mines farther west likewise got along independent of Cornish skill. In the early days of Butte one copper magnate did import Irishmen, and the other, Cornishmen, making these in 1900 the chief immigrant groups.[100] Utah and Arizona also had Cornish and Welsh miners early in the twentieth century. But carting away an exposed mountain of copper called for few rock tunnelers.[101] Even on the older ranges of Michigan, especially after the loss of a strike in 1895, working conditions were unsatisfactory. Emigrants from Cornwall went instead to the Witwatersrand, and Italians and Slavs filtered into the mines of the north country and the West.[102]

Thus in mining as in textiles British skill was vital in American industry's early days but lost importance after American techniques departed from the British model. British miners, like the textile operatives, moved up the ladder when unskilled laborers and new machines took over their old jobs. As foremen, mine captains, and inspectors, though seldom as owners, they long dominated the pits.

5

Furnace and Anvil

The American coal and ore which British miners had a hand in digging moved on through furnaces, forges, and foundries which likewise used British skill. For four-fifths of the nineteenth century the most important metallurgical advances originated in Great Britain and were copied in the United States. Although the American industry would have adopted these new processes even if no foreigners had come, British iron and steel workers did speed its growth. And no less than in textiles or mining, special skills won the British the best American jobs.

British ironmasters' technological leadership was due not only to England's long experience with small iron furnaces; colonial Americans had emulated these. But in the eighteenth and early nineteenth centuries the British industry, hampered by the shortage of timber, began to burn coal in place of charcoal.[1] But while the old-country iron and steel works rapidly expanded, America's inexhaustible forests kept her archaic charcoal furnaces aglow until the 1840's.[2]

When Americans at last turned to coal, British advice carried them over many hurdles. In 1783 three Scottish brothers built the first cold-blast furnace in Franklin County, Pennsylvania; the first Pittsburgh rolling mill, in 1812, was the work of an Englishman.[3] The Welshman Thomas Cotton Lewis in 1817 erected the first American mill for puddling and rolling bar iron and afterward built several more in Pennsylvania and Ohio.[4] Edward Nock, an Englishman who in Wales had learned the boiling method of puddling, introduced it to Pittsburgh in 1837.[5] In 1839 a Pennsylvania company hired a Welsh ironworks superintendent, David Thomas, who had mastered the hot-blast process in Scotland, to set up the first successful American furnace of this type.[6] William Firmstone, an English mill manager who immigrated in 1835, constructed early hot-blast furnaces in Ohio, Pennsylvania, and Kentucky. Both Firmstone and Thomas became leading pig-iron manufacturers.[7]

British experience with new fuels was also valuable. In the early 1830's Englishmen built the first Connellsville coke ovens.[8] At a cold-blast furnace Firmstone in 1835 pioneered in burning coke. He and Thomas also first fired American blast furnaces with anthracite.[9] In the Mahoning valley a Shropshire man, John Crowther, in 1846 used uncoked bituminous.[10]

The immigrants continued to pace the American industry through mid-century. In western Maryland an English company in 1844 rolled the first heavy iron railroad rails; the next year at Danville, Pennsylvania, a former English blacksmith, Benjamin Haywood, built the country's first rolls for making "T" rails and the first apparatus for sawing hot iron.[11] English workmen turned out the first American wrought-iron tube.[12] About 1867 John Player, an English manufacturer at West Conshohocken, introduced his improved hot-blast stove.[13] His countryman Samuel Broadmeadow made good blister steel in Pittsburgh about 1830, while at Cincinnati two years later William and John Garrard produced the first fine crucible steel.[14]

Several other technical innovations, perfected in the United States, were also the work of British-Americans. David Thomas about 1852 installed much stronger blowing engines than were used by British blast furnaces.[15] A Scot, Henry Burden, between 1825 and 1840 invented machinery for making spikes and horseshoes and for rolling iron.[16] During the 1850's Isaac Reese, son of a Llanelly ironworker, developed an improved firebrick; his brother Abram came forth with new rail-rolling equipment.[17] In Cincinnati in 1870 Samuel Danks from the Black Country devised a long-desired mechanical puddler which, though puddling itself was becoming outmoded, attracted the British industry's attention.[18]

Less ingenious immigrants than these, coming merely to do a job, were no less essential to the American industry. Iron puddlers without peer in the United Kingdom, Welshmen took ship along with their anthracite-mining countrymen during the 1830's and 1840's and soon were rabbling the red-hot pig in many a new American mill.[19] Soon others who had settled earlier on southern Ohio farms built their own charcoal-iron furnaces, drawing still more immigrants from Wales.[20] In new iron centers of the 1850's like Johnstown, the workingmen were chiefly Welsh.[21] Even in Richmond, Virginia, there were enough Welshmen at the Tredegar Forge and Rolling Mills for a rousing St. David's Day celebration in 1837.[22]

In 1857 a foreman in a South Wales ironworks told an American traveler that within the decade a score of men out of the mill's two hundred — "the pick of their workmen" — had left for the States; he himself "had many kindred in America and expected to join them in the spring." Welsh furnacemen could speak as familiarly about "Pottsville, and Catasauqua, Hanging Rock, or Johnstown as if those places were . . . Ebbw Vale, Ynyscedwyn, Pontypool, and Rhymney."[23] Immigrant guidebooks posted them on Pittsburgh wages, and Pittsburgh became "a good place for Welsh maidens."[24] As Youngstown or Trenton blew in new furnaces, skilled Englishmen and Scots also crossed the sea. Though Germans and Irishmen for the most part performed the rough labor in these early years, Irishmen who had learned the trade in Great Britain fared as well as the British.[25]

The latter continued to arrive in force during the Civil War and for more than two decades afterwards. British unions paid idle members' passage; American manufacturers recruited hands in England, Scotland, and also Germany; and trade journals demanded that arriving immigrants not be harassed even by the trifling head tax.[26] Thus the British turned up everywhere. A new Pittsburgh steel mill in the 1860's might get by with Pennsylvania Dutch laborers, but for skilled hands it hired Sheffield, Birmingham, and Manchester men.[27] In fact, ironmasters complained that native Americans were too apt to go back to the farm at harvest time.[28] At Knoxville a Welsh colony grew up around a Welsh-owned rolling mill.[29] In the 1870's the Welsh superintendent of a new Columbus steel-rail mill enlisted his crew chiefly from among his own former old-country employees and hired Welsh foremen, engineers, and even bookkeepers.[30] Other new works, down to an anachronistic charcoal furnace which went into blast on the wooded shore of Lake Superior in 1868, relied on Welshmen and Scots.[31]

During the long depression of the 1870's iron and steel workers, like others, practically ceased to immigrate. An English company in 1876 brought English workmen to its new Tennessee iron town of South Pittsburgh, and Scottish capitalists hired Scottish foremen to start mills in Tuscarawas County, Ohio, but both ventures failed.[32]

No sooner did the first rumors of reviving American prosperity reach the depressed iron and steel towns of Great Britain in 1879 than ironworkers again started across the Atlantic. Drawn by newspaper reports and steamship advertisements, some who could muster only the ocean fare were stranded in eastern ports, unable to reach the mills.[33] Many puddlers and rollers came under contract to American companies, despite the protests of men already employed; others made their way to Pittsburgh "on spec"—the hope of finding work.[34] The sudden influx was premature. Late in the year trade unions in both countries warned prospective emigrants that men were still out of work in the United States.[35] But as the American boom gathered momentum, and as British furnaces also were once more blown in, all found jobs.

The flood of newcomers in 1879 and the next few years was the last. Depression in 1884 again pinched off the movement. Furthermore, it was largely at the behest of the iron and steel workers' unions that Congress in 1885 forbade importation of contract laborers, who had been used as strikebreakers.[36]

More important, American manufacturers were ceasing to require foreign puddlers, rollers, heaters, and other skilled hands. To be sure, the revolutionary technological changes of the time still came from Britain. The Bessemer process began in England in 1858, the Siemens open hearth ten years later in South Wales, and the Gilchrist-Thomas basic process also in the United Kingdom in 1879.[37]

When Americans planned Bessemer works during the late 1860's, they pilgrimaged to England to study the new experiments there. But new processes no longer depended on immigrant British workingmen, who, in fact, now came to be regarded as a drag on further progress. Although a pioneer Bessemer plant near Harrisburg in 1865 planned to import a thousand skilled Englishmen, another at Johnstown started, according to one of its officials, "without a single man who had ever seen the outside of a Bessemer works" and with only a few who had any skills at all; most were simply "intelligent laborers . . . with no prejudice and without any reminiscences of what they had done in the old country." [38] Several early Bessemer steelmasters in America were British-born, but none had learned the process before immigrating.[39] Yet within a dozen years American mills' production records astonished British steelmen.[40] Outdoing the British in total output and inventiveness by 1890, the American industry no longer lived on foreign talents.[41]

American manufacturers disliked skilled British workers' wage demands no less than their conservatism. Carnegie's superintendent at Braddock, himself the son of a Welsh ironworker, said in 1875:

> We must steer clear as far as we can of Englishmen, who are great sticklers for high wages, small production and strikes. My experience has shown that Germans and Irish, Swedes and what I denominate 'Buckwheats' — young American country boys, judiciously mixed, make the most effective and tractable force you can find. Scotsmen do very well, are honest and faithful. But mark me, Englishmen have been the worst class of men I have had anything to do with.[42]

He put a young Welsh immigrant over his Bessemer department, but for ordinary hands it was cheaper to train European peasants who had no British preconceptions either of how to make steel or of proper hours and wages.[43]

Furthermore, here again British immigrants found an American industry less and less to their liking. The pace was too hectic. In the Pittsburgh mills in 1890 steelworkers earned more than men in England only because they had to work harder, produce more per hour, and go on for more hours a day than a British employer would dare demand. "I am quite a different man here," said one immigrant; "I can do more work; I feel that I have it in me, but . . . I shall be done in ten years." [44] Resistance was futile, especially after the steel workers lost their great strikes of 1892 and 1901.[45] Workingmen in Britain hesitated to emigrate to such a battlefield.

In 1890 the fifteen thousand British-born workers in the primary iron and steel industry were still a tenth of all employees and a quarter of the foreign-born.[46] British ironworkers still traveled back and forth as business improved in one country or the other, perhaps spending only the summer season in the United States.[47] Welsh colonies grew up in western iron centers such as Pueblo; in 1911 the opening of new mills was still welcome news in Welsh-American communities.[48] British experts continued to develop new methods for American companies, like Benjamin Talbot's continuous steel process of 1899 and the Roe puddler of 1902.[49]

But southern and eastern Europeans were flooding in. In most works built after 1900 few British immigrants were ever hired.[50] Similarly, since the Connellsville coke industry, in spite of its early inception by Englishmen, was a growth of the 1880's, it immediately acquired a "new immigrant" labor force.[51] The Polish, Hungarian, and Italian newcomers forced the British upward but not wholly out of the mills. Together with Germans, Scandinavians, and native white Americans, men from Birmingham or Sheffield held the better jobs down to the first World War.[52] At United States Steel's Homestead mill in 1910, British immigrants were 20 per cent of the skilled workers, 12 per cent of the semiskilled, and only 2 per cent of the unskilled. Of all the British, 47 per cent were skilled and 37 per cent semiskilled.[53]

"A considerable number of the heads of the American iron industry of today acquired their training, their knowledge, and their experience in British works," a visiting party of British ironmasters observed in 1901.[54] Some had come to America to establish mills for British capitalists or to invest their own money. Others had started work in American plants as superintendents. Skilled workingmen sometimes became superintendents and eventually owners. Perhaps a larger number, however, were born in Great Britain but grew up and learned the business in America; yet they — and others born in America of British parents — also acquired old-country experience from their fathers. As for the most famous British-born ironmaster, Andrew Carnegie, he never worked as heater, puddler, or roller in either country but happened to see his chance in a steel company's front office.[55] The English, Scottish, and Welsh immigrants who long were the linchpin of the American iron and steel industry were another breed.

One branch of that industry was torn from Great Britain during the 1890's and transplanted in tariff-fertilized American soil. Hitherto most of the world's tinned sheet iron had come from South Wales, the United States taking 70 per cent of it.[56] But tinplating was not profitable in America. In 1871 some Pittsburgh Welshmen, tinplaters in the old country, set up a small plant. Others manned new Ohio and Pennsylvania mills until South Wales cut prices ruinously during the hard times of the 1870's.[57] In the next decade such men again planned American works for which they recruited hands and bought machinery in the homeland; the Welsh union frowned on such schemes as a threat to their trade.[58]

After 1890 the McKinley tariff suddenly permitted new American tinplate mills to wrest the home market from South Wales. Although at first they had to import machinery, iron "black plates," and tin, Welsh-American ironworkers who had once been tinners were already on hand.[59] By 1892 American manufacturers were also importing workmen, and, with sixty mills and thousands of men suddenly idle in South Wales, large groups sailed of their own accord.[60] A few years later most Welsh works had shut down, while in the United States about forty mills were making and tinning their own black plates.[61] New tinplate towns like New Castle, Pennsylvania, suddenly rivaled Scranton and Pittsburgh as Welsh-American centers.[62] Welsh manufacturers moved all or parts of their plants to America, though, since the tariff protected only the final dipping process, many still imported all the materials from Wales.[63]

Whether owned by Welshmen or Americans, the early works relied on the skill of Welsh tinners using Welsh machinery and Welsh techniques. Within a few years, however, as equipment and methods were improved, Welsh workmen no longer were necessary nor, over-fond of time-honored ways, even desirable.[64] In one department of a large American plant in 1892 three gangs of Welsh and five of American tinplaters worked. The company asserted "that it was only a matter of honor on their part that they kept the Welshmen, as they got them for the purpose of starting the thing, but the American workmen were producing more from each mill." [65] Furthermore, as soon as the industry was well enough established for the law against alien contract labor to be applied, several Welshmen were turned back at the water's edge.[66] By 1906 the Welsh were a decreasing minority of the tinplate workers of Pennsylvania.[67] As South Wales found new markets in the following years, Welsh manufacturers even persuaded some of their old employees to return home.[68] Yet though new American mills imported no more hands from Wales, they frequently drew them from Welsh communities in the original American tinning centers, keeping up a lively Welsh-American interest in the state of employment in the industry.[69]

British immigrants held their place longer in those metalworking trades which required the highest proportion of skilled craftsmen.[70] Since foundries, machine shops, smithies, and the like were much smaller affairs than blast furnaces or rolling mills, the identity of their labor force is harder to trace. Yet many a Scot and Englishman did work for, and some owned, such companies.[71]

As the British shipbuilding industry shifted during the 1860's from the Thames north to the Tyne, Tees, Clyde, and other estuaries in the iron-producing districts, hundreds of wooden-shipwrights left southern England for America.[72] Before long there also appeared skilled iron-ship workers from the new yards of the north. The Irish-born shipbuilder on the Delaware, John Roach, preferred to hire American farmers and fishermen, who, though clumsy at the trade, would uncomplainingly work longer hours than the British.[73] Yet at a San Francisco yard in 1905 there was "hardly a man . . . from the chiefs to the workmen who [did] not speak with a strong Scottish accent." [74] George William Dickie, a California Scot whose forebears had been shipbuilders, became a noted marine-engine designer and steel-ship builder.[75]

The highly specialized steel trades of Sheffield and Birmingham trained many a man for American factories. Beginning to make saws in 1835, a Paterson manufacturer lured the essential men from Sheffield by offering high wages; immediately successful, he sent for more.[76] Between the 1840's and 1870's English and also German cutlers came to works in Pittsburgh and in Meriden, Bridgeport, and Waterbury, Connecticut.[77] American employers prized Sheffield workmen; "if from the factory of Rogers," an 1840 guidebook advised emigrants, "it is a sufficient introduction anywhere." [78] Urging a Sheffield blade forger to emigrate in 1867, a New York manufacturer requested, "Bring your hammers and other small tools and perhaps an Anvil or two." [79]

Hard times in the 1870's halved their wages in America, but in 1879 cutlers again came from Sheffield, where many were out of work. American duties against razors led a Sheffield manufacturer to pack both his workmen and his business off to the United States; the party even brought tubs of Sheffield water, believing no other suitable for hardening razors.[80] A Bridgeport cutlery works imported more than a hundred artisans, a remarkable sight as they transferred at New York to the Bridgeport ferry:

Some of [their luggage] was done up in bedquilts, and there were boxes of all conceivable sizes, colors, and modes of construction that must have descended from the fifteenth century, but scarcely a modern trunk among them all. It was primitive but picturesque — particularly as the stout, stolid-looking women made no more than the men of shouldering 25 cubic feet of box and carrying it as if it had been a band-box . . . Less surliness was never exhibited by a colony of immigrants. The men talked freely of their condition at home, of the cutlery business of Sheffield, and of the loss of prestige in the markets of the world which England has suffered of late.[81]

During the 1880's Sheffield trade unions assisted idle members to emigrate to American shops, which were glad to get rid of green hands who had not served an old-country apprenticeship.[82] But many cutlers of Sheffield, the American consul there reported, would never emigrate. "Though overcrowded, they love the old hive, their comparative freedom from strict rules, and their 'Saint Mondays' and many holidays." [83] Yet enough Englishmen did tear themselves away to form a quarter of the foreign-born "tool and cutlery makers" in America in 1890.[84]

Several lesser metal trades were built on immigrant skill. Weaving of wire cloth, used in paper making, was introduced to the United States in 1847 by an English manufacturer. This small industry attracted enough English and Scottish workmen to alarm the American wire-weavers' union.[85] When the Cornishman Richard Esterbrook organized his steel-pen company in Philadelphia in 1858, he brought artisans from Birmingham.[86] A Johnstown mill hired a crew of English wire drawers in 1879.[87] In Cleveland a chain and cable works boasted in 1873 that it had selected workmen "from some of the best shops in England." [88] Even the old American specialty of gunsmithing occasionally employed English craftsmen.[89]

The early growth of British textile manufacturing made Britain likewise the world's machine shop. Though spinners and weavers built their own early wooden jennies and looms, iron-machinery making soon became a trade in its own right.[90] The first American cotton and woolen mills ran on British-designed machinery, though they could not openly buy any until 1845, when Parliament repealed the ban on its export. Yankees also set up their own machine shops, at first copying smuggled British plans but soon outstripping their British rivals at many points.[91]

Throughout the century British machinists, or "engineers," brought their talents to American shops. An Englishman who emigrated in

1832 to manage a New York company took along Manchester "machine-makers, turners, filers, and fitters-up" with their tools.[92] An immigrant working at a Logansport railroad shop in 1873 wrote, "Our Formen here are nearly all English & Scotch men and many of the men also."[93] Though few British machine manufacturers moved to America, many an immigrant journeyman soon became a superintendent and within a few years had a shop of his own.[94] Staffordshire men and Welshmen headed a number of wrought-iron works in the 1840's.[95] Most machine-shop proprietors were native Americans, but Scots and Englishmen, like Richard Kitson in Lowell after 1849, were as famous.[96] Fifty years later on a tour of the States an English trade union official observed, "The first workshop I visited was . . . managed by a man from Manchester, in the second a Scotchman was foreman, and the third was controlled by a Crewe engineer."[97] Immigrating ironfounders and machinists were doubly in luck when they stumbled on such shops, where, a Fort Wayne Scot wrote in 1865, "the skilled British artizan will always get the leading work and the highest remuneration."[98]

British newcomers' superior skill annoyed some Americans. "Of course," said one employer in 1874, "if one has a pig-headed Englishman for a blacksmith, everything that does not come from Hengland is rubbish."[99] In 1865 a technical journal rebelled:

> English workmen are far behind our own, both in point of dispatch, accuracy of workmanship, personal cleanliness, and moral character. We judge from the samples we see among us. They are arrogant, boastful, uneducated, and continually prating about "the Clyde" and what wonderful achievements are performed on that classic stream, or else eternally sounding the praises of Maudsley and Fields, Napier-rs, etc. — to the disgust of our mechanics, who think, not unreasonably, that what "Napier" may do or not do is of very slight importance.[100]

On the other hand, to British workingmen accustomed to the engineering works of Birmingham a factory which might be the boast of Pittsburgh seemed no more than "the workshop of a locksmith."[101] But minor jealousies aside, their ability made British machinists welcome throughout America.

Depression or strikes in the engineering trades of Great Britain, unless paralleled in America, led machinists to emigrate. Men blacklisted during an 1852 lockout sailed for Australia or the States.[102] In the 1860's immigrant members of the Amalgamated Society of Engineers, the principal British union in the trade, organized their first American branches, expecting them to "prove of great service to many of our members who are emigrating to that country to seek employment, which . . . they cannot obtain in their mother country."[103]

American working conditions suited British machinists. Wages were higher than at home, jobs were steadier, and one could more easily find a new one when necessary. In 1904 a Yorkshire tool and die worker

> said that the majority of [American] firms would set a man on without fuss or trouble as to references, or even seeing him. For every job held he had merely written a letter offering his services, saying what he is expert in, and the salary he received at the last place.[104]

Yet rather than take a slightly strange job, many British immigrants when laid off were apt to return immediately to Great Britain.[105] Groups of machinists, molders, boilermakers, shipbuilders, and other metalworkers who had come from there, many — before 1885 — under contract, sailed home or on to Australia whenever hard times hit their particular callings.[106] At such times, furthermore, the American molders' and boilermakers' unions warned the British organizations against further immigration.[107]

When the depression of the 1870's lifted, American employers wrote to the British unions offering good wages to all comers.[108] Two or three hundred Bradford men who had lost their jobs in a strike left for Philadelphia.[109] During 1879 and 1880 membership in the North American branches of the A.S.E. nearly doubled.[110] The Engineers discontinued their emigration fund, however, expecting to see again many of the departed at the first reversal of the business cycle.[111]

In 1890 nearly a tenth of all machinists in the United States —

fully three-tenths of the foreign-born — were British immigrants.[112] During the next twenty-four years machinists and related craftsmen still crossed the Atlantic. In 1902 the A.S.E.'s American organizer advised them not to bother to negotiate for jobs before sailing: "You are only six days older when you land, and what is 3,000 or 4,000 miles for a young man? The way to get work is to go after it."[113] And go after it they did in good years, until in 1915 the war boom in British industry turned many homeward.[114]

Thus in certain American metal trades British training long remained in demand. Unlike the primary iron and steel processes, in which unskilled Europeans were so numerous by 1900, these callings required that the average workingman have a high degree of skill. Of course, as in other industries, employers preferred cheaper hands. They often hired British experts just long enough to teach their trade to lower-paid Americans; the latter advanced so rapidly that as early as 1840 a committee of the Commons heard that the Yankees "fancy we are out of date."[115] When the group of Sheffielders who went to Bridgeport in 1879 found that they were expected to instruct green and poorly paid Europeans, many threw up the job in disgust.[116] Like the finer textiles, however, these trades continued to need versatile craftsmen.

In the American iron and steel industry as a whole, British immigrants followed the same sort of cycle as textile operatives and miners. Indispensable when furnaces, foundries, and shops were first set up, their experience became outmoded — except in the most highly skilled crafts — as soon as the American industry could make its own way. But in the interval these trained English, Welsh, and Scottish hands were the puddler's rabble which stirred up the new heavy industry.

6

A Chest of Tools

Besides the three giants — textiles, mining, and heavy metals — several smaller but no less distinctively British trades contributed methods and men to nineteenth-century America. As these industries grew in the United States, some in their first uncertain decades and others over a longer period relied on British skill.

No British manufacture, however large, outshone the Potteries of Staffordshire.[1] American pottery, slowly outgrowing the artisan's workshop, attracted few immigrants before 1840. A Philadelphia porcelain manufacturer had English workmen in 1826. Eight years later a Liverpool man brought six hundred English white-ware workers to Troy, Indiana, but soon gave it up.[2]

An exodus from Staffordshire and the modern American pottery industry both began during the 1840's. English potters in 1844 were alarmed by unemployment and new labor-saving machinery. Though the offending devices were suppressed, the potters' union undertook to "make labor scarce" by sending idle members overseas. Not proposing to build an American rival to Staffordshire, the union planned to settle the emigrants on Wisconsin farms. Though this "Pottersville" scheme speedily collapsed, some emigrant potters did become farmers, and others started kilns in Illinois.[3]

At about this time East Liverpool, Ohio, and Trenton, New Jersey, commenced to share the title of the American Staffordshire. James Bennett, a Derbyshire potter, in 1841 discovered a suitable clay deposit along the Ohio and with his three brothers built the first East Liverpool kiln. They also started the smaller pottery industry of Baltimore.[4] A few years later another Englishman, James Taylor, who about 1832 was reputed "the first practical thrower upon the wheel" on "the English plan" in America, founded the Trenton works.[5] By the late 1860's Staffordshire immigrants manned thriving potteries, often replicas of those on the Trent, in both East Liverpool and Trenton. Besides importing English techniques, they worked under the English system whereby one workman hired and paid his helpers and contracted with the company for the group's piece rates.[6]

As in other manufactures, however, English skill soon passed to American laborers. Although many workmen at the twenty-four East Liverpool potteries in 1877 had served seven-year apprenticeships in Staffordshire, one employer observed that "our American boys seem to take hold without much teaching and in a few months become both expert and speedy." [7] New machinery also shouldered out old-country skills.[8] Nevertheless, to inaugurate some ware new to America or even to break a strike by their older workmen, manufacturers during the 1870's continued to import Englishmen.[9]

But a decade later few were leaving the Potteries for the United States. Tunstall folk told the American consul: "Oh, yes; a good many young fellows want to see the world and are led over by expectations and promises of high wages. But they always want to come back when trade is slack in the States." Some complained of frequent breakdowns and unsteady jobs in American works.[10] In 1890 there were only two thousand British-born potters in America, but they were a seventh of the total.[11] After 1900, except for "well-trained and experienced young managers from Stoke-on-Trent," they practically ceased to immigrate.[12] Through the years many Staffordshire operative potters became managers and owners in New Jersey and Ohio.[13] American manufacturers liked to recall their trade association's first meeting in 1878, when "old 'Jimmy' Godwin held up his glass and in his broad Staffordshire dialect asked the landlord if he did not have something bigger to drink champagne from." [14] The English Potteries left their stamp on the American industry's shops and front offices as well as on its tableware.

Only a small fraction of the immigrant skill which went into American glass was British. As early as 1808 a Pittsburgh company with English equipment and workmen started the first flint-glass furnace in Pennsylvania; an Englishman commenced making glass tableware there in 1820; and in Massachusetts in 1825 the Sandwich glass factory imported its first hands from England, Germany, and Belgium.[15] During the Civil War an agent recruiting soldiers for the North with false promises of jobs inveigled Ashton glassblowers to emigrate.[16] Later several new window-glass and plate-glass companies in Pennsylvania, Indiana, and Missouri imported crews from England, Belgium, Germany, and France.[17] An English trade union assisted unemployed Yorkshire glassblowers to leave the country; the American union, however, soon drove them home.[18]

As late as 1889 the dearth of skilled glassblowers forced a manufacturer at Jeannette, Pennsylvania, to import twenty-five Englishmen.[19] Throughout the American industry in 1890 the more than two thousand British glassworkers constituted 22 per cent of the foreign-born and 6 per cent of the entire labor force.[20] Within another ten years, however, skilled glassworkers, whatever their nationality, gave way to machinery run by unskilled Americans and southern and eastern Europeans.[21]

British immigrants were not essential to other American factory trades. Yet several large industries employed at least a few British specialists, and in several small ones a considerable proportion of the workers were British. During the 1840's Scots and Englishmen operated machinery in many an American paper mill.[22] Thirty years later George West, once a Devonshire paper worker, became the greatest paper manufacturer of the United States.[23] Several thousand boot and shoe makers from England and Scotland worked in America about 1890, though many returned home as machines supplanted custom work.[24] Yeovil glovemakers emigrated to Gloversville. In their small trade in 1890 British immigrants were 37 per cent of the foreign-born and 7 per cent of all employees; even twenty years later most of those still in the business had learned it in England.[25] Though negligible in American furniture-making, Englishmen and Scots appeared early at Grand Rapids, and as late as 1909 British craftsmen were brought there to make fine morocco-upholstered pieces.[26]

About 1840 American bank-note makers imported English copper-plate printers under contract. Such newcomers, "particularly if London workmen," an emigrant guidebook advised, "can invariably meet with employment immediately upon landing." The best lithographers hailed from London or Paris.[27] Experienced British printers — and green Canadian women compositors — were numerous enough during the 1880's to arouse the American unions to try to restrict further immigration.[28] Type founding in New York was said to be "almost exclusively in the hands of the Scotch artisans."[29] A few persons of British birth and training no doubt could have been found at any time in most other American industries, from cigar rolling to meat packing, but their skills were never indispensable.[30]

In this burgeoning industrial America where British immigrants ran factory machines and swung picks underground, the growing cities needed both skilled building tradesmen and men to fashion building materials. Among the latter, British workmen specialized in quarrying and cutting granite, freestone, and slate — stones common to the homeland. Their differing techniques and tools divided them into three distinct groups, and the geology of Britain determined their nationalities.

The quarries of North Wales made American slate the province of the Welsh. They worked slate on the lower Susquehanna as early as 1734, but for more than a century the tiny industry there was in native American hands too awkward for slate splitting. When after 1818 the United States imported slate from North Wales, the Caernarvonshire ships berthed Welsh families on top of their cargoes.[31] By 1845 skilled quarrymen from Blaenau Ffestiniog, directed by their countrymen who had leased likely sites, were exploiting the Peach Bottom slates of York, Lancaster, and Harford Counties.[32] At the same time Welshmen started quarrying in Northampton County in eastern Pennsylvania. Though by 1880

Germans and Irishmen performed the rougher labor, boom times soon brought more Welsh and English into Pen Argyl and Bangor.[33]

Welsh farmers in Maine in 1846 started a small slate industry, but New England's one great Welsh community sprang up on the Vermont–New York line, the third American slate belt.[34] Although quarrying began there in 1839, the industry practically dated from 1870. Welshmen were in the field as early as any. Pour into Poultney, Granville, West Pawlet, and Fair Haven though they did, during the 1880's and 1890's the quarry owners, many of whom were Welsh themselves, never could get enough of them. A twelve-year-old signal boy therefore earned more than his quarryman father had made in Wales, while the father himself enjoyed three times his old wages.[35] A severe slump in Wales after 1907 sent slateworkers swarming anew from Blaenau Ffestiniog, Bethesda, and Nantlle to the United States among other places.[36]

New England granite drew quarrymen and cutters from Cornwall and Devon and from Wales, but Scots, coming especially after the American tariff of the 1860's disrupted the great granite works of Aberdeenshire, made the trade their bailiwick.[37] During the later nineteenth century Scottish colonies gathered in such places as Quincy and Ware in Massachusetts, Vinalhaven and Rockland, Maine, and Concord, New Hampshire.[38] In 1906 a Scottish-American editor remarked:

> The Scotch community of Quincy is at present so intent upon their work of manufacturing granite tomb-stones and memorials . . . for the ensuing Decoration Day trade that little time is left for aught but counting profits . . . If the native population have had a feeling that the Scots are born into the world in a pall of gloom and have the blood frozen about their hearts, they are bound to be excused, for none of them ever saw a Scotsman enter their city who did not directly seek employment at the tomb-stone trade.[39]

During the 1880's the half dozen granite quarries of Barre, Vermont, became seventy; Scots kept their hand on every step from blasting to the delicate carving in the "stone sheds."[40] In quarries as far west as Wisconsin and in urban cutting shops everywhere

Scots, Englishmen, and Welshmen raised the granite and fashioned it with hammer and chisel at the "banker." [41] Since a small stone-dressing shop called for little capital, many an immigrant soon had his own.[42] At one in Quincy three Scots in 1869 introduced polishing machinery to America.[43]

In quarrying and working the soft freestones, other British immigrants brought their skills to the United States. Among the early nineteenth-century Welsh farmers of Oneida County, New York, were old stonecutters who soon turned their hands to the local limestone.[44] In northern Ohio during the 1860's the Englishman John Worthington, once a workman on the new Houses of Parliament and then a Toronto contractor, employed hundreds of Scots in his huge sandstone quarries.[45] At about the same time another English stonecutter, John Rawle of Chicago, exploited the Bedford limestone of southern Indiana.[46] In the event of strikes by the granite or stonecutters, their employers sometimes secured strikebreakers by advertising for skilled hands in Scottish, English, and Canadian newspapers or, after the contract-labor law of 1885, at least by recruiting them at Castle Garden.[47]

American unions objected to the Scots less because a few came under contract than because their sudden mass appearance each spring during the 1880's and 1890's dashed hopes of labor shortage and high wages. American winters shut down quarries and the open cutting sheds for three or four months a year; in Great Britain a man could work in any season, though for lower wages. The steamship gave the answer. In March and April crowds of Scotsmen landed at Boston and New York, worked through the season, and sailed back about Christmas "with a good bag o' siller for their mothers and sweethearts." [48] Should the American season turn out poorly, they left earlier and empty-handed.[49]

Union men who were year-round residents, not a few of them also Scottish immigrants, complained that these interlopers worked for "whatever wages they can get."

> Then they boast in Scotland of the big wages they got in New York, but which they certainly never received nor had the courage to demand.

This sort of thing is repeated year after year until the term of "greenhorn" is a bye-word and a reproach among Scotsmen who work here all the year round.[50]

But there was not enough winter work for all, and a British banker-hand seeking other labor might be told, "You have a trade and make good wages in summer." [51] Nova Scotians and New Brunswickers similarly worked in the Maine quarries during most of each year and went north to the lumber camps in the winter.[52] After 1890 the American unions gradually reduced all this seasonal migration by demanding exorbitant initiation fees from foreigners.[53]

In all branches of the American stone industry in 1890 there were nearly eight thousand British immigrants, 28 per cent of the foreign-born or 13 per cent of all. Nearly half were Scots. Since these census figures include both the slate, granite, and freestone trades, in which the British specialized, and others such as marble in which they did not, their proportion in their own trades alone was even greater.[54]

Before 1890 many native Americans and Italians, Scandinavians, and other immigrants, both skilled and unskilled, also entered the granite and freestone industries.[55] Thereafter the proportion of unskilled hands increased, most rapidly in freestone. Until nearly the end of the century all stone dressers were artists with their hand tools, but between 1895 and 1915 planing machinery displaced most soft-stone cutters. Pneumatic quarrying tools and sawing and polishing machinery also became common in granite, but carving this refractory stone still required old-fashioned handwork as well. Slate, which had to be deftly split, likewise defied machinery. Thus Britiish workmen held their place longer in American slate and granite than in freestone.[56]

British building tradesmen were even more migratory than the stonecutters. Bricklayers, stonemasons, carpenters, and painters drifted wherever new buildings were going up. Their skills were hardly strange to America, though an English steeplejack had to be hired to repair Fall River mill chimneys in 1885.[57] Yet they came on many an immigrant ship. American employers facing labor shortages or strikes during the 1860's advertised in British papers or sent agents to hire bricklayers and carpenters.[58] House carpenters from Canada and the Maritime Provinces often undercut union wages in New York and Boston.[59] As long as wooden ships were still built on the east coast, furthermore, ship carpenters and caulkers came from the Maritimes to yards in East Boston and other ports.[60]

"It's guid pay in summer, but in winter ye can walk the streets in New York."[61] Thrown out of work each winter like the stonecutters, many building tradesmen after the 1860's became seasonal migrants. In 1885 a New York bricklayer complained that seven or eight hundred English and Scottish competitors for jobs arrived every year: "In the winter you can't see none of them; they work their way over here on the steamers . . . What they can earn in one week will carry them back again."[62] The summer's savings and the short, cheap steerage passage permitted a man a thrifty winter back home even if unemployed. A Lancashire bricklayer whose wife and children "lived 'ome" said as he sailed from New York in 1887, "I goes 'ome every year and takes five 'undred dollars with me."[63] Stonemasons' wages in American cities being two or three times those in Britain, a season in New York might leave nearly half the summer's $700 in a man's pocket as he stepped ashore at Glasgow or Liverpool.[64] After a particularly dull winter in the Scottish trade, nearly every stonemason who could scrape together the passage money emigrated to recoup his fortunes. Two thousand landed in New York during six weeks of the spring of 1887, overcrowding the labor market there for lack of rail fare to inland cities.[65] British house decorators were said to have three seasons: America each spring; Scotland during the summer, when the upper classes were in London; and London in the autumn, when owners of town houses went to shoot in Scotland.[66]

American builders' unions at first welcomed the flood of initiation fees, which, by requiring members to renew their cards four times a year or even monthly, they extracted from seasonal migrants on each arrival.[67] Such devices frankly aimed at limiting the size of the labor force; aliens had to pay a higher scale of dues.[68] In 1890, however, fifty-two thousand British immigrants made up 17 per cent of the foreign-born building tradesmen, and thirty-two thousand British Canadians were another 11 per cent, respectively 5 and 3 per cent of all such workers.[69] And English, Scottish, and Canadian masons, carpenters, bricklayers, plasterers, painters, and plumbers continued to flock to American jobs.[70] Within two years after the San Francisco earthquake of 1906, for example, enough members of the British carpenters' union arrived there to support eight locals instead of the previous two.[71] Thus British building tradesmen, like quarrymen and some others, formed an international labor pool from which American employers could draw trained hands.

A few other British skills were in demand in America. Sailors from Britain and the Maritimes sometimes manned American vessels. After the Civil War the reviving Boston and Gloucester fishery brought as many as a thousand Bluenoses south each year for the season.[72] English sailors came to United States ports on the Great Lakes for the seven ice-free months of high wages.[73] The coasting trade and the lack of any Anglo-American agreement on maritime deserters further encouraged hundreds of British mariners to jump ship in American ports each year. "Fighting" second mates and boatswains drove them to desert, especially from Nova Scotian and New Brunswick vessels, "on board of which," a British consul reported in 1878, "'lime juice' and 'Act of Parliament' ships — by which is meant ships whose crews are regulated by law and not by brass knuckles and belaying pins — are held in high contempt." [74] British sailors often accused captains of virtually forcing them ashore in order to avoid paying their wages; most deserters in any case desired not to settle in the United States but only to find better berths.[75]

During the 1880's and 1890's British cotton merchants yearly brought hundreds of Canadian stevedores to Southern ports to load Liverpool ships. After working as "jammers" and "headers" at Norfolk, Savannah, or Pensacola from fall to spring, the longshoremen returned by train to New York, Boston, or Buffalo and thence home by water to load lumber vessels during the summer.[76] Forty years earlier many skilled lumberjacks in Michigan, Wisconsin, and Minnesota likewise had been Canadian and British immigrants, veterans of the New Brunswick and Maine camps.[77]

Among immigrant domestic servants, although some were disappointed not to find British conditions of service in the republic, none were more prized than English men and girls.[78] The New York police asserted in 1902 that in most cases of robbery by servants "the butlers, footmen, or valets . . . were formerly employed in English houses. It would appear that English servants . . . are . . . often engaged here with a minimum of inquiry or investigation." [79]

A few thousand agricultural specialists came to the United States. New private estates and public parks hired foreign gardeners and nurserymen. While Englishmen were more numerous, Scottish gardeners were especially esteemed. One Glasgow ship in 1884 brought a hundred such Scots, for most of whom jobs waited.[80] Some of the oldest seed houses in the country were founded by Scotsmen early in the nineteenth century; Calvert Vaux, one of the two designers of New York's Central Park in 1859, was an English landscape gardener; and hardly a city during the next fifty years lacked Scottish superintendents of parks, cemeteries, or private grounds.[81] A Somerset landscape gardener, John Davey, dignified "tree surgery" into an American profession.[82] And traveling through Kansas in 1885 with two pairs of ferrets, one old Englishman exterminated prairie dogs at one cent a head, making his own distinctively British contribution to the American economy.[83]

Together, these separate accounts of the American industries which made good use of those peculiarly British immigrants, the skilled industrial workers, indicate the special economic forces which led them to migrate. Of course the general state of America's economic health also touched them as it did peasants and laborers who lacked training valuable in the new country. In prosperous years it was westward ho! In lean years many returned home, where others deferred an American venture until better times. But having served industrial apprenticeships, the British followed a more precise pattern of movement. Reluctant to take up new trades, they kept a weather eye out for chances in their own both at home and abroad.

These skilled hands came from industries in which Great Britain led the world. Racing to match her, America required a direct transfer of British experience. Immigration could bring it. To start a gingham mill, a carpet factory, a tinplate works, or a pottery, or to open a coal, ore, or stone field, employers liked to have a leavening of foreign — usually British — workingmen, foremen, and superintendents. In the early days of such industries in the United States, British immigrants won wages and responsibilities unattainable at home. Thus they immigrated even when their trades were also flourishing in Britain, but especially if foreign — largely American — competition undermined them. As migration became easier, even men whose skills were already well known in the States responded to any sudden demand for them there. All in all, as a British workingman observed after a tour of American factories in 1903, "The more I saw the more convinced I became that America even today is largely dependent upon British-trained skilled labor in almost every department of industry." [84]

On the other hand, in an industry like gunsmithing, in which America was the leader, foreign training was neither essential nor much used. And even those industries which originally were based on immigrant skill ceased, once they became solidly entrenched, to call for foreign experts, preferring to train less troublesome and more adaptable European peasants or American farm boys. Thus in 1895 a Russian-American employer remarked that although his skilled English artisans

> were excellent workmen and perhaps in cleanliness and fineness of work surpassed the Americans, they were inferior to the latter in every other way — difficult at making a beginning, extremely conservative in their mode of work, and always exceedingly specialized. [They] knew a certain part of the job; nothing else interested them. In the great majority of cases they learned nothing else; as they left their training, so will they die.[85]

As American manufacturers adopted labor-saving machinery—"a matter not so much attended to in England as its importance deserves," a British visitor lamented—British workers clinging to painstaking, almost handicraft methods were a brake on progress.[86]

After 1890 it was probably not so much any great lessening of the American wage advantage which discouraged British workingmen from immigrating as it was American employers' preference for unskilled new hands. In fact, American technical progress after 1890 in, for instance, the cotton mills, by raising the individual's output, actually increased this wage differential.[87] Furthermore, in British industries generally the decade after 1900 saw wage rates stagnate and the cost of living rise.[88] Sluggishly rising real wages in some American industries perhaps did dampen British interest in emigrating.[89] Only the highest American wages could overcome dislike for the long hours, fast pace, and unregulated working conditions.

> Many of these workmen informed me [reported the working-class visitor of 1903] that they would have preferred to remain in the old country. Several expressed a wish that they were returning with me, but all admitted that there are openings in America which would never occur in England, and as their skill was their only capital, they felt compelled to accept the opportunity.[90]

Wherever American industry continued to need and to welcome with high pay their old-country skills, they were still willing to put up with American working conditions.

Emancipated from the skilled craftsman by machinery, in 1885 American employers were undismayed by the new union-sponsored law against recruiting labor abroad.[91] But the new red tape discouraged the British. Of Ellis Island in 1903 a machinist complained:

> We were so hungry, but nothing could be had. After parading past the doctors and getting our passes stamped, we arrived at a desk attended by a clerk and an interpreter, who inquired in five tongues, 'How much money have you?' 'What nationality are you?' 'Where are you going and who to?' These and a host of other questions were asked, and with

scant courtesy . . . Although no doubt the U. S. A. system is smart, yet civility should be practised by the officials.[92]

An occasional skilled workingman, deported upon arrival merely for having corresponded with friends in America about prospects for work, returned loudly denouncing Yankee officialdom.[93] Whether American employers wanted them or not, British emigrants now thought twice before casting their lot in the United States.

Thus in most American industries — iron and steel by 1870, coal and iron mining by 1880, most textile processes by 1900, and even upstarts like tinplating by 1905 — the original English, Welsh, and Scottish skilled hands lost their place to peasant greenhorns, Irish or French Canadians before 1880, southern and eastern Europeans thereafter. Many were able to move up into managerial jobs or even ownership, but, for their countrymen who might have followed them to America, opportunities were drying up. After the 1880's British immigration no longer kept pace with the expansion of American industry and population. Though between 1903 and 1914 more Britons annually sailed from the United Kingdom than during any previous dozen years, not a third went to the United States.[94] Thus ended not simply another phase in the old immigration cycle but a whole era during which British immigrants had helped a score of American industries to dwarf those of Great Britain herself.

7

The Rights of Craftsmen

The dexterity with shuttle, pick, or chisel which raised British immigrants to the top of the nineteenth-century American working class also made them leaders of the trade-union movement. Having already tested the bargaining strength of their indispensable skills in Great Britain, in the United States these craftsmen once again fought for their own interests. Of course the American labor movement, like that of France or Germany, would have grown even without the personal guidance of British unionists. In every country workingmen had to band together against great, impersonal corporate employers. But it was British immigrants, in the American trades in which they worked, who both formed the nucleus of the skilled working class which first turned to unionism and also infused into the new labor movement the essence of British trade unionism.

British craftsmen had long been more attuned than Americans to the idea of collective action. If a Yankee disliked the way his boss ran the shop, he either quit, turning his hand to some new calling, or stuck it out in hope of becoming a boss himself. "The young American mechanic of ideas," a Boston editor wrote in 1877, "[looks] out for Number One. He is not so anxious about the number of hours he shall work, or the pay he shall receive, or the privileges he shall enjoy." But the young English workingman thought of "association for the benefit of his class."[1] Born into a society in which classes had always been more rigidly fixed than those of the New World, he was content to defend the accustomed rights of his station and calling. An American journalist noted in 1875 that a Lancashire cotton weaver of Fall River who felt oppressed remains in Fall River; he does not attempt any other work; he is simply a Fall River weaver and stands and suffers on that ground . . . He means to be a weaver, and at the bottom of his heart he stoutly believes that the world owes him such a living as he fancies by weaving, and that if he does not get it somebody is wronging him.[2]

While other European immigrants shared this outlook, most of them, lacking industrial training and thus having to start in America as unskilled laborers, could not enforce their wishes on their employers. But in the early years of many an American industry, British hands had things their own way. In 1829, three years after English colliers first arrived in the Pennsylvania anthracite fields, the mine owners complained: "Their high wages pamper them with the idea of still obtaining more, and knowing their very limited number, they spend the greater part of their time in wandering from one mine to another." [3]

Thus even while welcoming the British immigrants' industrial skill, American employers frowned on their trade-union notions. Not that the British labor movement was much older than the American. The Combination Acts stifled British unionism during the first quarter of the nineteenth century, and during the 1830's unions flourished alike in both countries. But in the 1840's and 1850's British unions grew more rapidly and steadily.[4] Then and later, as skilled hands poured by the tens of thousands from Britain to America, they were more fitted than any other group to join and to lead the labor movement.[5] Not only were many of them experienced unionists, but some, unemployed or blacklisted at home, had immigrated at their old unions' expense.[6]

Only two crafts actually transplanted their old-country unions to the States. Members of the Amalgamated Society of Engineers and of the Amalgamated Society of Carpenters and Joiners set up their first American branches in 1861 and 1867.[7] (The Steam Engine Makers' Society, a small rival of the A.S.E., also maintained a New York bridgehead.[8]) Down to the first World War the Engineers had about forty American locals and two thousand members; the Carpenters were about as strong until after the 1890's, when they increased to some sixty branches and four to eight thousand card-holders.[9] Obviously by no means all immigrant British machinists or carpenters joined the 'Mals, nor was either union restricted to British artisans; the Engineers in 1902 organized a German-speaking branch in Chicago.[10] But most of their members were men who, having belonged in the old country, clung to their share in the benefit funds for sickness, unemployment, old age, and death.[11] After 1890 the much larger rival American unions, the International Association of Machinists and the Brotherhood of Carpenters and Joiners, battled to suppress or absorb the Amalgamateds. In 1913 the Amalgamated Carpenters submitted to the Brotherhood but kept their own benefit system. The Engineers held aloof from the I.A.M. until 1920.[12]

These transplanted British unions swung little weight in the American labor movement. Without them, British carpenters and machinists probably would have taken a leading part in the Brotherhood and the I.A.M. Many immigrant engineers did join the Machinists. Despite the A.S.E., in 1901 the I.A.M. claimed that there was "a complete assimilation between the machinists who come from the British Isles and from Sweden with the American organization, since such immigrants have had the experience of the strong organizations of those countries." [13] An Englishman, George Preston, was for a number of years secretary of the I.A.M.[14] And except for the Amalgamated Carpenters on one hand and nonunion Nova Scotian carpenters in Boston on the other, English and Scottish building trades workers, it was said in 1901, "have strong unions in their own country and readily abide by the [American] union rules when they migrate." [15]

Apart from the Amalgamateds, it is difficult to measure the British share in the early American labor movement. Because of language, many other foreigners had separate unions or their own branches of American organizations, but the British mingled with native Americans in "English" branches — meaning English-speaking. In union records their names do not readily distinguish them from old-stock Americans, while labor newspapers avoided the divisive matter of national origins. Thus meaningful statistics do not exist. Nevertheless, it is clear that in nearly every trade with British immigrants, they had a hand in the indigenous American unions.

When Welsh, English, and Scottish coal miners arrived in the United States, they had a militant, though hardly triumphant, union history behind them. In England and Scotland strong county-wide unions federated in 1841 as the Miners' Association of Great Britain and Ireland. Although this collapsed within seven years, in 1863 Alexander Macdonald regrafted the scattered branches into the Miners' National Union, which during the 1870's shared the field with the Amalgamated Association of Miners. Split again during the 1880's, the colliers in 1889 reunited solidly in the Miners' Federation of Great Britain.[16] Thus coal miners who emigrated during these decades included men well versed in labor leadership. In fact, until Parliament in 1871 conceded the right of collective bargaining, many a blacklisted agitator left the country. South Walians thus barred from their trade in the Principality and unwilling to move to Lancashire or Durham took their mining skill and union principles to the Susquehanna or the Mahoning.[17]

It was an Englishman, John Bates, with Welsh, English, and Irish assistants, who in 1849 organized the first union in the Pennsylvania anthracite fields. Though this lasted no longer than the first abortive strike, small local groups carried on a twenty years' intermittent struggle in the region.[18] When the Maryland soft coal miners — many of them Scots — struck in 1850, they secured a former Lanarkshire union leader, William Clachan, to guide them.[19] In southwestern Illinois in 1861 two Staffordshire miners, Daniel Weaver and Thomas Lloyd, united the bituminous colliers into the nucleus of a national union, the American Miners' Association. John Hinchcliffe, English tailor turned American lawyer, was its president before its demise in 1868.[20] The only colliers who resisted the Missouri mine operators in the 1860's and 1870's were the Welsh and English at Bevier.[21]

In 1868 the center of miners' unionism swung back to eastern Pennsylvania. John Siney's Workingmen's Benevolent Association, known after 1870 as the Miners' and Laborers' Benevolent Association, has frequently been confused with the secret fraternity called the Molly Maguires. The Mollies, however, were Irish mineworkers who avenged wronged Irishmen, while Siney led English, Welsh, and German colliers as well as Irish. Siney, to be sure, was born in the Queen's County in Ireland, but he grew up in the Lancashire town of Wigan and organized a brickmakers' union there. Coming to Pennsylvania in 1863, he first hewed coal the next year at St. Clair.[22] Like most Irish-Americans, Siney was a Catholic and a Democrat, but in 1874 a Carbon County paper said, "He looks and talks like a Scotch-Irishman." [23] Actually he was a Lancashire Irishman, one of many who coupled Irish birth or parentage with English industrial and trade-union experience.

Whatever Siney was, he was no Molly Maguire. His lieutenant in the W.B.A.'s strike of 1870, John Parker, was English.[24] Welsh, English, Irish, and German union members all took part in this strike.[25] About half the delegates to the council of the union, which by 1872 had branches in the eastern bituminous fields, seem to have been Irish; the rest, English and Welsh.[26] Although an operators' journal periodically announced the imminent rebellion of the English, Welsh, and Germans against their Irish Catholic leaders, in 1875 it had to admit that neither religion nor nationality had been at issue in a recent strike. The Irish struck "to get the upper hand not of the Protestant Church but of the Philadelphia and Reading Coal and Iron Company. Moreover, Irish Orangemen were also engaged in the strike, and so were English Episcopalians, Welsh Baptists, German Lutherans, and many more." [27] In 1873 the striking Blossburg local marched behind a Scottish bagpiper blowing "The Macgregors' Gathering." [28]

In other American coal fields many a union leader was indisputably British. John Pollock, born in Northern Ireland and reared in the mines of Scotland, and Chris Evans, who came from England, spoke for the Tuscarawas and Hocking valley miners during the 1870's and 1880's. In Illinois, Daniel McLaughlin and John James, henchmen of Macdonald before they left Scotland, led the colliers of Braidwood and later of the state. Siney, Pollock, and James signed the call to, and McLaughlin and Evans attended, the Youngstown convention of 1873 which organized the Miners' National Association of the United States, a second short-lived attempt at a national union. James patterned its constitution after Macdonald's British organization. The names of the thirty-three delegates to the first convention suggest that a third were at least by ancestry English, another third Irish, and the rest Scottish and Welsh.[29]

Evans, McLaughlin, and other British miners were leaders of the National Federation of Miners and Mine Laborers of 1885, of its 1889 successor the National Progressive Union — which also took in the rival Knights of Labor's National Trade Assembly No. 135 — and finally in 1890 of the United Mine Workers of America.[30] William T. Lewis, who had come from Wales at an early age, had been Master Workman of the miners' section of the Knights; his brother Thomas L. Lewis became a leader of the U.M.W.[31] This new group's first president was a Scot, John Rae, and the first secretary, Robert Watchorn, a Derbyshire collier.[32] In Illinois, William Scaife, formerly an official of a Durham local, and Lanarkshire-born John M. Hunter led the state union.[33] The Englishman John Kane was vice-president of the national organization and editor of its journal.[34] The Alabama miners after 1893 followed William Fairley, an experienced Durham unionist.[35] Two Irish veterans of the pits of Scotland, Patrick McBryde and Patrick Dolan, were U.M.W. officials; Dolan challenged John Mitchell for the presidency.[36] Mitchell, the perennial Moses of the U.M.W., was American-born but of Orange Irish parents; his Scottish stepmother reared him in the Scottish and English mining village of Braidwood, Illinois.[37] The Welshman Edwin Perry was secretary-treasurer of the U.M.W. shortly before the first World War.[38]

Was it mere coincidence that British colliers were unionists both in the homeland and abroad? When they organized, did they reflect merely American conditions? The Cornish iron and copper diggers show the reverse of the coin. In Cornwall, largely because of the contract system which in effect made each miner his own boss, they had known neither labor unions nor strikes.[39] Cornishmen brought the system to northern Michigan, where, despite the lack of the old personal ties between miners and owners, they remained indifferent to collective action.[40] The two thousand miners who struck on the Marquette range in 1874 were Swedes and Norwegians; the Cornish and Irish did not join them.[41] Yet a lost strike in 1895 and poor working conditions thereafter led many Englishmen to abandon the Marquette and Menominee.[42] In 1895, in fact, it was a Lancashire iron miner, Robert Askew of Ishpeming, who organized and led the Northern Mine Workers; later he was an organizer for the American Federation of Labor.[43] But the Western Federation of Miners' great Michigan copper strike of 1914 was carried on by Finns, Slavs, and Italians, who in general were not skilled miners and who furthermore objected to Cornish foremen's discrimination against them.[44] Thus in their own way the Cornish reflected their British background no less than did their coal-mining countrymen.

Like the colliers, British-American ironworkers stood up for their right to organize. At an Allentown mill in 1875 "the ironclad [open-shop contract] was signed by a few Germans . . . The Irish, Welsh, and English put the dampers down" and won their case.[45] But despite their numbers, iron and steel workers from South Wales, the Lowlands, and the Black Country were weak unionists. In the homeland their organizations had been local affairs; the National Amalgamated Association of Ironworkers of 1862 could never muster much power.[46] Although American unions might accept as full members British newcomers with old-country cards, their leaders were oftener Irish than British by birth or recent ancestry. In the 1870's most delegates to the National Forge of the United Sons of Vulcan, which had begun in 1858, had Irish names; others were perhaps English, Welsh, and Scottish.[47]

Not a few key officials of various ironworkers' organizations, however, were British-bred. Both John Edwards, president of the Sons of Vulcan for several terms, and John Jarrett, a vice-president, were

Welshmen.[48] The organizer and head of the Associated Brotherhood of Iron and Steel Heaters, Boilers, and Roughers of the United States in 1872 was Thomas P. Jones, a Glamorgan man who had learned his trade and led strikes in Scotland.[49] William Martin of the Iron and Steel Roll Hands was born in Scotland of English parents.[50] In 1876 these three unions combined as the Amalgamated Association of Iron and Steel Workers; of its four presidents and three secretaries down to 1893 three were American-born, two were Irish, Jarrett was Welsh, and Martin was a Scot.[51] The names of the fifty-three locals' secretaries and of the thirteen national officers in 1877 indicate that half may have been English, at least by descent, perhaps a fifth were Irish and as many Welsh, and a few Scottish and German, but how many had come from British ironworks and unions it is impossible to guess.[52] The union gained strength as Welsh tinplaters arrived in the 1890's but waned after losing the great strikes of 1892 and 1901; American steelworkers remained practically unorganized until the 1930's.[53]

Before the first World War the textile workers of the United States had no strong national unions nor, in most mill towns, even effective locals. But the "walking delegate" did flourish where there were colonies of English and Scottish operatives. Scottish carpet weavers at Thompsonville called a strike as early as 1833, and skilled men from Kidderminster soon set up unions in other New England and Philadelphia carpet centers. Others freshly imported for new branches of the American trade soon launched their own organizations.[54] Most of the 1,300 members of the Power Loom Brussels Carpet Weavers' Mutual Defense and Benefit Association, which began about 1880 and included the bulk of the weavers, were English.[55] In 1885 Philadelphians jokingly spoke of a Yorkshiremen's group, the "Order of George III," supposed to devote itself to keeping Yankees out of the carpet mills.[56] Nottingham lace workers who came in the 1880's and 1890's at first held to their old English union but soon struck out on their own.[57] In the silk industry of Paterson, with its German, French, Swiss, and Italian as well as English hands, unions were weak but fared best among highly skilled men like the horizontal warpers, the loom fixers, and the dyers, many of whom were Macclesfielders.[58] And when in the 1890's silk manufacturers moved their mills to the anthracite region to exploit the unoccupied female labor there, they discovered that miners' daughters could become just as good unionists as their fathers.[59]

In both England and New England it was the Lancashire cotton weavers and mule spinners to whom "a strike was as natural as a day's rest on Sunday."[60] Fall River and New Bedford, where they hived, inevitably felt their sting. Although Lancashire unions probably never set up branches in America, certainly their onetime members banded together early in their Fall River career. Though they lost one union in the strike of 1850, the mule spinners were seldom unorganized after 1858.[61]

Fall River mill owners even suspected that their Lancashire competitors had sent the most fiery agitators across the ocean to disrupt American production.[62] Even docile French Canadian and Irish hands could be stirred up by the English with "their peculiar ideas of their rights and the machinery of their home style of agitation."[63] When a party of Lancashire operatives was reported to have landed at New York, a Fall River employer remarked, "Well, we shall have a lot of greenhorns here tomorrow." An overseer replied ruefully, "Yes, but you'll find that they have brought their horns with them."[64] A most un-American lot they seemed. "Whatever they might do in England," the mill owners warned, "interference with the right of free labor [will] not for an hour be tolerated in America."[65]

The operatives themselves blamed capitalist intransigence for the endemic strife in Fall River.[66] A local clergyman agreed, finding the operatives "very much indisposed to submit to injustice, prompt to contend for what they consider their right, and determined to improve their condition as fast as possible, [but] also . . . a peaceable and law-abiding class."[67]

Whoever was to blame, the great Fall River strikes of the 1870's were Lancashire affairs. In 1875 the weavers twice struck unsuccessfully against wage cuts and joined with other Massachusetts and Rhode Island cotton and woolen operatives in a "national" union.[68]

The spinners' union helped some members to return to England during these strikes, and many weavers also went back.[69] More sailed in 1877, when Fall River unionists lent a hand to striking English and Irish operatives at New Bedford.[70]

At the storm center stood a Stockport immigrant of 1874, George Gunton. Blacklisted after the 1875 strikes, he soon reappeared in Fall River as editor of the *Labor Standard*. Mill owners all across the North learned to fear his Lancashire oratory. To protest new wage reductions in 1878, Gunton got up a mass demonstration which he marshaled, by his own account, "mounted on a fine spirited grey charger, uniformed with military coat, sword, and a brass helmet with plumes." His enemies thought the headdress remarkably like an inverted coal scuttle.[71]

After leading another weavers' strike in 1879, Gunton abandoned the Fall River operatives, but another Stockport man, Robert Howard, who before emigrating in 1873 had led a spinners' union in the Cheshire town, took command. Despite lost strikes in 1879 and 1884, Howard held the reins not only of the local unions but also of the National Mule Spinners' Union, formed in 1885 about a Fall River core.[72] He was another Lancashire Irishman whose trade and trade unionism were English. He even spoke "in the choppy dialect of old England," and when he revisited Lancashire, the *Manchester Guardian* thought him an Englishman.[73] Howard's successor in the Fall River unions, James Tansey, similarly was Rochdale-born of Mayo parents, and, although always considering himself Irish, he learned carding and first served as a union official in Lancashire.[74] Many other Fall River cotton trade-union officers were English by ancestry as well as by birthplace and training.[75] In New Bedford in 1899 the unions were "almost entirely in the hands of the English and Irish." Even the handful of Scottish operatives supplied nearly as many union leaders as the teeming French Canadians.[76]

On the other hand, in New England cotton and woolen towns which had few British-trained operatives, unions made little headway. Mill owners in one isolated valley, having held wages below the Fall River level, had attracted few Englishmen. Lacking Lancashire guidance, the French Canadian and Irish hands could not unite; in 1880 the district had yet to see a serious labor disturbance.[77] So too in Rhode Island.[78] In 1883 a mill agent of Manchester, New Hampshire, could recall only one brief strike in that town, where English operatives had seldom sought work except when the Fall River mills were idle. Fall River men had been behind attempts to organize Manchester.[79] In Lawrence two Englishmen, Robert Bower and Richard Hinchcliffe (brother of the Illinois miners' leader), kept the cause alive in the 1870's with their labor weekly, the *Lawrence Journal*.[80] But neither Lawrence nor Lowell, where most mill hands were French Canadians and Irish, had active unions in the early 1880's.[81] In Fall River itself even those French Canadians and Portuguese who acquired skilled trades banded together far more reluctantly than the British and Lancashire Irish.[82] Many a newcomer from Quebec first entered the mills as a "knobstick"—strikebreaker in the Lancashire lingo of the striking regular hands.[83]

When the United Textile Workers of America, the first important national union in the trade, was formed in 1901, Fall River and New Bedford men were its mainstay. Tansey was the first president, and the two other principal officers were Englishmen.[84] John Golden, the perennial president, was Lancashire Irish and was said to have left England after a blacklisting for union agitation.[85] Most of his lieutenants seem to have been British or Irish.[86]

The Englishmen, Scots, and Irishmen in the American stonecutting trades likewise were strong unionists. The Granite Cutters, organized nationally in 1877, had for secretary in their early years a Cornish artisan, Josiah B. Dyer, and later as president a Scot, James Duncan.[87] In such places as Barre and Quincy, where most granite cutters were Scotsmen, they dominated the locals; elsewhere Irishmen, Italians, and Scandinavians had a larger share.[88] The Quarrymen's, the Journeymen Stone Cutters', and the Paving Block Cutters' national unions had similar memberships.[89] On the other hand, the slate quarrymen never had strong unions in America, though in

1874 they contributed to the strike fund of their more militant countrymen in North Wales.[90]

As for the Trenton potters, when they struck in 1877, they turned for aid first to their countrymen back in Staffordshire.[91] And one of the three leaders of the New England shoemakers' strike of 1860 — "the greatest strike in American history before the Civil War" — was James Dillon, a Cheshire man.[92]

These men also looked across their craft boundaries. Several British immigrants were pillars of the National Labor Union of the late 1860's: John Hinchcliffe of the miners; Richard F. Trevellick, Cornish-born head of the International Union of Ship Carpenters and Caulkers; and Andrew Carr Cameron, the Berwick printer who edited the Chicago *Workingman's Advocate*.[93] George Gunton threw his Fall River operatives into the short-lived International Labor Union of 1878 and 1879.[94] In the Knights of Labor, though probably the British were relatively as numerous as they were in the trade unions, they had little to do with its leadership.[95]

But the American Federation of Labor was another story. The fact that Samuel Gompers, for decades its head, was London-born was unimportant: his parents were Dutch Jews, he came to America when a boy, and his trade of cigar making was not one which many British entered in America.[96] But more typical British immigrants like John Jarrett, Robert Howard, Dan McLaughlin, William Martin, and Chris Evans were Federation stalwarts from the start; James Duncan was for thirty years one of Gompers' chief lieutenants.[97]

Modeled after the Trades Union Congress, this federation of craft unions suited the British better than an "industrial" catch-all like the Knights of Labor. Even those who did join assemblies of the Knights — notably pottery, silk, and carpet workers — were as skilled as any craft unionists.[98] Likewise most of the coal mineworkers, in the days when they established their tradition of industrial unionism, were highly skilled men.[99] Like the leaders of the labor movement in Britain itself until late in the century, the skilled immigrants fought for their own immediate welfare rather than that of the mass of laborers.[100] Of course the similarity between British and American craft unionism was the result not merely of immigration; even in industries without British hands, workingmen followed the pattern of organization which had succeeded in England.[101] Yet Americans were influenced directly by the benefit systems which the Amalgamated Carpenters and the Engineers brought to the United States. To the lack of such a scheme the collapse of an American carpenters' national organization in 1872 could be attributed.[102] The Granite Cutters, with their many Scottish and English members, in 1877 were "the first important union" to adopt strike benefits.[103] After the 1880's most American craft groups followed suit.[104]

While craft unionism was the rule, some British workingmen in the United States heeded the new-model unionism which reached out to the general laborers in the homeland after the late 1880's.[105] In 1915 John Golden observed that although many textile operatives who had come from Britain long before still prattled of "the weaver for the weaver" and "the spinner for the spinner," the new British example had converted him to industrial unionism.[106] But the Fall River craftsmen rebelled against his attempts to welcome all mill hands into the U.T.W.[107] Golden himself excoriated the Industrial Workers of the World for their unorthodox methods and nondescript followers in the Lawrence and New Bedford strikes of 1912.[108]

A handful of I.W.W. leaders at Lawrence were British-born operatives, but their countrymen had small use for such extremists.[109] In 1905 the I.W.W. briefly and anomalously included the four thousand machinists of the Amalgamated Society of Engineers, suspended by the A.F. of L. during their jurisdictional fight with the I.A.M. Despite their socialist leader Isaac Cowen, however, the A.S.E. soon dropped out of the syndicalist organization at the behest of the executive council in London.[110] Though by this time many newcomers in both the Engineers and the Amalgamated Society of Carpenters were socialists, most British-Americans clung to their ancient craft sectionalism.[111]

Their bargaining tactics were equally conservative. Daniel Weaver of the American Miners' Association in 1861 condemned "that reckless zeal and mad, headlong precipitancy which invariably obstructs or ultimately annihilates the cause it is intended to promote . . . It is not wise at all times to demand at once all that is due, but what is attainable."[112] Mine owners might call John Siney a firebrand, but actually he preferred to come to friendly annual wage agreements with them and ended his career exhorting his rebellious followers not to strike during the depression of the late 1870's.[113] Between 1886 and 1889 miners and operators held yearly national conferences to compose their differences.[114] Even the ironmasters' journal praised John Jarrett as one "who can look on both sides of a controversy; who can mediate as well as fight; who can, when both capital and labor are at boiling heat, give the soft answer that turneth away wrath."[115] In 1875 George Gunton and other Lancashire union leaders harangued the Fall River operatives against foolishly striking for better pay in the face of an empty treasury and a falling market.[116] Robert Howard and James Tansey usually got along peacefully with the mill owners by informal bargaining rather than by threats or strikes.[117]

Measures more radical than craft unionism never attracted many British immigrants. Some hoped to recast the system of production and distribution in the mold of the English coöperative movement. Like trade unionism, however, coöperation in the United States owed as much to the British example at Rochdale as to British immigrants. Most of the several hundred American coöperative stores and the occasional coöperative factories were not set up in places where many British people lived.[118] But English workingmen, appalled at the cost of living in the States, did start some of these ventures.

In 1867 Lancashire mill hands organized the Fall River Workingmen's Coöperative Association, which prospered so well that by 1881 its store covered an entire block.[119] The mule spinners in 1869 started their own "dividing store." Each member contributed a monthly sum for his family's food, and one man bought at wholesale for all.[120] Operatives in New Bedford and other mill towns soon did the same. Unfortunately their treasurers, usually poor weavers or spinners who suddenly found their hands full of greenbacks, were prone to abscond, leaving their hapless fellows to have their wages trusteed by the wholesale merchants.[121] In 1881 the *Labor Standard* observed that "the little huts built by enthusiastic operatives in which to divide butter and beans can now be seen near the back doors of corporation tenements, used as pig-stys and hen coops."[122] In Lawrence, however, the Arlington Mill's employees ran a far-famed store with an English-trained manager; Englishmen supported smaller projects in Philadelphia and Trenton.[123] During the heyday of John Siney's union in the early 1870's, anthracite miners escaped the coal companies' "pluck me" stores through their own coöperatives.[124]

A few English workmen also essayed coöperative production. Refusing to furnish their own tools at a Waterbury cutlery works, sixteen Sheffielders in 1852 quit to set up their own company.[125] Hard times and wage cuts in Fall River during the 1870's and 1880's inspired Lancashire operatives to sell stock in coöperative mills, which, however, they never succeeded in building.[126] After strikes in Philadelphia in 1884, English carpet and damask weavers operated works of their own.[127]

In neither Britain nor America did coöperation succeed in undermining capitalism. But workingmen won less sweeping victories at the ballot box and in legislative lobbies. Until 1867, however, only in the United States could all of them vote. Thus by 1874, when the first labor members were elected to Parliament, British workingmen were already deep in the politics of the republic. Andrew Cameron's *Workingman's Advocate* spoke for the Greenback Party in 1867; Cameron himself was secretary of the National Labor Party convention of 1872.[128] John Siney and John Hinchcliffe were delegates to several Greenback conventions; Richard Trevellick presided over those of 1878 and 1880.[129]

These men and the Massachusetts labor leaders took part in the campaign of the 1870's for short-hour laws. The Shropshire-born editor of the Fall River *Labor Journal*, Henry Sevey, and Robert Bower and several other Englishmen helped secure the state's ten-hour law of 1874.[130] Weaver-editor George Gunton, a prime mover of the Boston Eight Hour League, in 1877 forced prosecution of Fall River mill owners for violating this act and in 1880 became secretary of the National Ten Hours League.[131]

In Fall River the backbone of the Greenback and labor-reform movements of the late 1870's and early 1880's were the Lancashire union men. They annually delivered the city to Ben Butler, the labor-reform candidate for governor, and in 1879 elected one of their own number, Thomas Webb, to the state senate despite whispers that he was "one of these low-lived, fire-eating, Communistic labor reformers that had cursed Fall River by their destructive and pestilential influence."[132] In 1880 the Labor Campaign Club and the Greenback Labor Party nominated Gunton for the legislature, but he ran a poor sixth, since both major parties, seeing which way the wind was blowing, had put up spinner Robert Howard.[133] Elected to the state senate as a Democrat in 1885, Howard served eight terms as labor's spokesman on Beacon Hill and, as Democratic candidate for Congress in 1894, carried Fall River but not his entire district.[134] In 1884 he was a leader of the state labor party which, dissatisfied with Butler's record as governor and regarding Cleveland as anti-labor, swung Fall River to Blaine.[135] When the New Bedford representative in the legislature voted against a labor bill in 1885, the spinners' and weavers' unions urged their members, only half of whom could vote, to become citizens; eventually Samuel Ross, the English head of the spinners, took the offender's seat.[136] The labor reformers of Lawrence sent Robert Bower to the State House in the early 1870's.[137]

In Illinois the St. Clair County colliers in 1870 elected John Hinchcliffe to the legislature, where he sponsored the state's first mine-safety law; Walton Rutledge, the English miner who drafted it, became state mine inspector.[138] Other mine-union leaders in the assembly, David Ross and William Scaife, secured stronger amendments in 1889 and 1891.[139] In Pennsylvania a miners' lobby obtained an inspection act in 1869.[140] A Scottish miner and self-taught geologist, Andrew Roy, wrote Ohio's first safety act and became the official inspector.[141] From mining villages in Scotland and Pennsylvania William B. Wilson rose through the U.M.W. to Congress and served under President Woodrow Wilson as the first Secretary of Labor.[142]

In bold contrast to the run of British-American workingmen with their cautious unionism and limited economic and political aims were a handful of radicals. If old enough, they usually boasted of Chartist exploits during the 1830's and 1840's, when some active Chartists, fearing imprisonment, did flee to the western republic.[143] Nevertheless, George Julian Harney, probably the most notable Chartist who settled there, took no part in American affairs.[144] Nor did the Scot David Johnston, sometime overseer of the poor of Camberwell, who left England when Chartism collapsed in 1848.[145] Finding the Charter's suffrage reforms already embodied in the constitution of the new state of Wisconsin, Matthew Mark Trumbull emigrated; forty years later, a conservative Chicago lawyer, he defied public hysteria by demanding clemency for the wrongfully convicted Haymarket anarchists.[146]

Two English-American workingmen outside the organized labor movement advocated "labor reform." A member of the Leeds Working Men's Association of the 1830's, John Francis Bray lived out his last fifty years on a hardscrabble Michigan farm of which the principal crop was socialist polemics, printed in labor journals all over the country.[147] William Dealtry, an English cabinetmaker of Cincinnati who found no publisher for his rambling treatise on the inequities of the economic system, set up and printed it himself.[148] Coming to New York in 1902, a young self-educated Tolstoyan anarchist of Leeds, William MacQueen, soon landed in jail, nominally for inciting Italian and Hungarian weavers of Paterson to violence.[149]

Several British socialists became leaders of the American party which took root after the 1890's. In fact, Andrew Cameron had already represented the National Labor Union at the Basle convention of Marx's International Working-Men's Association in 1869.[150] But American socialism owed far more to radicals from the continent than to the British. John Spargo later recalled:

When I came to America early in 1901 and joined in the creation of the present Socialist Party — it was then known as the Social Democratic Party — there was not a branch to which I could belong at which the business was wholly transacted in English! . . . As a result only those English-speaking members who were specially fond of associating with the Germans and those who possessed an unlimited amount of patience stayed in the movement for long.[151]

A Cornishman who in England had served several years on the national executive of the Social Democratic Federation and had helped organize industrial unions, Spargo was for a dozen years a leader of the American party. In 1917 he broke with it over its pacifist and, he believed, pro-German policy.[152] Thomas J. Morgan of Chicago, who in 1893 urged the A.F. of L. convention to set up an independent labor party on the British model, and Owen Bowen, a Welshman of Martin's Ferry, were lesser lights.[153] But though Paterson mill owners might think that all English immigrants were "tainted with a communistic spirit," it was neither "labor reform" nor socialism but the craft unionism of skilled artisans which was the typical British immigrant's answer to the challenge of industrial America.[154]

Thus whether concerned with labor in politics or the politics of labor, British immigrants put their old-country union experience to good use. Even after 1900, when other foreigners overran their trades, English-speaking men were still the best fitted to conduct union affairs.[155] It was said in 1900 of the coal mineworkers' locals, "Usually the president is English, Irish, or Welsh, and the other officers are Italian, Polish, Slovak, Lithuanian." [156]

On the other hand, men who in Britain would have stayed within the ranks of labor found jumping to the other side of the fence much easier in America. Having talents valuable to American industry, potential union leaders and "labor reformers" instead became foremen, superintendents, and owners of companies.[157] Unionism and labor parties thrived best among the cotton operatives of Fall River and the coal miners, hardly any of whom could hope to become capitalists. But elsewhere the weakness of American class barriers tempted trade-union officials to forget class loyalty and climb as high as they could. The iron and steel workers' chief, John Jarrett, resigned in 1883 to become secretary of the manufacturers' American Tinned Plate Association, narrowly lost an appointment as Chief of the Bureau of Labor Statistics, served as consul at Birmingham, and finally went into business in Pittsburgh.[158] Even Henry Sevey and George Gunton abandoned Fall River labor journalism, Sevey to report for a conservative Providence newspaper and "Professor" Gunton to conduct a New York institute of social economics where he preached the happy inevitability of large combinations both of labor and of capital.[159]

In or out of the labor movement, British-Americans were a conservative lot. While they helped at many points to revolutionize American industrial technology, their skill was their capital, and they fought like any capitalists to prevent its depreciation. Attached to tried and true methods of work, they likewise clung, with "the old Lancashire tenacity that never yields," to the trade unionism which had suited their craft interests at home.[160] Since one tradition endeared them to American employers no more than the other, their unionism further reduced the demand for British immigrants after 1890. They seemed to be eternally "kicking against foremen, kicking against rules, kicking against everything."[161] Few Americans, however, feared that they had any violent ends in view. No matter how alien some thought their trade unionism, it was no more than a function of the favored position in the American economy which their industrial skills had won them.

8

Countrymen and Fortune Seekers

By no means all British-Americans had been trained in the homeland's factories or mines for specific American jobs. Nonindustrial British immigrants, like the mass of Irish and continental Europeans who came in the same years — and like their own countrymen who had first settled the American colonies — found the new world strange. They were a mixed lot: farmers, rural and urban laborers, clerks, and merely ambitious — or idle — young men. Although most knew some British calling, America's peculiar farming or mercantile practices forced them to learn it afresh or to labor at whatever new job the country chanced to offer. Expecting no sure niche in the American economy, such newcomers hoped somehow to make their fortunes.

Before the late 1820's, when depression in British trade first drove abroad swarms of skilled artisans, probably the great majority of British emigrants had been farmers, peasants, and village craftsmen.[1] During the seventeenth and eighteenth centuries they sailed from an island still field and pasture to a yet more rustic land. America did not draw them then so much as Britain forced them to flee. In the late eighteenth and the early nineteenth centuries an agrarian revolution disrupted the British countryside. Landlords who divided up and enclosed within hedgerows the archaic open and common fields, in order to inaugurate scientific "high farming," upset English, Welsh, and Scottish rural society and, when they turned arable into pasture, hired one shepherd where several plowmen had plodded. In the Highland glens recurrent potato shortages and the final collapse of the clans uprooted crofters. As the Irish multiplied on potatoes and milk, cottagers willing to pay exorbitant rents for tiny plots displaced prosperous tenant farmers. Occasional general crises in agriculture — depression after the Napoleonic war boom and, thirty years later, merely the fear that a slump would follow repeal of the duties on imported grain — swelled the rural exodus. Some of the displaced sailed to America hoping for new farms, and more trudged to the new industrial districts of England, Scotland, and Wales.[2]

Repeal of the protective Corn Laws in the late 1840's did not immediately ruin agriculture; indeed, the next quarter-century was its golden age. Then a succession of bad harvests, culminating in the disastrously wet summer of 1879, struck just as railways and steamships opened the British market to the farmers and cattlemen of the American prairies and plains. The countryside stagnated until the end of the century.[3]

These vicissitudes variously affected the different classes on the land. The soil of Britain belonged principally to the nobility and country gentry, their thousand-year predominance strengthened by enclosure of open fields and commons into tenant farms. But as prices — and rents — fell after 1880, so did landlords' income. The English yeomanry of small freeholders having long since disappeared, most farmers in all parts of Britain were leaseholders who, despite rent adjustments, now also lost heavily. At the bottom of the scale the landless agricultural laborers' real wages did rise during the later nineteenth century. But since machinery was beginning to supplant laborers, they and their better-educated sons and daughters more than ever were apt to forsake the soil for the towns or to seek land in broader and freer countries.[4]

Canada also had agricultural emigrants eager to go to the United States. In fact, westward-moving farmers, Canadian or American, ignored the continental boundary. From the late 1830's until the mid-1890's, Canadian farmers found that the best new land lay below the border. Thus when the plow was breaking new prairie sod, they settled from Ohio to Dakota. Then during the next two decades the farming frontier, and with it both native and immigrant Americans, moved northwestward across the Canadian prairie provinces. The nations were two; the land was one.[5]

By 1860 the frontier had not advanced beyond eastern Kansas and Nebraska nor into northwestern Iowa and the northern parts of Minnesota, Wisconsin, and Michigan. But already the virgin country lay a long and expensive journey westward from the seaports. Furthermore, as the frontier moved on across the Great Plains toward the mountain mining camps during the 1870's and 1880's, the acres open to homesteaders would support cattle but few men. On the other hand, in the rear of the frontier line much new land remained either unclaimed or in the hands of speculators. And everywhere, east and west, there were American farmers anxious to sell their fields, stock, and buildings and pull up stakes for the West.[6]

To be lord of his own acres — that universal ambition in a country like Britain where land signified rank — was the dream which turned the British countryman, whether laborer, tenant, or younger son of the gentry, toward America. An English farmer in New Jersey said in 1879:

> Here we buy land at what is paid annually for rent in England, viz., $25 per acre, so . . . an industrious man may raise himself to a point of independence and own the soil he tills. There is nothing so elevating as a man working and thinking for himself; it expands his mind; he takes a broader view of the world and humanity; he raises himself from an automaton (for whom others think) to a man.[7]

Another English immigrant the same year boasted of the good fortune of his brother-in-law and sister, who by working for a Connecticut farmer had saved enough to buy a Kansas farm:

> Kate and John is quite aristocrats at least they would think themselves so if they were in England and had a hundred & sixty acers of land and a house of their own and twenty acers of wheat and two horses and a cow and kill all our own game plenty of hares rabbits prairie chickens geese & wild ducks.[8]

But American agriculture, particularly in the West, baffled many English-bred farmers.[9] The Kansas couple, so prosperous in 1879, were nearly penniless after the ensuing nine years of drought, blasted crops, and low prices. "I often tell him," the wife wrote, "we should have more pleasure of our life if we lived in Old England even if he only had his days labour for he got payed for it but we work many a month and don't get any pay."[10] A disgruntled Englishman in North Dakota in 1885 warned people at home against risking the West:

> The climate is far more severe and uncertain than I thought it would be; the living is dear beyond our worst expectations; and, most important of all, *capital* is needed here if anything substantial is to be realized. Farming and cultivation must be carried out on a far larger scale than we were led to expect, if it is to pay at all.[11]

Wherever the immigrant chose to settle, the low price of the virgin land offered by the government or by the land-grant railroads was a minor part of the cost of farming. An Englishman who lived in Minnesota during the 1870's advised his countrymen not to emigrate with less than £500 nor to attempt to buy or farm more than eighty acres; not more than a fourth of an immigrant's capital should go for the soil itself. "The possession of land so impossible at home and so easily obtainable in America," he cautioned, "is the ruinous snare into which too many fall."[12] Evidently only persons in comfortable circumstances at home could hope at once to succeed as American landowners. Consequently, although the depression in British farming drove many to Canada, Australia, and other emptier lands, the late nineteenth century saw the virtual end of British migration into American agriculture.

Yet while the West discouraged many, other British farmers took up older acres in the East for more congenial market gardening or dairying. In 1890 over half the ninety-two thousand British-born farmers in the country and roughly half the fifty-six thousand British Canadians lived east of the Mississippi. Outside the South there were thousands in every agricultural state.[13]

Exactly where in each state most of them settled is indeterminable. Unlike German or Scandinavian farmers in the Middle West, the English, Scots, or Canadians seldom huddled in communities of their own kind. Those who did band together are quickly listed. Most British-American rural colonies antedated the Civil War:

Albion, Illinois, founded in 1817 by Morris Birkbeck;[14] Carlyle, Illinois;[15] Arena, Wisconsin, to which the British Temperance Emigration Society sent Liverpool mechanics in the 1840's;[16] and Welton, Iowa, similarly settled in 1850.[17] Scots came about 1820 to Caledonia, LeRoy, and Scottsville in western New York.[18] A group of Kintyre families thrived at Argyle, Illinois, from the late 1830's.[19] There were other prosperous colonies of Scottish farmers at Dundee and in Will, Boone, and LaSalle Counties, Illinois,[20] near Janesville and Portage City, Wisconsin,[21] in northern Tama County in Iowa,[22] and even in Walton County, Florida.[23] Canadian farmers moved into Polo and Farina, Illinois, in the 1830's and the 1850's.[24]

Like other foreign-language groups, the Welsh settled together to a much greater degree than the rest of the British. Their rural communities in Oneida County, New York — which made "Welsh butter" famous — and in Cambria County, Pennsylvania, took root in the 1790's. In Ohio within a few years Welsh families, some from Pennsylvania and others directly from Wales, farmed at Paddy's Run in Butler County, the "Welsh Hills" of Licking County, several spots in Gallia and Jackson Counties, at Gomer in Allen County, and at Radnor in Delaware County.[25] During the 1830's Welsh Ohioans who revisited the homeland renewed the America fever there.[26] For another twenty years families from Wales and from the eastern Welsh settlements spread to new colonies in Waukesha, Columbia, LaCrosse, and Winnebago Counties, Wisconsin, in Blue Earth and Fillmore Counties, Minnesota, in Howard and Iowa Counties, Iowa, in northern Missouri, and even in Tennessee.[27] Besides the countrymen from North Wales, some South Wales miners and ironworkers turned to farming in the United States.[28]

After the Civil War the railroads and other land speculators recruited — among other peoples — Englishmen, Scots, and Canadians for all parts of the West.[29] The Pennsylvania Railroad and several western lines in 1870 opened a London agency to sell "cheap and comfortable" passage to the West and to help immigrants to select farms.[30] The Santa Fe set up the Anglo-American Agricultural Company to dispose of some of its lands.[31] In 1883, at the height of the Northern Pacific's colonization campaign, that railroad employed throughout the United Kingdom more than eight hundred agents to recruit emigrants at town markets and country fairs.[32] The American Land Company of London advertised a hundred thousand acres in southwest Minnesota in 1876, and the Land Colonisation and Banking Company of London in 1879 offered twenty thousand acres complete with town sites and grain elevators in Minnesota and Iowa.[33] Similar companies brought British farmers to Kansas, Dakota, and Oregon.[34]

Once again only a few British herded together. During the late 1860's and early 1870's English farmers settled whole villages in Kansas; state officials hired several men to go back home as recruiting agents.[35] In 1870 a band of three hundred Sussex emigrants came to Geary County.[36] The Burlington and Missouri Railroad organized a colony of English farmers. Sailing in 1872, the majority as steerage passengers, the 145 settlers included blacksmiths, wheelwrights, and a clergyman and brought £10,000 capital.[37] Scots in 1871 established a western Minnesota colony for raising purebred cattle.[38] In 1873 several hundred Somerset, Devon, and Yorkshire farmers and artisans, shepherded by a Dorset Congregational minister, took up eight townships of Northern Pacific and homestead land in Clay County, Minnesota, and gave their colony the Somerset name Yeovil.[39] The "Furness colony" in Wadena County was planted on forty-two thousand railroad acres in 1873 and 1874 by a tightly knit group of several hundred prosperous North of England farmers and tradesmen.[40] New Welsh farming communities sprang up at New Cambria and Dawn in Missouri, Arvonia and Bala in Kansas, Prairie Union in Nebraska, and in Washington Territory.[41] Even northeastern Pennsylvania got a new colony of sixty Scots in 1882.[42]

Ignorant of speculators' wiles, some British settlers failed to distinguish good land from bad. Texas disappointed English farmers in 1879, when several land companies were urging them to emigrate.[43] The Texas Freehold Farm and Emigration Union, agent of a railroad in the state, operated a lottery which promised each winner a house, eighty fenced acres, stock, tools, and provisions on several years' credit. Although the company attracted several parties from Yorkshire and Durham, they complained that land advertised as arable was in fact poor grazing country.[44] Outright swindlers snared others. Until extradited to America for forgery, one English shark offered his fellow countrymen land around the well-named but nonexistent Texas towns of Manchester, Brighton, Birmingham, and Glasgow.[45] Of Texas, even when land there was sold in good faith, the *London Standard* warned in 1879 that

> neither the climate of much of it, the people, nor the present state of the country will suit the class of emigrants who in the present depression are apt to leap before looking and with their circumscribed ideas are inclined to believe that one piece of Texas is like all the rest . . . The emigrants who have already been induced to go out . . . declare they were deceived and that the country is unfitted for English settlers of the better class.[46]

During the 1880's the British consul at Galveston advised farmers with little capital not to risk Texas agriculture.[47]

Arid California land, often purchased by British farmers before they emigrated, was equally risky.[48] Unprepared for the difficult soil and climate, even the wealthy Englishmen who tried to grow oranges during the 1890's under the guidance of the Kern County Land Company failed after a few years.[49] English farmers in southern California found sugar beets unprofitable.[50] Wiser immigrants learned local methods by two or three years' work before purchasing their own land.[51] Some prospered, and, despite failures and recurrent charges of fraud, land companies continued to bring families out to English settlements.[52]

In the South, its agriculture disrupted by the Civil War, land speculators and state governments hoped to attract immigrant farmers. Besides Texas, only the Old Dominion got many. Between 1866 and 1874 several English and Scottish gentlemen brought groups of their countrymen to south-central Virginia.[53] After 1906 the state secured a few hundred British settlers for the Piedmont.[54] In Florida during the 1880's an English land company promoted immigration, while two hundred Scots struggled with the sands of Sarasota.[55] But British consuls, pointing to the sad lot of the few British farmers who had tried the South, warned others away.[56]

Probably no foreigners ever were worse adapted for American life and yet more famous than a certain few hundred young British immigrants of the 1870's and 1880's. Many a landed English or Scottish family, its income falling during the agricultural depression, sought any haven for its younger sons. Educated at public schools and universities the same as the heir to the family estates but gradually losing their traditional refuges in government, the army, or the church, such young gentlemen aroused much concern. Perhaps the wilds of America could make them self-reliant and even wealthy, while by banding in their own settlements they might preserve the amenities of caste though surrounded by republicans. Thus began the bizarre careers of LeMars, Iowa; Rugby, Tennessee; and Victoria, Kansas.[57]

A Scottish silk merchant of London in 1873 planted the Victoria colony on seventy thousand acres purchased from the Kansas Pacific. In spite of bitter winters, dry summers, grasshopper plagues, and the well-bred "younger sons'" fondness for the Fort Hays saloons, in five years Victoria boasted thousands of imported hogs, sheep, horses, and the country's first Aberdeen Angus cattle. But the founder's death and the droughts of the 1880's scattered the colonists; a more industrious group of Volga Germans took the land.[58]

Thomas Hughes, apotheosizer of the English public-school boy, guided the Tennessee settlement. Liberally supported by prominent Englishmen, his company bought a broad tract in eastern Tennessee in 1880, laid out town site and farms, built a store, a saw mill, a brick kiln, a library, and the Hotel Tabard, and offered land on three years' credit at $1.70 an acre. The place was as congenial a retreat as Tennessee could offer. A Scottish traveler observed:

In Rugby town there is the rare advantage of a little good society. In passing many of the houses pretty British faces appear at the windows, smart young Oxonians meet you, and the good dress and manners of the men must impress their American brethren. Soft music floats from under verandahs, and at the store or post-office you . . . hear refined language; rather rare in western towns.[59]

But the soil was sterile and heavily wooded, and tennis, football, cricket, or lounging about booted, spurred, and festooned with bowie knives and pistols intrigued the lads more than following the plow-tail. The visiting Scot lamented:

> Young men work here for one dollar per day . . . clearing land, cutting down wood, and forming roads, ditches, &c. — the common work of a labourer. Those I met with are well-educated gentlemen and quite unfit for such labour. They complain that they expected to get experience in stock-farming . . . Coloured men work with them, and this is objectionable from many points.[60]

Since Hughes sparingly doled out the allowances provided by their parents, some Rugbeians resorted to selling their clothes to the "natives." After trying grain-growing, dairying, and a cannery, most of them deserted the place within two years. Despite a modest revival in 1886, the company ten years later sold the land.[61]

Favored with excellent soil, LeMars was begun in 1879 by three brothers, Cambridge crewmen turned land speculators. Hundreds of young upper-class Englishmen took farms. Here sports and gracious living did not wholly displace work. As an English visitor observed:

> The young fellows have about them the unmistakable hall-mark of the public schools, the universities, the services; and the hard work that is performed bears more the air of pleasurable picnic roughing-it than genuine toil. No caste is lost by the young man who, dissatisfied with the slower returns of farming, engages in any of the numerous occupations — we should call them trades — of a new colony. The auctioneer, the butcher, the livery-stable keeper, provided they are recognized by society at Le Mars as gentlemen, are not considered to degrade their good old names by such experiments in new enterprise, and continue on the footing of gentlemen with the young farmers. You see the heir-apparent to an old English earldom mowing, assisted by the two sons of a viscount; you can watch the brother of an earl feeding the thrashing-machine. The happy sunburnt faces of the well set-up, strong-backed, young Britishers are pleasant features in the rich, agricultural landscape.[62]

But though some succeeded at stock-raising, within a few years LeMars lost its distinctive atmosphere as others sold out and drifted off to the cities or to England.[63] Other groups of middle- and upper-class Englishmen settled at Decorah, Iowa, in the late 1860's and at Fairmont, Minnesota, a decade later.[64]

Some young immigrants came expecting American farmers to initiate them into the mysteries of the country gentleman's life as pursued in the States. For "tuition" of £30 to £150, agencies in London contracted to place them as pupils on Western farms. One advertisement read:

> Englishman (in London for a few weeks) having large prosperous estate in California Northern, will receive a few sons of gentlemen desiring to learn mixed and fruit farming and stock raising. At expiration of term very moderate amount of capital will ensure independent livelihood; exceptional facilities offered; advertiser having numerous interests can guarantee his pupils remunerative positions on certain conditions, or is open to leasing, or selling on easy terms, blocks of suitable land; best of living; perfect climate; good hunting, fishing, riding, &c. Moderate premium.[65]

Many wealthy English parents bit on such dubious propositions. The "farm pupils," however, soon rebelled against paying for the right to do farmers' chores. For twenty years the West from Minnesota and Kansas to California seemed to be full of runaway farm apprentices. Lacking professional or technical training, they lived on whatever their parents might send and drifted disheartened and helpless.[66] One of their brethren who eventually made his American fortune thought that these "remittance men" and "thousand pounders" were "the greatest curse to the English name in the United States . . . They cannot find work that a gentleman could do and would not think of taking other work, as they have the family name in their keeping. They are the laughing-stock of the communities in which they live."[67]

At least one well-born young man carved out his own American barony. John Sutherland Sinclair emigrated in 1875 at seventeen; when in 1891 he unexpectedly inherited the landless earldom of

Caithness, he was farming "an enormous acreage" in North Dakota. Though during the next twenty years he often visited Great Britain and voted as a Scottish peer, he preferred to live near the source of his fortune and finally retired incognito to Los Angeles.[68]

On the Great Plains the range-cattle industry of the 1870's and 1880's promised both profits for British investors and excitement for young horsemen. In 1884 about thirty British syndicates owned twenty million acres of range from Texas and New Mexico to Wyoming. Several sent out British managers and herdsmen.[69] In Ellis County, Kansas, the small English settlement of Silverdale began with a group of immigrant hands whom an English rancher brought over during the 1880's.[70] Young gentlemen took to cowpunching as they never did to plowing. In 1885 an American observed that it was common "for young English university graduates of high social position to lead for a year or two the rough life of a hired cowboy on a ranch, to learn the cattle business and be competent to manage a large herd to be purchased with the capital of friends at home."[71] A disastrous career as a sheep rancher in arid southern California in the 1870's could not daunt one young Englishman or his wife, who exclaimed, "It was glorious fun, like pic-nics always."[72] The younger son of the Earl of Airlie raised cattle and horses on Colorado land given him by his father.[73] Although only a few hundred Englishmen and Scots became Western ranchmen and cowhands, they at least were better suited to their American life than were most upper-class British immigrants.[74]

Before the Civil War even British urban workers sometimes took up land in America. On his Wisconsin farm in 1848 a onetime woolen operative rejoiced: "Thank god I have not to rouse my chilldren at the sound of a bell from their beds and Drag them through the pelting storm of a Dark winters morning to earn a small pitance at a factory."[75] At Canton, Illinois, in 1851 many of the English farmers had been textile hands in Lancashire. One settler even remarked, "It is very rare that I come across an Englishman who follows farming that followed the same occupation in England; they are generally from the manufacturing districts."[76] But as more and more capital was necessary to realize the dream of land ownership in America, poor men among the agricultural classes of England, Scotland, and Wales no longer attempted it. Furthermore, American rural society, thinly scattered over broad expanses, lacked the close community life of British villages and hamlets. Nor did American acres bring the prestige of a British squire. Thus many immigrant crofters and farm laborers lost interest in acquiring farms and, like other European peasants, looked for work in the cities; even those who hoped to save the price of a farm were apt never to return to the soil.

In the Old World too, peasants were migrating into industrial and urban centers; whether they went ten or a hundred miles or crossed the ocean to find a new job, the goal was a city. Many choices lay before the British agricultural laborer. A short journey would take him to some manufacturing or mining town.[77] Government or some philanthropist might pay his passage to Canada, Australia, New Zealand, or South Africa; South America also offered cheap land.[78] Joseph Arch, leader of the British Agricultural Labourers' Union of the 1870's, encouraged emigrating members to go to Canada, and union funds sent hundreds to New Zealand.[79] Impoverished Highland crofters also went to the colonies.[80] The fact that many agricultural laborers sailed to new lands within the Empire or trooped into the mines and factories of the homeland accentuated the industrial character of the British who did go to the United States.

How many laborers came to America directly from the British countryside is problematic. Between 1873 and 1918 not 2 per cent of the immigrating English, Scottish, and Welsh with occupations stated that they had been farm laborers. Fully a quarter, however, were recorded as laborers; they probably included countrymen as well as urban workers.[81] Whether plowman or docker, Hodge or proletarian, apparently the British laborer improved his status in the United States. In 1890 the census listed specifically as agricultural laborers only 3 per cent of the working male English, Scottish, and Welsh immigrants and as laborers of any type only another 7 per cent.[82]

Many British Canadians likewise came to American cities as unskilled laborers. Like rural Britain, the farms of Nova Scotia, Prince Edward Island, and New Brunswick suffered from the competition of the prairies and plains. Ambitious farmers' sons and daughters from the Maritimes struck out for the cities of New England, which needed the girls as domestic servants and the lads in many unskilled jobs.[83] In 1900 four steamship lines were engaged in ferrying them for a few dollars from Halifax or Yarmouth to Boston.[84] As the "Boston States" attracted young Maritimers in quest of fortune, so Chicago, Detroit, and other midwestern cities drew emigrants from Ontario.[85] The census of 1890 described only about 6 per cent of the male British Canadians in the United States as agricultural laborers, though another 10 per cent were unskilled hands of some kind.[86]

In a sense, America offered even more to laborers than to skilled craftsmen. While the latter had their good jobs and might rise in their own industries, unskilled greenhorns with native ability, ambition, a "willingness to work and to take the work which presents itself," and a bit of luck could go high as any.[87] Several eulogistic books and articles have listed, almost at random, English, Scottish, Welsh, and Canadian immigrants who made their mark and their fortune.[88] About such diverse individuals it is difficult to say more. The crude occupational categories of the census, while useful for industrial workers, cast little light on men in mercantile and financial callings.[89]

It is doubtful whether successful immigrants owed much to old-country mercantile experience. The colonies of English and Scottish merchants in American ports early in the nineteenth century no doubt did, but afterwards British bookkeepers or clerks found the old practices out of fashion in the United States.[90] There, British consuls warned,

> British training, even the best, is looked upon as a positive disadvantage. A trained British clerk has to unlearn all that he has learned at home before he can conduct business on American methods . . . Employers prefer to take on an untrained boy and start him from the bottom of the ladder . . .
>
> In the large cities there are a number of immigrants who have come

to this country seeking clerical work, and, running short of funds, have gradually got to looking shabby and find that the addressing of envelopes or other low-paid work is all they can get . . . These men soon drift into the 'down-and-out' class.[91]

On the other hand, many bookkeepers, salesmen, buyers, and exporters and importers were British and Irish.[92] A group of British-born Wall Street brokers sent Queen Victoria annual birthday messages during the 1880's.[93]

Although many inexperienced British newcomers eventually became successful merchants, the only commercial business in which the British were conspicuous as a group was one for which many had been trained at home. Young men who had learned the drapery trade in Scotland — especially Glasgow — worked in, and perhaps eventually set up their own, dry-goods stores from Boston to San Francisco. During the 1880's and 1890's these expanded into modern department stores, where young Scottish immigrants who knew or wished to learn the business could always find a berth. A Scottish merchant of Worcester in the 1880's combined a dozen Eastern and Middle Western stores into a "Scotch syndicate."[94]

In businesses in which the British as a group were not so conspicuous many individuals could be mentioned; a few will serve as prime examples. Samuel Insull was a lower-middle-class Londoner who, having gone to work at fourteen as an apprentice clerk, emigrated in 1881 — seven years later — to become Thomas Edison's secretary. Within eleven years manager of the Chicago Edison Company, he went on to monopolize the public utilities of the Middle West.[95] Erastus Wiman came from Ontario by way of the Toronto and Montreal branches of the Dun mercantile agency to New York, where he managed the central office for twenty-five years, got control of various telegraph interests, and devoted himself to developing Staten Island.[96] None, of course, matched the success of Andrew Carnegie, the Dunfermline boy whose canny calculation of his chances brought him to the peak of the booming steel industry.[97] Late nineteenth-century America set no limit on men like these.

The same was true of professional men and women. In 1890 much higher proportions of British and British Canadian immigrants than of other foreigners worked in the professions (Table 7). Yet whether

Table 7.

Per Cent of Working Population of Each Nationality in Professional Occupations, 1890.*

Nationality	Males	Females
English and Welsh	3.5	5.0
Scots	3.1	3.6
British Canadian	3.8	6.7
All other foreign-born	1.8	1.7
German	*2.1*	*2.3*
Irish	*1.7*	*1.4*
Total foreign-born	2.2	2.5
Native white of white parents	6.7	15.6

* *Eleventh Census of the U.S.* (1890), II, 354, 484–485.

most English- and Scottish-born physicians, teachers, journalists, or lawyers had had British or American training is indeterminable. Statistics of clergymen of certain denominations may indicate the answer. Of more than four thousand Protestant Episcopal clergymen in the United States in 1898, over 15 per cent were natives of the United Kingdom or some part of the Empire. But about three-fifths of these, having gotten their theological education or ordination in the United States, probably had immigrated when children and were essentially Americans.[98] Among Northern Presbyterian ministers in 1897 about 11 per cent were British-born; again, more than two-thirds had prepared for their calling in the States.[99] Since these two American churches were the closest to their British coreligionists, in other sects the proportion of British-born and especially of British-trained clergymen may well have been still smaller. At any rate, few British professional men sailed as immigrants for America between 1871 and 1918.[100]

But if most British-born professional people in the United States were not British-trained, only a few seem to have been adult workingmen when they immigrated, among them such self-made men as

Matthew Mark Trumbull, brickyard laborer turned lawyer, and Robert Collyer, the blacksmith who became a famous preacher.[101] More than four hundred English, Scottish, Welsh, and Protestant Irish nineteenth-century immigrants became renowned enough to be listed in the *Dictionary of American Biography*, but nearly half of them, having been brought to America when children, probably grew up more American than British.

British-American farmers, laborers, and even merchants and professional men were less essential to the United States than skilled miners and factory workers. But to all these newcomers the American economy presented amazing opportunities. Individuals of other nationalities — Italian stonecutters or French silk-weavers, Irish or Scandinavian laborers — might also make fortunes. But in practically every American field which they entered, the British enjoyed the highest status and rose most easily.

Part II. The Cultural Adjustment

9

"In a Foreign Land Amongst Strangers"

Good jobs were only half of British immigrants' good fortune. Their cultural background made the New World less bewildering than it was to other foreigners. As their new neighbors assumed, the "assimilation" or "Americanization" of the British was relatively easy. With folkways and habits of thought acceptable to Americans, they enjoyed a unique advantage over most newcomers.

High wages did give most of them an especially troublefree time of it. Unlike Irish, Italian, or Slavic peasants whose American careers began and often ended with shovel or broom, they could escape the social barriers which starvation wages imposed. During depression years they might have to return home or tramp the country, but in good times, when many other immigrants could make only a slum living, they stood as high on the country's economic ladder as most native Americans.

There were a few unhappy exceptions. In mid-nineteenth-century mill towns or colliery villages where British workmen filled the ordinary as well as the best jobs, their lower ranks felt oppressed. Fall River cotton operatives who toiled from dawn to dark six days a week and lived in dirty corporation tenements, or coal miners' families who endured ramshackle company houses and perennial debt to the company store, thought the land of promise of the 1870's shabby enough.[1] But within a few years in Fall River as other nationalities pushed them up out of the lower-paid mill jobs, English operatives became known as "house-proud" people who "like to live in a good house and have nice furniture and will pay high rents." [2] Among the anthracite miners of Carbondale, the Welsh stood out for their "neat and comfortable homes." [3]

Most British-American workingmen were glad to squander their unaccustomed wages on material comforts. "They can make at least one half as much again here as in England," remarked a Paterson mill owner in 1880, "but then they do not live in the same penurious manner. They come here to enjoy rich food, and want meat three times a day, whereas in England they would be satisfied with cheese and porridge." [4] The Staffordshire potter who had worn "a flannel shirt and a handkerchief around his neck from one week's end to another" soon bought "a white shirt and a white collar and a nice necktie and a pair of patent-leather shoes." [5] The English textile operatives of Philadelphia, the British consul observed in 1880, lived very high indeed for industrial workingmen.[6] During the Homestead steel strike of 1892 a reporter found the family of a "sober and thrifty" Welsh striker living in "a large, handsome cottage in the Queen Anne style, gaily painted," with heavy carpets, upholstered furniture, electric lights, and a parlor organ.[7] Actually, it seldom occurred to social workers or official commissions to describe the quarters of British immigrants. Though sumptuous only in comparison with the standards of Lancashire, Ayrshire, or Glamorgan, their homes were too like the average American one to be singled out.[8]

Prairies and plains might make British farmers and ranchers long for the tidier landscapes of home, but in eastern Pennsylvania the weathered mountains and valleys above the anthracite measures suited Welsh miners, and Appalachian slate villages resembled those of Snowdonia.[9] Isolated and monotonous as an American mill town might be with its single industry, it did bear a family resemblance to Preston, Birmingham, or Merthyr Tydfil. Only Boston really suggested an English town, but immigrants who had grown up amid stone and brick — unlike onetime peasants trapped in some American slum — at least did not miss the open countryside.[10]

No place in America wholly baffled British newcomers. To many an Englishman or Scot lugging his chest down the gangplank at New York or Boston and to many a British Canadian crossing the border, the new country must have seemed rather like the old. Despite two centuries in a new environment, Americans still showed their British origins.

Even the "American language" puzzled the newcomer no more than the accents of some far corner of his own island. Unless he was a Welshman, he was sure to speak intelligible English. Although Gaelic still flourished in the Scottish Highlands and the Maritime Provinces, most Scots who came to the mines and mills of America were Lowlanders whose ancestors' only speech for centuries had been the "broad Scots" dialect of English. Newark with its thread mills had "plenty of Scots from Paisley, Glasgow, and Kirkcaldy, but none from the Hielan' hills, who can speak the Gaelic." [11] Of course, a newcomer's accent and intonation marked his origin. American machinists might be amused at a Scot's worry over "boch losh" in the gears, and it took practice for many an Englishman to pronounce "Ohio" with "a short quick O and with big aspirate *h*io." [12] But they were spared the foreigner's usual struggle to master a whole new language.

Although in elementary schools Britain lagged behind the United States, most English working-class immigrants could at least read and write. In Scotland a strong tradition of nearly universal and largely public-supported schooling ensured popular literacy. Welsh secular schools might be rudimentary, but the vigorous Nonconformist Sunday Schools taught both child and great-grandmother to read the Scriptures. After 1880 compulsory universal elementary education wiped out illiteracy in the new generation. Since most emigrants were young persons from the skilled urban working class, they were likely to have been better educated than the average.[13]

British immigrant workingmen may not have read much of the common literature of the English-speaking countries, but they shared many ways of thought with Americans. They were Protestants. The number of Roman Catholics in Great Britain increased tenfold between 1829 and 1929, but most of them were immigrant Irishmen rather than native English and Highland Catholics or the famous converts of the time.[14] The many Lancashire or Glasgow Irishmen who moved on to America with British industrial training were still

Catholics, a group apart. But (with the exception of the Welsh) the British, unlike Lutherans, Catholics, and most other immigrants, usually could join well-established congregations — Episcopal, Methodist, Presbyterian, Baptist, Congregational — with services in their own tongue. Doctrine and practice ran the gamut from high ritualism through liberal rationalism to fundamentalist evangelism, but no phase of one country's religious tradition was unknown in the other. British immigrants were never suspect in America on account of exotic faith or polity.

Nor did their economic notions — excepting trade unionism — startle Americans. The static outlook of their village forebears long since shattered, British urban workers accepted American belief in the inevitability of progress more easily than did peasants from other nations. Perhaps Americans preached *laissez faire* more wholeheartedly. The early growth of British industry led a shocked Parliament — where traditions of *noblesse* still lived — to regulate intolerable factory working conditions as early as the 1830's. Not for several decades did American state legislatures begin to interfere with hours and safety hazards in mills and mines.[15] But neither country was yet in a mood to move far in this direction; both disclaimed the state's old responsibility for prices, wages, and standards. The ambitious American's watchword was the same self-help which Samuel Smiles recommended to Englishmen.[16] Like a native of the United States, a nineteenth-century British immigrant workingman wished only a fair field and no favor. It was no accident that the son of one such newcomer became the leading American theorist of *laissez faire*, William Graham Sumner.[17]

For all the similarities, no American believed that his country was only another England. Did not the young republic's constitution forbid titles of nobility and enforce legal equality? Was not England saddled with royalty, peers, and paupers? Such differences, however, had little to do with the immigrants. The New World had never attracted many from the upper ranks of the mother country; most Americans were descendants of middle- and lower-class immigrants. Thus the nineteenth-century working-class newcomers found America more congenial than did their wealthy countrymen who wrote so many books about their jaunts through that curious republic. One of the travelers concluded in 1910 that "the Englishman or Scotchman of the lower middle classes . . . most easily adopts the United States as his home. He falls exactly into American ways." Untrammeled in a land of middle-class outlook, he became "twice the man he was in his cramped British environment." [18] Indeed, who was more American than such an ambitious foreigner?

Even well-born English immigrants observed that although British-Americans were not "altogether of the kind you would have associated with in England, . . . you will find that the majority improve very much when they become their own masters and get a home they can call their own." [19] Some workingmen clung to old terms to describe their new status. An American editor was amused by a Fall River Englishman who, having prospered through "hard labor, frugality, and fortunate investment," testified in court that for five years he had been following the occupation of "gentleman." [20] Most were glad to adopt American equalitarian notions. In 1880 an English visitor met immigrant workingmen whom he had known at home:

> They were no longer the same men. Here [in England] their employers seldom or never spoke to them, and the workmen were rather glad, as they feared the communication would relate to a reduction of wages. They thought it hardly prudent to look a foreman or overseer in the face . . . In Lancashire it never entered their heads to introduce me to their employers. But when I met them in America they instantly proposed to introduce me to the mayor of the city. This surprised me very much, for when they were in England they could not have introduced me to the relieving-officer of their parish, with any advantage to me, had I needed to know him. These men were still workmen, and they did introduce me to the mayor as a 'friend of theirs' . . . in an easy, confident manner, as one gentleman would speak to another.[21]

As their economic position assisted their social adjustment to America, so the British immigrants' cultural background contributed to their material fortunes. Language enabled them to go wherever an American might go; they were not limited to dealing with their fellow countrymen in the United States. British clergymen filled pulpits in many a church with a native American congregation.[22] American newspapers were glad to hire British journalists.[23] Dozens of English actors and actresses, intoxicated by American applause and dollars, cast their lot with the country.[24] Even men who started in America as laborers might rise at least as easily as the same sort of native Americans. Indeed, it is the great diversity of the fields in which the British were able to achieve success which makes many of them difficult to classify.

Englishmen were disconcerted, of course, to find that in Yankee breasts a family grudge rankled against the old mother country. "The instant they find you are English they immediately drop all other topics of conversation to refer to the time 'we licked you badly,' or to discuss the degeneracy of the House of Lords, or some other topic which they think will be of interest to you." [25] (Welshmen thus accosted were likely to startle Americans by most heartily seconding the indictment of England! [26]) American Anglophobia had many sources: old wars against redcoats, the Irish bias of the press, manufacturers' dread of free trade, free-silverites' fear of London bankers, and behind all a lingering sense of colonial inferiority.[27] During the 1860's an English-American warned against ruffling this tuft in the Yankee plumage:

> I would advise new settlers not to meddle with politics, nor to speak with disparagement of either the people or their country; never give their own country the least advantage when comparing it with America; never tell their neighbors that they neither like America nor her institutions — or that they wish themselves at home again. The American people are exceedingly sensitive, about both themselves and their favoured land, and they are seldom troubled with anything like squeamishness in thinking aloud in the presence of strangers. Englishmen in particular would do well not to brag about the "Flag that's braved a thousand years," nor of the land where the great Charter of the Constitution acknowledges every man's house his castle; neither should they boast of England being the birthplace and the cradle of social liberty! [28]

But although some lamented that this Anglophobia alarmed British emigrants into going to Canada or Australia instead of to the

United States, it was John Bull whom Americans abhorred and not the actual Welshman, Scot, Canadian, or even Englishman in their midst.[29] Politicians might twist the lion's tail to please Irish constituents, but an Englishman who had lived several years in America remarked, "The speakers that denounced Great Britain, as a general rule, like Englishmen greatly, and did not hesitate to admit to us in private that the whole business was electioneering clap-trap." [30] Not immigrants but symbols of British power goaded Americans to fury. The *Elmira Telegram* in 1890 objected to the singing of "God Save the Queen" in the United States as "a sacrilege . . . disgusting and odious to every good citizen." [31] When a New Brunswick schooner put into Bridgeport in 1892 flying the Union Jack at her masthead instead of the customary flag of the country, a thousand persons thronged the dock while the revolver-brandishing captain — one O'Grady — drove off a company of militiamen who had threatened to strike his colors.[32] Even the sporadic antagonism of skilled American workmen toward British competitors for jobs included no personal dislike.[33] The rival Amalgamated Society of Engineers might seem "an institution whose principles are antagonistic to American ideas," but the Machinists' and Blacksmiths' Union in 1871 invited the English engineers themselves to join them.[34]

At the opposite pole, the Anglomania of some Americans had equally little to do with the immigrants. Newly created industrial and commercial barons — or their wives — aped the English aristocracy.[35] English tailors, their shops emblazoned with British coats of arms, outfitted the four hundred's daughters.[36] New York hotels adopted stylish British names.[37] A British title assured its bearer — frequently an imposter — unlimited credit or even a rich wife from the gullible republicans.[38] American "admiration for the Queen is remarkable, even to English people," a British visitor commented in 1882.[39] All classes loved to trace their British ancestry.[40] In North Carolina the descendants of colonial Highlanders had their corner of the state reorganized as "Scotland County." [41]

But those British who settled among the Americans passed almost unnoticed. They hardly seemed to be "immigrants" in the usual condescending sense of the word. The "immigrant problem" had nothing to do with prosaic English, Scots, and Canadians, or even the more clannish and foreign-speaking Welsh.[42]

Thus the British escaped the usual American ridicule of foreigners, and they themselves saw nothing ludicrous in their place in American society. On the vaudeville stage the caricature of the Irishman, German, Jew, or Italian was an exaggeration of an actual lower-class type which any immigrant or city-bred American could recognize. The "stage Englishman," however, was a titled fop, "vulgarly overdressed, almost invariably wearing white spats over his boots, with a single eye-glass, with a walking stick, and silk hat. Whatever his class in life he uses no h's and repeatedly exclaims, 'Don't you know,' 'deucedly clever,' and the word 'blooming' in every other sentence."[43] This incongruous dandy hardly represented anyone's notion — except for the "h's" — of the miners and mill hands who settled in America.[44]

Nor did Americans tag the British with opprobrious names as they did "micks," "dagoes," "hunkies," and the rest. One who argued loudly for England might be called "John Bull" — hardly likely to offend him.[45] "Cousin Jack," the Cornish miner's sobriquet on Lake Superior, he himself had imported from Cornwall.[46] Although a Welshman might object that such names as "Taffy" or "goat" were the subject of "jests by cheap wits," these also had the respectability of long usage in the old country.[47] A Scot would feel more surprise than hurt if some American knew enough to call him "Jock" or "Sandy." As for the English, the British naval and merchant marine ration of lime juice to prevent scurvy inspired "lime-juicer" or "limey," but these were not widely used, except for sailors, before the first World War.[48] In Fall River the name "jick," implying more contempt than any of the others, was coined by Portuguese mill laborers who resented their Lancashire overlords.[49] But few Americans used any such terms; they seldom thought of their English, Welsh, or Scottish neighbors as foreigners.

And to the latter the United States did not seem a "foreign" country so much as "this 'Greater Britain' in which we have made our home." [50] Emigrant workingmen cared little whether the British flag or the American flew over them; the long voyage to Australia gave a greater sense of expatriation than did the Atlantic crossing.[51] "An Englishman never means the natives of the United States when he speaks of 'foreigners,' " a British traveler remarked; "he reserves that epithet for non-English-speaking races." [52]

The British in fact shared native Americans' "racial" prejudices. When "a quantity of Dutch people" settled near an English farmer in Wisconsin in 1847, he complained, "I Do not like them as well as English for one thing theire are principaly Catholics." [53] A young Scottish granite cutter working in Pennsylvania in 1885 refused to "be bossed by a nigger." [54] As for the "new immigrants," there were British-American editors who opposed the coming of "thousands of hungry starving Italians, Hungarians," and other "general pests" or who justified Russian pogroms as no more than the Jews deserved.[55] George Gunton attacked the "jew clothiers" of Fall River and dismissed Disraeli as "the Dizz Jew." [56] The bias of the English often thwarted trade-union leaders who tried to unite them with foreign-speaking workmen. At an operatives' meeting in Fall River in 1878 a French Canadian who briefly addressed his fellow countrymen in French "was repeatedly insulted by the English-speaking audience, being hissed and hooted and laughed at." [57]

Skilled British craft unionists particularly disliked the European laborers who, sometimes as strikebreakers, after 1880 gradually took their places in American industry.[58] John Golden, the Lancashire Irish leader of the United Textile Workers, in 1906 contrasted "the English-speaking people" with "the foreign elements" overrunning the mills.[59] Indeed, dislike for the "new immigrants" discouraged British colliers from entering American mining, which by 1910 seemed "a Hunkey's job." [60] The early-twentieth-century rule that every newcomer to the mines had to work two years as a laborer made things still worse. As a visitor to Scranton observed: "It goes against the grain in an English-speaking man to fetch and carry for a Slovak or a Pole." [61]

The British sense of kinship with Americans was expressed in many ways. Except for the Welsh, British-Americans intermarried with native Americans to a greater degree than did other immigrants.[62] They would have agreed with the Parliamentary report which lumped native Americans and British and Canadian immigrants together as one "American-British" race.[63] British Canadians were indeed as "American" as the Americans; until their own nationalism took root late in the nineteenth century, many looked forward with equanimity to the Dominion's inevitable annexation to her southern neighbor.[64]

And the British seldom lived apart from native Americans. Of the farmers, only the Welsh generally chose to band together in their own communities.[65] Except in places like Fall River or Scranton where some industry drew men together, American towns and cities had no British Canadian, English, Scottish, or even Welsh districts to equal the Irish, French Canadian, Italian, or Polish neighborhoods. No native American discrimination compelled the British to live by themselves. To be sure, the Welsh and the Scots, and to a lesser degree the English, were apt to gravitate to a few wards of a city. Columbus had its "Welshburg" and "Jonesborough." [66] In New York about the middle of the century some spoke of a "Scotch quarter," but actually this stretched along the uncrowded upper west side of the island.[67] In most cities neither the Welsh nor the Scots were as concentrated as Irish or German immigrants — far less so than the "new immigrants" who came after 1880. Although they usually did not disperse through a city quite on the pattern of old-stock Americans, the British were segregated only in the sense that Americans were — outside the "foreign" districts.[68] In Fall River the English moved out of sections where incoming French Canadians or Portuguese settled. Their own ability to pay high rents was not the only reason; they were uncomfortable living too close to the "foreigners." [69]

"Englishmen assimilate quickly and easily," a Parliamentary report concluded in 1906. "At the same time there is no tendency among Americans to reproach a man with foreign, least of all British, birth or make it stand in his way." [70] What happier lot could a man ask who had left his old haunts to make his way under strange skies?

But no matter how favored by American economic and cultural circumstances, the British could tell a hawk from a handsaw and the eagle from the trident. If they arrived assuming that an English-speaking country must be much like home, they soon discovered that it was "hard work for an Individual to leave the social circle of freinds and aquaintances and seek a new home in a forigen land amongs strangers." [71] Torrid summers and arctic winters which could sallow even "the rosy cheeks of Wales" were not the worst of it.[72] It was the un-Britishness of American society which most often outweighed the fat new pay envelope. Men could strike against long working hours, but what could they do when American food, no matter how abundant, failed to appease hunger? Boarding-house cooks, knowing nothing of "the substantial joint," served up "made dishes" in "a miserable caricature of a French dinner." [73] For newly arrived Englishmen "nothing semed to Digest properly." [74]

Many grieved also to hear the "couthy, kindly, musical" accents of the homeland fading away into Yankee monotones.[75] In 1866 a Scottish-American deplored the tendency of a few of his fellows

> to nibble their words, to try to smooth down the rough Doric of their Northern tongue, and to lisp or sniffle out the natural speech with which the Creator has endowed them. They would just as soon have people believe that they had been born on this side of the Atlantic and that their grandfather had signed the Declaration of Independence as that they came direct from Drumclog with the parish minister's certificate that their luckie-daddy was ruling elder for forty years.[76]

But though some might thus "out-Herod Herod in Yankee swagger and arrogance," most clung to their own ways.[77] In Lawrence, a Scot observed in 1888, "the ladies especially appear[ed] to have a contempt for the American 'twang,' for they spoke as though they had just come newly over from Paisley or Hawick, the Carse o' Gowrie, or the windings of the silvery Forth." [78] In Chicago even a Canadian stood out in a crowd with the "'mutton-chop' cut of his whiskers," his tweed sacque suit, and his briar pipe.[79]

Americans' informal manners often irritated Englishmen of those classes which expected deference from inferiors. Returning to England in the late 1830's, a gentleman farmer complained of American notions of equality "between the servant and the master, the two working together, eating together, and associating together—a daughter of an Independent Freeholder rising from the table to make room for the servant. Was there ever such a thing? I could not abide it."[80] On Western cattle ranches in the 1880's, a traveler warned,

> the English settler will for some time sadly miss the social laws which govern the intercourse of different classes in the old world. At first he will not like the independence of the cowboy under him, who by look and manner will let him know that the question who is the better man of the two has long been settled in his own mind. His hands will itch when some saucy 'Do it yourself' is the only answer he receives to some order concerning a matter not quite within the scope of his 'help's' duties.[81]

The higher in the British social scale a man stood, the less likely was he to accept American culture.[82]

Of course most British immigrants, who as workingmen had derived least benefit from the homeland's class structure, were glad to leave off cap-touching and forelock-tugging and let their "elbow joint stiffen."[83] Yet even they grumbled that in this free and easy country their own children showed them little of the proper respect.[84] Furthermore, British artisans, accustomed to recognition for such status as they had achieved, were annoyed by American employers who, not having mastered the trade themselves, did not honor a journeyman's ability or position.[85] Some British-American labor leaders distrusted schemes, successful in the old country, for arbitration of disputes between masters and men. In Britain one could rely on the upper classes, from whom arbitrators were often drawn, to uphold the tradition of disinterested responsibility; parvenu American aristocrats were too biased.[86] And in this land of equality and hard work, the immigrants sensed a paradoxical contempt for men who failed to rise above manual labor. "My financial condition may be a trifle better," said a Wisconsin Englishman, "but my social condition was much better in England. There a mechanic is respected." [87]

In fact, in all things but money and quick promotion, British-Americans thought the United States a debased copy of their homeland. Many seemingly familiar customs and institutions had lost their British essence. "The Land of Slipshod," one immigrant in 1885 called the country, its language not English but "a silly idiotic jargon — a mere jumble of German idioms and popular solecisms, savored by a few Irish blunders," the enforcement of its basically English legal code "totally farcical," and its children half-educated, spoiled, and unruly. America resembled

> a big, ungainly youth who had run away from home when little more than a child; being compelled to earn his own living prematurely, he had subsequently no small amount of conceit at the phenomenal prosperity attained at so early an age. As the scramble, however, in order to secure this success, had been arduous in the extreme, the enterprising youth in question had not found time or opportunity to study out thoroughly all the fundamental principles of things.[88]

In 1875 another wrote from Indiana to his sister at home, "*Oh I should be very happy* to have you come over here, but my poor Mother was so disgusted with this Country that I am afraid to say come to you." [89] An Englishman, struggling with a Wisconsin farm in the 1840's for the sake of his children's future, sighed that "the woemen in general are the most Disatisfied with theire situation." His wife bore this out: "As for saying how I like the cuntry all I can Say is I am Happy with a good husband and I know it is my Duty to strive to make him happy also." [90] From a Kansas farm forty years later another Englishwoman, fondly recalling the old village church, asked, "Who is choir master now do you sing yet. Our children have no notion of singing. But I blame the schools for that. There is nothing like there is in England." [91]

Many returned home discontented with "the manners and habits of the people." Only memories of America's high wages and full dinner tables could draw them back there again.[92] In 1883 a silk dyer returning to Paterson from a visit to his native Macclesfield admitted that although he preferred to live in the Cheshire town, he could not resist American pay.[93] Twenty years later an English visitor to a Fall River mill talked with a Darwen weaver of the same mind:

> "This is the right side of the water," he cried into my ear through the din of the looms.
>
> "Do you mean better to live in?" I replied.
>
> "No," was the answer, "better for making money. I would sooner live in England, and if I can save enough to keep me out of the mill, I'll go home before I die." [94]

There were more things in life than dollars. "I can live poor on little wages in England," a Paterson silk operative concluded, "but a man wants some additional inducements to remain in this country." [95]

Although as the years passed the immigrants' personal ties came to be in America rather than in Britain, their fondness for and pride in the old country waxed. British travelers found them everywhere, "British in heart and memory, . . . always with a touch of the exile eager to see an English face and to hear an English voice!"

> "I just thought I'd come and meet someone from the old country," is the way they put it. Or if he is a Yorkshire man then rather wistfully, "And how may they be doing up Bradford way?" Or if he be a Lancashire man — "Do you happen to have been down Manchester of late?" Or if he be from Somerset, he grips me with both hands and smiles all over his face when he hears that my native town is Bath.[96]

In Pittsburgh in 1904 a Scottish visitor, meeting a group of his former countrymen, was touched "to see eyes glitter over songs that have the 'sough o' hame' in them and to find that after half a century, perhaps, Scotland is still the land of dreams to many, although the steel corner of Pennsylvania is the land of dollars." [97] In 1890 the visit of a party of Welsh ironmasters stirred Pittsburgh workingmen from Swansea, Morriston, and Llanelly to troop down to the Monongahela House with patriotic greetings.[98] However firmly rooted in the United States, British immigrants all hoped for an eventual Whitsuntide and summer at home.[99] And most of the good in America was British. "I shall never forget," a traveler wrote,

> one enthusiastic Scot in the West who seemed to regard America as another Scotland on a large scale and who, after speaking of the Scotsmen, from Hamilton to Andrew Carnegie, who had helped to make America what it is, declared, as he thumped the table emphatically with his fist, that America would have a poor show if it had not been for the Scottish.[100]

Love of the homeland was of course not peculiar to British immigrants. But they suffered no economic and psychological buffeting such as sharpened most other nationalities' nostalgia. Their wages were the highest; no artificial barriers kept wealth and recognition from them; Americans accepted them as equals. Yet they too clung to old loyalties. The bond was not merely sentimental or figurative. British-Americans were sure to answer the cries of British soldiers wounded in the Crimean War or of victims of a Welsh mine disaster or a Lancashire or Highland depression by raising relief funds of several thousand dollars.[101]

Most significantly, even after years in the United States subjects of the Queen disliked to renounce their old allegiance and to become American citizens. When war between the two countries threatened in 1842, even British sailors who had served several years in the Yankee navy departed for Liverpool.[102] During the 1860's an English-American observed of his countrymen generally, "They are patriotic John Bulls. They take British papers, frequent British beerhouses, drink British ale, and are proud and happy to call themselves 'British residents.'"[103] And after 1870, when an Anglo-American naturalization treaty was finally adopted, they could no longer continue to claim British citizenship once they had taken out American papers.[104]

Naturalization statistics are late and inadequate. In 1900, by which time special circumstances had led many to become voters, adult male British immigrants who had not applied for their first papers included 13 per cent of both the English and the Scots and 21 per cent of the British Canadians, though only 7 per cent of the Welsh. Among other immigrant groups who had come to America over approximately the same period the proportion of aliens was somewhat smaller: 10 per cent of the Irish, 8 per cent of the Germans, and 11 per cent of the Scandinavians.[105] The census of 1920 exhibits the same pattern. Of male immigrants of voting age, 15 per cent of the English and the Scots, 22 per cent of the British Canadians, and 9 per cent of the Welsh had not begun the naturalization process, as against only 11 per cent of the Irish, 9 per cent of the Germans, and 12 per cent of the Scandinavians. While these differences are not extreme, before 1890 the lag may well have been considerably greater.[106]

The Welsh, however, did not share this British characteristic; in both 1900 and 1920 no immigrant nationality had a higher proportion of fully naturalized citizens. The Welsh-Americans were no less attached to their own homeland — Wales — than were the English or the Scots to theirs. But they were not equally loyal to the "Queen of England." [107]

Only on this question of naturalization did American Anglophobia directly touch the immigrants. Americans were particularly concerned that the British become citizens; aloofness seemed to challenge the boasted superiority of American political institutions.[108] British subjects could not understand this American fetish — a ceremony unrequired by any other nation and unnecessary in the dominions, the lands most like the United States. One Englishman remonstrated in 1916:

> If circumstances lead me to Mexico, Turkey, or Germany, to South America or to China, am I to give up my birthright and become a subject of Mexico, Turkey, or Germany or any other power? Your suggestion that unless a Briton is prepared to give up his nationality he should stay at home seems to me utterly preposterous . . . An American living in England is never pestered to become a British subject . . . May I ask, therefore, why an Englishman over here should be heckled into becoming an American citizen.[109]

Some objected to the form of the naturalization oath, by which one forswore the Queen by name and pledged to fight against, perhaps, the mother country.[110] Others, both workingmen and employers, wanted no such ties, as they expected to leave America at the first sign of hard times.[111] But probably most felt just as Americans feared they did; granting the United States' material advantages, Britons of all people could hardly subscribe to the fantasy that constitutional government and individual freedom were American inventions or monopolies. The idea that justice and public integrity were purer in the States, with every newspaper full of stories of corrupt city bosses, fraudulent government contracts, venal judges, and lynch law, than in the Britain of Gladstone seemed to them unusually perverse.[112]

The naturalization process itself was apt to exhibit American officialdom at its worst. In 1906 one would-be citizen, the Cornish socialist John Spargo, described his ordeal. The clerk, a

> young man of a class closely related to the yahoo and the hoodlum, . . . [regarded] the applicants for citizenship . . . as his inferiors, to be mocked by him at will. I felt angry — all the more because I knew that an indictment for participation in election frauds loomed before him. And I could not help thinking that in the land whose citizenship I was relinquishing there would have been no possibility of such disgraceful conduct toward applicants for anything. . .
>
> And such questions! Some of them absolutely horrified me. I had been in lands where one had to have passports to travel and where life is spent under very strict government surveillance, but never where the lines were more tightly drawn around one's personal liberty. I thought of Russia and then of the England I had already renounced. Did I really want to give up English freedom for citizenship in a land where I could not be free to read what books I liked or to attend public meetings of all kinds?

Appalled by signs of "pull" by certain applicants, Spargo sympathized with an old Scot who the previous week had flung his naturalization certificate on the clerk's desk, exclaiming, "Take this paper. I do not want it, for I am sick of the corruption and favoritism shown everywhere. I don't want to be a citizen in a land where there is no justice."[113]

Thus while British immigrants found America a fine place to make their fortunes and while they felt more at home there than any other foreigners, few doubted that for a proper life the old country was, after all, the only land.

10

Old Ways and New Ties

Like all other immigrants whose hearts were still at home, British-Americans strove to preserve what they could of the familiar ways of the old country. At whatever points America seemed lacking they banded together in their own social institutions. Thus linked, they were an autonomous community like those Irish-American or Polish-American enclaves which native Americans thought so insidious. But while the strange and unfriendly environment helped drive Irish or Polish newcomers in upon themselves, the British were quite free to enter American affairs. Nor did their voluntary banding together cut off either English, Scots, or Welsh from the broader society about them. Yet even they, prizing their peculiar cultural identity in the midst of the new world, could hardly live without social institutions of their own.

What the British could not bring with them to the United States they at least remembered fondly. British public personages still seemed more real than the ludicrous statesmen of Yankeeland. Apart from that ostentatious republican Andrew Carnegie, a few radicals, and a handful of eccentric Boston Jacobites, Englishmen and Scotsmen of every class revered the Queen and her family.[1] In 1900 one observed, "Nothing . . . develops the loyalty of an Englishman to his Sovereign to such an extent as expatriation." [2] Schism rent an English club in Philadelphia during the 1850's after a banquet toastmaster dared to pledge the President of the United States before the Queen.[3]

When Victoria was married in 1840, the British of New York celebrated for two days, regaling several hundred poor English, Scottish, and Irish widows of the city with a roast ox and a thousand-pound wedding cake.[4] The Queen's subjects and former subjects throughout the country annually banqueted on her birthday, May 24, and perpetuated it after her death as Empire Day.[5] To commemorate her Jubilees in 1887 and 1897 every town with enough British-Americans to form a committee had its special church services, processions, outings, and banquets. During the 1887 festivities in New York two thousand persons attended services at Trinity Church, four thousand packed the Metropolitan Opera House for a musical program, and twenty thousand went to Staten Island for games and fireworks.[6]

When the old Queen died in 1901, British-Americans thronged churches all across the North and West.[7] They turned out again the next year to mark her son's coronation and thereafter to commemorate his birthdays, his death in 1910, and the crowning of George V.[8] Other joyful milestones in the royal family's course, such as the marriage of Princess Louise in 1871, they marked with dinners and balls; unhappy events, like the death of the Prince Consort in 1861 and of the Duke of Clarence in 1892, with condoling messages.[9] When Prince Arthur visited the United States in 1870, the British residents of New York, Boston, and other cities offered addresses of welcome.[10] Other notables likewise got warm greetings from deputations such as the Scots who honored the Duke of Argyll in 1879 or those who sailed to New Brunswick in 1901 to see the future King George and Queen Mary.[11]

During most of the nineteenth century the reigning house reminded the Welsh only of their long-lost independence; they had small love for the "scandalous" Albert Edward — "Prince of Wales, indeed!" [12] But the ceremony at Caernarvon castle in 1911, when a boyish and more winning prince assumed the title, fired their hearts.[13]

From across the ocean British politicians' struggles appeared more titanic than ever. What were paltry Yankee politics alongside the battles which Gladstone waged with Disraeli or Chamberlain? After Disraeli in 1878 plucked Peace with Honor out of the Eastern Question, the California British rewarded him with another trophy, "a silver brick adorned with quartz specimens."[14] In later years the fondest dream of Welsh-Americans was a visit by the — to them — incomparable Lloyd George.[15] So too when British squadrons put into American ports, their officers could count on a banquet with their expatriate countrymen.[16] The leading British residents of Boston entertained the band of the Grenadier Guards in 1872 and the Honourable Artillery Company of London in 1903.[17]

British tavern-keepers in American cities catered to their fellow exiles' home thoughts under such signboards as the "Robin Hood," the "Dog and Partridge," the "St. George's and Cambrian," and the "Carnarvon Castle." In New York in the 1830's Luke Shaw's Eagle Porter House advertised — besides its skittle alley — that "a *free and easy* takes place every Tuesday evening in the old English style," and for the Welsh the Owain Glyndŵr Tavern kept a harp to accompany its weekly "harmonic meeting."[18] At such houses an immigrant, free from Yankee censure, could "enjoy himself in the true 'Old Country' fashion, taking his pipe instead of cigar, his jug of ale or beer, sitting also to regale himself instead of standing." The host dispensed "the best of malt liquors" and served up "a variety of English relishes in first-rate style, as Welch rare-bits, chops, steaks, ham and beef" — a good English supper hours after American boardinghouse mistresses had doled out their last meal for the day.[19] In Chicago the Round of Beef House announced in 1870 that it would mark the Queen's birthday with "a match at quoits for a silver goblet" and then provide "a mammoth English Round of Beef."[20] Scots in Chicago could play shuffleboard and quoits at the Caledonian or in later years in New York savor the "musty ale and mutton pie" of the Old Grapevine.[21] In Boston the landlord of the Park House in 1882 regaled his British friends with an "old style English Christmas lunch" for which he had imported a quarter of English beef.[22] Boston Scots met at the Breadalbane Dining Rooms.[23]

In the large cities Scottish-American households relied on grocers who imported Edinburgh oatmeal, Glasgow peasemeal, Lochfyne herrings, finnan haddies, and Dundee marmalade and on bakers who made "oat cakes, soda scones, Abernethy biscuits, shortbread, mutton pies, and other national dainties." [24] As for drink, though Bourbon might be tolerated, Scotch and Irish whiskies were preferred; importers also advertised Scotch ale and Dublin porter.[25] A party of Scots who toured the States in 1883 could find nothing worthy of the name of usquebaugh except in their countrymen's homes; at Milwaukee they complained, "We had nae whiskey since we landed — only something ca'd 'rye'." [26] The eventual American popularity of Scotch may have begun among the immigrants. "Some say," a British consul observed in 1901, "that it came into fashion with golf." [27]

With such tastes British workingmen seemed to Americans to be sots who "just filled up their time betwixt the workshop and the beershop." [28] At Paterson an American asserted in 1832 that the English mill hands, usually drunken and unruly, were "the most beastly people I have seen." [29] The first Staffordshire potters to come to Trenton appeared to include "hardly a sober man." [30] In New Bedford the English cotton operatives, an eye out for the police, brewed their bitter in the company tenements.[31] During the 1870's it was not alone the high wages of the hand-jack spinners which led the woolen mills to adopt automatic machinery instead; they still had "the disorderly habits of English workmen. Often on a Monday morning half of them would be absent from the mill in consequence of the Sunday's dissipation." [32]

Pennsylvania anthracite towns in the 1870's had dozens of "saloons *Cymreig*." The preoccupation of Welsh-American communities with the temperance movement only reflected the fact that the miners and mill hands "had learned in Aberdare, Merthyr, Rhymney, &c., to drink beer like water, to get as drunk as tinkers, to swear and curse worse than the demons of the bottomless pit." [33]

Some excused their drinking as an antidote to the exhausting labor in American mines and factories.[34] Others on Middle Western farms thought beer prevented the ague.[35] But, unlike Americans' reckless whiskey guzzling, most of the immigrants' beer drinking was harmless enough — "an old English custom introduced by old-country people like myself," a respectable Fall River Englishman said in 1885:

In England, where I was reared, the habit was for a man, when he drew his pay every Saturday night, to go in and enjoy himself. He was not considered a drunkard; neither do I consider the people of Fall River drunkards. They go in and get their glass of beer as they do in the old country. In this country there has perhaps been some spirits introduced, but the people are not anything like drunkards.[36]

The immigrant artisans to whom beer was so essential long held that America could never hope to make steel to match the English — she " 'adn't the 'ops, you know." [37]

Though tastes in drink differed, Americans shared most of the chief holidays of the British calendar. But Christmas, struggling free from Calvinist inhibitions, lacked the English Yuletide traditions. Among the English-speaking Protestants of New York as late as the 1860's only the Episcopalians held Christmas services.[38] When a party of English farmers celebrated their first Wisconsin Christmas Eve in 1843 by midnight caroling through the village, some startled Americans rushed out in their nightshirts, sure the Indians were attacking.[39] Such ignorance bothered the immigrants not a bit. During the 1870's Fall River stores offered them "your Christmas beef and goose" and "the genuine English plum pudding," and the operatives decked the mill halls with evergreen boughs, ate oranges and apples, and sang, danced, and feasted.[40] In later years an American noted:

The English trim their churches with their own hands — it is no meaningless ceremony with them; they gather the greens and wreathe the holly to welcome the coming of the Christ Child. On Christmas Eve the candles are lighted in many homes and shine a welcome through the windows to the wayfarers; and, best of all, after the midnight service in the church, the waits go about the sleeping city — no whir of spindles or clatter of looms is heard — singing carols.[41]

Early in the twentieth century a party of Fall River Lancashire folk yearly came to Boston to carol through the Back Bay, accept the hospitality of its mansions, and collect money for their parish fund.[42]

But while Americans were assimilating such customs, Boxing Day and the rest of the English season fell before the exigencies of American jobs.

Although in Scotland as in New England dour Calvinists long had ignored Christmas, during the late nineteenth century the Scots gradually softened.[43] But the real holiday of their season was Hogmanay — New Year's Eve. Then in the old country the people gathered at village and town crossroads to consign the old year to "Auld Lang Syne" while guizards, like English waits, went about singing for gifts. The next day brought the "first fittin'," somewhat like the New Year's calls which mid-nineteenth-century Americans paid each other. While Scottish-Americans gradually dropped the old drunkenness of the day, Hogmanay remained their chief festival.[44] Some English immigrants observed the tradition of sweeping out the old year and carrying the new over the threshold.[45] Until late in the century Scots also celebrated Auld Handsel Monday, about ten days after the "new style" New Year's Day.[46]

Scottish immigrants' Hallowe'en traditions probably helped fix that night's American form, though it had long been known in some parts of the country. In 1891 a Scottish-American editor called it

> a festival about which, outside Scottish circles, comparatively little is known in the New World, but . . . if it could only be celebrated in regular old-fashioned style with a blazing fire in the open grate, and on the fire a big pot full of potatoes, and round the fire a wheen lads and lasses trying their fortunes by putting nuts on the live coals, with the younger members of the family dookin' for apples in the dimly lighted background, and all the other accompaniments of covered looking-glasses, turnip lanterns and flickering shadows, we fancy it would be a popular entertainment with other nationalities besides the Scotch.[47]

While Americans did not take up such other British holidays as Whitsuntide, the immigrants soon added American festivals to their calendar.[48] A Waterbury cutler in 1850 explained to friends back in Sheffield, "We have a day that they call thanksgiving & if there is any person that has not a turkey that day they are thought nothing of. That day is on the 29 november so you see we was forced to have one."[49] But the most warmly enjoyed days were those which awakened memories of the homeland.

However America may have won its battles, it was not upon any playing fields. The United Kingdom, however, was swept during the mid-nineteenth century by a gospel of sport preaching the moral virtues of cricket, football, and other games of villagers and public school boys. To Americans, however, such play was a waste of God-given time.[50] In 1840 an emigrant guidebook warned the English workingman that Americans knew

> none of those sports, pastimes, amusements, and recreations such as he has been accustomed to in his own country, as cricket, quoits, rackets, fives, &c., although many attempts have been made on the part of 'old country' people to establish them; to walk much about the city is contrary to general custom and therefore only renders him singular; few, if any, Americans doing so for mere pleasure, Sundays perhaps excepted, and then only for a few hours in the middle of the day, never in the latter part of it.[51]

Americans might be all business, but English newcomers preferred an afternoon of cricket. During the 1830's the knitters and weavers of Philadelphia mills organized cricket clubs; mill proprietors played alongside their workmen. As in England, cricket was equally a game for "gentlemen" amateurs; in Philadelphia, New York, Brooklyn, Boston, Lawrence, and Lowell certain cricket clubs were begun in the 1840's and 1850's by well-to-do English merchants and professional men, and others by workingmen.[52] Fascinated, young Americans soon took the field. Before long a cricket team might include either English veterans or American novices, or both. After the 1840's baseball seduced all Americans except a few snobs and Anglophiles.[53] But on any summer's Saturday afternoon from the 1850's through the 1890's the anthracite miners of Schuylkill county, the English hotelkeepers of New York and Brooklyn, the textile operatives of half a dozen Massachusetts and Rhode Island mill towns, and almost any twenty-two Englishmen in the East, the Middle West, or on the Pacific coast were likely to be found on some level piece of ground with bat, ball, and wickets.[54] "Gentlemen's" clubs, both English and American, also carried on in several cities.[55]

Now and then an "All-England," Irish, Canadian, Australian, or West Indian team thought matches with these cricketers worth a tour of the States.[56] An All-American team which paid a return visit necessarily included several English-born players.[57] Sometimes an American club hired an English expert for the season; eleven such professionals played eleven "gentlemen" of Philadelphia in 1880.[58] But cricket remained an exotic. As British immigration slackened after 1890, each year saw fewer matches. Furthermore, English, Irish, and Welsh immigrants and their children eventually turned to baseball.[59] In fact, the organizer of the first professional baseball team, the Cincinnati Red Stockings, was Sheffield-born Harry Wright, who had been professional bowler of the St. George's Cricket Club of New York.[60]

British football ran a similar course. The United States saw its first rugby and association football during the 1870's. Though American college boys soon adopted a form of the rib-smashing rugger, immigrant workingmen, only part-time athletes, preferred soccer.[61] Since by this time soccer was as well known in Scotland, Wales, and Ireland as in England, men from all corners of the United Kingdom played it.[62] No sooner did a new mill go up than the English or Scottish operatives organized an eleven. During the 1880's clubs took the field in New York and in Fall River, Newark, Paterson, and other textile centers; they battled annually for the championship of the American Football Association.[63] In 1890 there were about twenty-five soccer clubs in Fall River, where two thousand persons might turn out to see a game, and Philadelphia had seven clubs made up almost entirely of British immigrants.[64] Miners, steelworkers, and stonecutters across the country organized football clubs and leagues.[65] Their sons, eyes on the famous personages who played for American colleges, gradually drifted away from soccer.[66] But since it was becoming a European favorite, by 1910 the leagues included teams of Scandinavians, Hungarians, and Czechs as well as British immigrants. Thus the game continued to thrive.[67]

American athletes appropriated the favorite sport of the Scottish immigrants. In Scotland each year many a rural community held its day of "games" — a rudimentary track and field meet — and the best men competed at the great Highland gatherings. In 1836 the Highland Society of New York held its "First Sportive Meeting." [68] Within the next thirty years Scots in Boston, Philadelphia, and several other cities likewise staged Highland games. Caledonian clubs sprang up to manage these patriotic and profitable field days, with all the old contests: "throwing the heavy hammer," "putting the heavy stone," "tossing the caber," "vaulting with the pole," "the running high leap," "the long jump," "the hitch and kick," "the hop, step, and leap," "hurdle races," the tug o' war, and races of 100 yards to a mile. Americans as well as Scots soon flocked by the thousands to Caledonian games in cities the country over. If the Scots frowned on these motley crowds, they welcomed the flood of silver at the gates and soon threw the competitions open to all athletes, be they Scots, Americans, Irish, Germans, or Negroes. Down to the 1870's, however, practiced Scotsmen won most of the prizes. After the Philadelphia games of 1866, they could boast that in the hammer throw "a number of robust men entered, but their awkward style of throwing showed clearly that they had no experience in the art of throwing. Scotland beat the field." [69] The champions of Scotland itself, those braw lads Donald Dinnie and James Fleming, came over in the 1870's for a triumphant and profitable circuit of the Scottish-American games.[70]

By this time the Caledonian clubs had to compete for public favor with American imitators. In fact, the modern American track and field meet evolved directly from the games of the immigrants. The New York Athletic Club ("athletics" then meaning only track and field events) started "handicap Scottish games" in 1868, and Princeton, a Presbyterian college with a Scottish president, held its first "Caledonian Games" in 1873 with a Scottish athlete from Montreal, George Goldie, as gymnastics instructor.[71] Americans abandoned some too peculiarly Scottish events like caber-tossing and — more suitable for picnics — the three-legged and sack races. Objecting to

American semiprofessionalism and preoccupation with "records," the young Scottish workingmen of the Caledonian clubs kept up their games in the old tradition, in several cities to this day.[72] English and Welsh immigrants sponsored less variegated field days.[73]

Scotsmen's "ain game," however, was curling. On many a frozen American pond broom-wielding Scots and Canadians could be seen frantically sweeping the way before a granite "hog" which their skip had sent skimming down the ice. Regular matches between the stonecutters and stonesetters of New York or Chicago suggested the forgotten origins of the game. Nearly every Scottish settlement in the North had its curling club. In New York and the Middle West their leagues held annual bonspiels and challenged visiting rinks from Ontario. The Grand National Curling Club, formed in 1867, during the next fifty years included as many as thirty local clubs. When a mild winter south of the Canadian border gave them only a few days of the sport, curlers nevertheless sat down to a supper of beef and greens and recounted the deeds of skips and sweeps of the past. Though others occasionally joined them in the "roarin' game," curling remained a Scottish and Canadian crotchet. During the summer the Scots played quoits, bowls, and shuffleboard, outdoor games with some elements of curling; they organized a few quoiting and bowling clubs.[74]

On the American copper and iron ranges Cornish miners in rope-trimmed canvas jackets enjoyed their old-style wrestling.[75] A few Scots had shinty teams.[76] During the 1870's in the West, hunting and shooting were popular alike among English gentlemen farmers and coal miners.[77] At the fashionable Illinois shooting resort of Wilmington, where "a tough wiry Englishman" kept bird dogs, there were "so many Britishers about that the place [was] called Little Britain." [78]

In 1873 a Chicago Scot "returned from a visit to Scotland with a knobby set of golf sticks and commenced knocking the 'gutty' balls around a field . . . to the amusement of his neighbors and the joyous sneers of the hoodlums." [79] Shortly after a few Scotsmen started playing golf in a vacant Yonkers lot in 1887, the first club in the country was formed there under the august name of St. Andrew's.[80] In ten years more than a hundred clubs — most of their members wealthy Americans — sprang up; Scots started a few, and many employed Scottish professionals.[81]

Other British sports such as lawn tennis, polo, and yachting were likewise fads of the rich and not of immigrants, and only college boys rowed four- or eight-oared shells. The blue-blooded Englishmen of LeMars did play polo.[82] But British workingmen were at least vicarious sportsmen. The *Labor Standard* kept Fall River mill operatives abreast of New Bedford yachting; the hopes of all the Scots in America sailed with the Clyde-built *Thistle* when she raced for the *America's* cup in 1887.[83] After Harvard oarsmen unsuccessfully challenged Oxford on the Thames in 1869, immigrants in New York — especially "the frequenters of the English alehouses in Bleecker and Houston streets" — pocketed wagers on their countrymen.[84]

Some newcomers were glad to find that horse racing on the English model was already popular in the States. English bookies in 1879 "almost monopolized the straight book-betting business" at Saratoga.[85] The young English gentlemen riders of LeMars formed a Jockey Club before their first year there was out; those of Fairmont, clad in homemade pinks, introduced hurdle jumping to the Minnesota state fair; and even Lancashire colliers wasted no time in clearing Wyoming sage brush for a quarter-mile track.[86]

As mid-nineteenth-century English magistrates suppressed the old prize ring, bare-knuckle fighters — "lusty, low-browed, short-cropped, broken-nosed" — emigrated to America.[87] But the day of the disciples of Bendigo and Gentleman John Jackson was done even there. After the 1880's, when American pugilism adopted the Marquess of Queensberry's boxing rules and gloves, the hardest hitters were generally Americans. In 1897, however, Cornish–New Zealander Bob Fitzsimmons won the heavyweight championship in the United States.[88]

Immigrants from "Our Lady of the Snows" won Americans' fancy with their tobogganing, snowshoeing, and hockey clubs.[89] The Canadians also played lacrosse after the late 1860's; some American colleges took up the game.[90] Even the indigenous American game of basketball was conceived by a Scottish-Canadian immigrant, James Naismith, as an indoor combination of soccer and a game called "duck on the rock" which he had played when a boy in northern Ontario.[91] But however British sports might be altered by Americans, they also flourished unchanged as long as there were young immigrants to play them.

To many British-Americans Saturday afternoon's pastimes mattered less than Sunday's institutions. To be sure, during the nineteenth century few emigrants left Great Britain for religious reasons. Parliament freed even Roman Catholics and Jews from their old civil disabilities, and, though the Anglican establishment offended Nonconformists, old and new forms of dissent flowered as freely in Britain as in America. A few tiny groups did hope to set up their own Bible commonwealths on American soil, among them John Alexander Dowie's disciples at Zion City, Illinois, and some Scottish families who went to Maine in 1904 to establish "the Corporation of the Kingdom." [92] But other British-inspired religious movements in the United States, such as the Y.M.C.A. and the Salvation Army, involved at most only a few immigrant missionaries.[93] Although American Mormons between 1840 and the 1880's persuaded tens of thousands of converts in England, Wales, and Scotland to come to Utah, the vision of land ownership probably moved these immigrants no less than spiritual faith.[94]

If few British came to America expressly to plant their faith, most did wish to worship as they had in the homeland. Since American sects rested on the same doctrinal and ecclesiastical foundations as British churches and chapels, immigrants were likely to find their particular denominations wherever they settled. Nevertheless, in places where they did not or where they swamped the existing congregation, they created their own churches — "immigrant churches" no less than the Irish Catholic, Swedish Lutheran, and other national groups even stranger to native Americans.

Most English immigrants were, if anything, either Anglicans or Methodists. Although the Church of England had long neglected the growing industrial population, many workingmen held to the faith and forms which their village forebears had known. Other Protestant Episcopalians immigrated from Ireland and Canada. But the Episcopal church which they found in the United States, though the well-to-do often patronized it, was a minor sect unprepared for so many new communicants.[95]

When Lancashire cotton workers started to come to Fall River, the town had only one Episcopal church. In the 1870's most English operatives there had no church to which to go. Even if they could find a pew, they "were made to feel the difference between a good coat and a poor one." One explained:

> I was brought up to go to Sunday school and to church, and went in England, but after I got here, folks were different. I suppose if I was going to die, I should have to own to some kind of belief, but as churches run here, I don't like to go. If working people were always treated kindly by those above them, they would go; but as it is these folks that run the churches take no pains whatever to elevate us in any way.[96]

Some operatives joined other Protestant denominations.[97] But old ties were strong. Between 1878 and 1900 Episcopal authorities responded to the Fall River mill hands' desires by creating six new churches or missions; even the original one became known as "the church of the English operatives."[98]

Many Gloucester fishermen from the Maritime Provinces were Anglicans, and towns and villages in mining or farming districts where British people settled soon had their Episcopal churches. In many an American industrial center the spread of this faith was far more the work of English workingmen than of the fashionable newly rich.[99] In a mill town with no Episcopal church a new cricket club was a signal to diocesan authorities that an "English remnant" awaited rescue.[100] If many immigrant Episcopalians resorted to their churches only for marriages, baptisms, and burials, others even after eleven hours' labor in the mill liked to spend their evenings improving their new church building.[101] The more the structures, furnishings, and services resembled those of England, with bells in the steeples and surpliced choirs, the more fond of them the immigrants became.[102]

In eighteenth- and nineteenth-century English industrial towns Methodism provided the emotional fervor and the chapels that the Church of England was slow to give the urban proletariat.[103] Staffordshire miners, among whom were "a good many Methodees," had daily prayers underground.[104] Thus many an English immigrant was an ardent Wesleyan. In a few places in the United States, such as isolated mining villages, Methodist congregations may have been mostly English. But since theirs was a major American sect, Methodists were likely to be swallowed up among their American fellow believers. And so were Baptists, Congregationalists, and other Nonconformists.

One group on the fringe of English Methodism, though originally inspired by an American evangelist, was unknown in the United States when immigrant members first arrived. The camp-meeting fervor of these Primitive Methodists or Ranters had taken English miners and urban workingmen by storm. After the 1820's their little meetinghouses sprang up in coal and ore towns as soon as Englishmen — particularly Cornishmen — appeared. But the Primitive Methodists never numbered more than a few thousand in the United States.[105]

Most newcomers from Scotland and Ulster, like their predecessors of colonial days, were Presbyterians of some stripe. Recurrent schisms had proliferated many rival shoots from the main stem alike in Scotland, Ireland, Canada, and the United States. Nevertheless, since families of Scottish or Scotch-Irish stock had planted their churches all through the frontier West, an immigrant Presbyterian could usually present his certificate to some American congregation.[106] In New England, however, the Congregationalists had absorbed the few Scotch-Irishmen who had settled there in the eighteenth century. Rather than join them, the Scots, Ulstermen, and Scottish Canadians who came to Yankee towns to weave, dress granite, build houses, or sell dry goods at the same time replanted the Presbyterian polity. By 1904 they had nearly fifty New England churches, with more than ten thousand members.[107] Furthermore, even in New York, Jersey City, Detroit, Chicago and other places where American Presbyterians abounded, the immigrants organized churches which were "Scotch" both in name and in membership.[108]

Wherever they went, Scots were bound to maintain their kirk no matter whether the minister's clerical robes and the mode of worship surprised American Presbyterians.[109] Although Taunton, Massachusetts, in 1887 already had fifteen Protestant churches, twenty Scots appealed for funds to put up a building of their own, saying that they, "still adhering to the faith of their fathers, 'do not feel at home' in any other church, and consequently have neglected attending any public place of worship." A Presbyterian minister of New York objected; one could remain true to the Westminster Confession within the existing Congregational churches. "If people who come to our country from Scotland, Ireland, Germany, or anywhere else do not like things as they find them when they get here," he admonished, "they had better either adjust themselves to the situation or go home." But the Scots persevered. Their countryman Robert Gilchrist, the Boston department-store owner, helped found several new churches; without them, he feared, Scottish-Americans would think only of money-making.[110]

Members of the smaller and more austere Presbyterian sects maintained to the last jot and tittle their mode of worship. In Cambridge, Massachusetts, a group of Prince Edward Islanders in 1895 organized the unique American congregation of MacDonaldites, a sect peculiar to their province, and modestly named it "the Church of Scotland." [111] Adamant against singing hymns to an organ or other instrumental accompaniment in the lax fashion of most American Presbyterians, such minor sects as the Covenanters, most of whom came from Ulster or the Maritimes, lined out metrical paraphrases of the psalms in tones that made even the minister think of untuned bagpipes.[112] Covenanters refused to vote in a nation whose constitution did not explicitly acknowledge Christ as king.[113] In so rigorous a congregation the way of the transgressor was hard indeed. Even though he had sinned — and escaped punishment — long before leaving the old country, the session of elders rebuked him and on the Sabbath held him up to public scorn. When called to account for Sunday tippling or football, immigrant Presbyterians were likely to grumble against "Holy Willies" and the "unco' guid" and to seek a more liberal church.[114] But while America gradually softened the rigors of northern Calvinism, most Scottish immigrants were no rebels. They preserved old sectarian loyalties even after the parent groups in the homeland had reunited.[115]

To the few Scottish Presbyterians who thought and spoke in Gaelic, distinct church services were vital. A Highland colony at Elmira, Illinois, in 1864 affiliated with the Canadian Presbyterian Church and, to choose a minister, heard fifteen sermons by applicants who claimed to have the Gaelic.[116] In Boston, where many Highlanders from Cape Breton and Prince Edward Island settled, the Catholics among them apparently lost their separate identity in the Irish parishes. But in 1871 the United Presbyterian Church started Gaelic prayer meetings.[117] Sixteen years later a Nova Scotian minister organized the Scotch Presbyterian Church, which held two Gaelic services each week.[118] Several other Presbyterian churches in Boston, New York, and Chicago ministered to Highlanders whose English was poor.[119]

Because of language, Welsh-Americans had to establish their own churches everywhere they settled. Those begun in the late seventeenth century by Welsh Quakers and Baptists near Philadelphia no longer worshiped *yn Gymraeg*. In the last century, moreover, Wales had been swept by a religious revolution. A new sect of Calvinistic Methodists — actually Presbyterians — had sprung up, and new fervor had entered the older Baptists and Independents (Congregationalists). Most Welshmen now belonged to these three sects. Anglicans were generally the gentry, who did not emigrate; Wesleyan Methodists and Unitarians were small groups. The large Welsh exodus of the early nineteenth century occurred at the height of the evangelical movement; in fact, discontent with the privileges of the established Church of England was at least a minor cause of emigration.[120]

Thus religion pitched the tone of Welsh-American culture. In 1885 an immigrant remarked:

> The genuine *Cymro* can not talk two minutes with you about the pedigree of a horse, the points of a good cow, or the best method of tillage, but he can sit on his heels by the hour and with beaming countenance tell the points of a good sermon or argue a knotty theological dogma.[121]

In new Welsh-American settlements of the early nineteenth century the immigrants' *hiraeth* (homesickness) was more for the chapels and preachers of the old country than for its scenery.[122] "I wish to request someone who is coming over to this valley from the old country," a Gallia County farmer wrote in 1851, ". . . to bring a large Peter Williams Bible."[123]

As soon as possible Welsh farmers, miners, or ironworkers commenced prayer meetings, a Sunday school, and a Bible society and built a union meeting house. Usually within a few years the Calvinistic Methodists, the Congregationalists, and the Baptists each put up their own building.[124] In Pennsylvania and the Middle West, which American Congregationalists had left to the Presbyterians, the Welsh Congregationalists — like Scottish Presbyterians in New England — in effect reintroduced their form of ecclesiastical polity.[125] In the entire country in 1839, an immigrant minister estimated, there were 46 Welsh churches, of which 16 were Congregational, 13 Baptist, 12 Calvinistic Methodist, 3 Wesleyan Methodist, and 2 Episcopalian.[126] Thirty-three years later, besides more than ten union congregations and two or three Episcopal churches, 384 chapels were counted: 154 Congregational, 152 Calvinistic Methodist, 71 Baptist, and 7 Wesleyan.[127] Though many chapels disbanded, their number increased slightly through the rest of the century.[128] Each sect organized state associations; in 1869 the Calvinistic Methodists united theirs in a general assembly.[129]

Welsh chapels were distinct not merely because their congregations punctuated sermons with spontaneous cries of "*gogoniant*" when English-speaking evangelicals would shout "glory." [130] Among what other people did a preacher have that "weird, peculiar intonation of his sermon . . . often strange and objectionable" to non-Welsh ears — the *hwyl*? [131]

> The judicious use of it is confined to the more passionate or pathetic parts of a sermon. It differs entirely from that monotonous tone that is often heard in English churches or the chromatic chanting of the mass before papal altars; it is a *melody* of the purest nature . . . in which the minister pours forth his pathetic passages when under "full canvas" . . . It is the application of sentences in a chanting style to portions of the minor scale . . . The sentence is started, for instance, on E minor. The minister has his own peculiar melody. It ranges here and there from the first to the fifth, often reaching the octave, and then descending and ending in sweet cadence on the key-note . . . The introduction and the deliberative parts are in the major, and the voice continues thus until the emotional point is reached; then it glides triumphantly into a thrilling minor, which generally continues to the close.[132]

Such eloquence made a *cymanfa bregethu* (preaching assembly), whether of a local chapel or one of the large associations, an annual red-letter event for a Welsh sect. Lasting two days or even a week if the *hwyl* started a revival, a *cymanfa* included a whole series of sermons, with prayers and hymns between, by a battery of ministers.[133]

As austere as the Scots, Welsh chapel-goers long abjured organ music in their services, kept the Sabbath strictly, and condemned idle amusements. In the southern Ohio settlements, "parting the hair was looked upon . . . as a sign of too much pride. The men combed their hair straight down over their foreheads." [134] Such extreme piety gradually relaxed as the American-born generations lost command of the Welsh language. In fact, their sects could continue only as long as the *hen iaith* survived. The dearth of books in Welsh handicapped their Sunday schools during the 1850's, but soon Welsh-American printers in Utica and New York brought out tracts, hymnals, volumes of sermons, and lives of preachers.[135] As among other non-English-speaking foreigners in the country, the older immigrants who controlled church affairs long resisted the use of English. Having always heard the gospel in Welsh and suspecting in their children's secular interests a lapse from grace, they felt that *Cymraeg* was inherently more religious than *Saesneg*: "The English language is so used in business and earthly bargains of all kinds, high and low, that it is hardly fit to go to church and chapel on Sunday." [136] An old Ohio Welshman complained, "When English came into the settlement, religion went out of it." [137]

But when at last the choice lay between conducting Sunday schools and services in English and allowing the second and third generations to grow up ignorant of the scriptures and indifferent to the churches, bilingual and then only English services were held.[138] In fact, it was difficult to find an American-born preacher fluent in Welsh, while a man from Wales might not suit the new generation.[139] Thus as men and women who had grown up speaking Welsh passed off the scene, their congregations either melted away into American churches or themselves became virtually indistinguishable from their American fellow believers.[140] In 1919 the Calvinistic Methodists voted to merge their general assembly with the Northern Presbyterians; the state *cymanfaoedd* maintained their identity until the 1930's.[141] Not that the Welsh were wholly submerged; in 1913 the choir of the largest Presbyterian church in Racine was solidly Welsh.[142] But for immigrants who had known the valleys of Wales, their own chapels, whatever the language used, were always the strongest institutional link with the dearly remembered land of their fathers.

In the pages of their own newspapers and magazines British immigrants' old loyalties also shone. Like the churches, the Welsh-American press flourished while Welshmen still spoke their own language. From about 1840 through the rest of the century their three major sects each published monthly magazines of sermons and church news. Most notable were the Calvinistic Methodists' *Cyfaill o'r Hen Wlad* (Friend from the Old Country) and the Congregationalists' *Cenhadwr Americanaidd* (American Missionary). Commencing with the *Cymro America* (Welshman of America) of New

York in 1832, more than a dozen secular weeklies, fortnightlies, monthlies, and quarterlies — leaning heavily on the literary journals of the homeland — appeared at New York, Utica, Scranton, Pittsburgh, and other Welsh centers. There were a few musical papers and even two humorous magazines. Only the religious papers, however, survived more than five years.[143]

At New York in 1851 the first number of *Y Drych* (Mirror) began an unbroken century of Welsh journalism. Moving to Utica in 1861, along its course it absorbed several rival weeklies: *Baner America* (Banner of America) of Scranton, 1866 to 1877; *Y Wasg* (Press) of Pittsburgh, 1871 to 1890; and the *Columbia* of Emporia, Kansas, and later Chicago, 1883 to 1894. At its peak at the end of the nineteenth century the *Drych* claimed twelve thousand subscribers.[144]

Though the gradual decline of the Welsh language in the United States put an end by 1907 to all these periodicals except *Y Cyfaill* and *Y Drych*, several printed in English took their place. First and longest-lived was the *Cambrian*, a literary journal which began in 1880 at Cincinnati as a monthly and later appeared fortnightly at Utica. Besides providing for Welsh immigrants and their descendants who knew more English than Welsh, its founder aimed to record his people's history in America "in a language which shall not be an unknown tongue to future historians." [145] The *Cambrian* suspended in 1919. After 1907 an English-language weekly, the *Druid* of Scranton and Pittsburgh, had nearly as many readers as *Y Drych*. Even the latter, which after 1939 was the only surviving Welsh-American periodical, in recent years likewise has printed most of its news in English.[146]

Thus while language accounted for the profusion of periodicals in the small Welsh-American community, it was not the only reason for an immigrant press. Scots, Englishmen, and Canadians looked in vain in American papers for the news which interested them most — word from home. The first British-American newspapers, the *Albion* (1822 to 1876), the *Old Countryman* and the *Emigrant* (appearing separately or combined between 1829 and 1848), the *Scottish Patriot* (1840 to 1842), and the *Anglo-American*

(1843 to 1847) reprinted news from the latest British papers to reach New York by packet ship.

After 1850, however, the rising immigrant community became as interested in news of its own doings as in the state of trade in Lancashire, some new sensation from the Old Bailey, or the Queen's latest excursion to Balmoral. Thus both *Y Drych* and the *Druid* were truly Welsh-American newspapers. The Scots stood next to the Welsh, in proportion to their numbers in the United States, as publishers and readers of their own papers. From 1857 until 1919 the *Scottish-American Journal*, owned and edited for almost its entire span by Archibald M. Stewart, served as many as fifteen thousand subscribers throughout the country.[147] A New York rival, the *Scotsman* (apparently combined with the *Caledonian Advertiser* in 1874), survived only from 1869 until 1886, and another weekly, John Adamson's *Boston Scotsman*, from 1906 until 1914. A literary monthly, the *Caledonian*, appeared between 1901 and 1923.[148]

No newspapers designed solely for English immigrants lasted long. The New York *English-American* suspended in 1885 after only a year; two *Anglo-Americans*, one in Lawrence in the 1870's and the other in Boston between about 1899 and 1906, did little better.[149] Several weeklies, however, catered to all British immigrants. A Chicago *British-American* appeared in 1864. The Queen's Jubilees first inspired the *British-American Citizen* of Boston (1887 to 1913), the *Western British-American* of Chicago (1888 to 1922), the *British-American* of New York and Philadelphia (1887 to 1919), and two monthlies, the *British Californian* of San Francisco (1897 to 1931) and the *British World* of Chicago (1898 to 1905). The first three each claimed as many as five to twenty thousand subscribers.[150]

Besides these general sheets, Canadian immigrants read the *American Canadian* of Boston (1874 to 1876) and the *Provincialist*, which merged with the *British-American Citizen* in 1887. More than ten thousand subscribed to the *Canadian American*, published at Minneapolis and Chicago (1883 to 1934).[151] Several British-American magazines were published, including the *Anglo-American Magazine* (1899 to 1902) and the *Canadian* (1904 to 1905), both in New York, and the *Inter-Nation*, a Boston Canadian journal (1905 to 1907). Although there were no periodicals for Scottish- or Anglo-Irish immigrants as such, the other papers printed news of them and of Protestant Ireland.

Most of these newspapers, whether Welsh, Scottish, Canadian, or British, were eight-page weeklies. A typical issue culled a page or two of provincial news from the press of the United Kingdom and Canada and eked out a few more with British and American literary excerpts; but it concentrated — especially if a Welsh paper — on the immigrant community in the United States. For British immigrants no longer merely looked back to the old country. They had found their own identity, neither wholly British nor wholly American, but instead Welsh-American, Scottish-American, Canadian-American, or, at least among the English, simply British-American.

11

National Cultures and Immigrants' Societies

The yearly banquet on the Queen's birthday could be left to a temporary committee; a man could now and then visit a tavern kept by a countryman; with cricket or football it was the game rather than the team which went on year after year; the immigrant church cared for one side of life; the British-American weekly came to thousands of individual homes. But for a full sense of belonging to a group with common origins, traditions, and outlook, immigrants needed something more. Here again like other foreigners, therefore, the British carried on their national culture in societies of their own.[1]

Their earliest societies, however, limited themselves to relieving destitute countrymen stranded in American seaports — and to maintaining their country's good name which such paupers threatened. The first was the Scots' Charitable Society of Boston, founded in 1657; during the eighteenth and early nineteenth centuries others began in New York, Philadelphia, Charleston, Savannah, and wherever else the need was endemic. Usually they took the name of their national patron saint: St. George for the English, St. Andrew for the Scots, and for the Welsh, St. David. In the larger cities the St. George's and St. Andrew's societies accumulated endowments and annually dispensed several thousand dollars among hundreds of persons for food and fuel, passage back to Liverpool, or railroad fare to look for jobs elsewhere.[2] The English organizations in the United States and Canada federated in 1875 as the North American St. George's Union and held annual conventions during the next three decades.[3]

Before the 1850's the charitable societies were virtually the only permanent British-American organizations. Gradually their annual banquets became as trenchant a reason for being as was their benevolence. These feasts, with toasts to Queen, President, "the land of our birth," "the land we live in," and so on down the calendar, usually fell on the holiday of the saint whose banner they bore. Though in the old country they had been only dimly aware of these dates, the immigrants made St. George's Day (April 23), St. Andrew's Day (November 30), or St. David's Day (March 1) the great patriotic occasion of their year.[4]

As thousands of British workingmen clustered about American mills and mines and cities, the yearly conviviality of a small philanthropic clique no longer sufficed. During the 1850's they too began to band together to uphold the popular culture of the homeland. But that land was not the United Kingdom. The immigrants redivided the Union Jack once more into the red cross of St. George and the white saltire of St. Andrew — or replaced it altogether with the dragon banner of the ancient princes of Wales. The societies did not admit Britons — only Englishmen, Scots, or Welshmen.

Scotsmen were sure to meet only with brother Scots. Despite their oft-remarked affinity for American ways, their pride in the "land of brown heath and shaggy wood, land of the mountain and the flood" — mill villagers though they might be — burned even brighter on foreign shores. Their ardor fired a fellow Scot on his travels through the United States:

> Scotland is indefinable; it has no unity except upon the map. Two languages, many dialects, innumerable forms of piety, and countless local patriotisms and prejudices part us among ourselves more widely than the extreme east and west of that great continent of America. When I am at home, I feel a man from Glasgow to be something of a rival, a man from Barra to be more than half a foreigner. Yet let us meet in some far country, and, whether we hail from the braes of Manor or the braes of Mar, some ready-made affection joins us on the instant. It is not race. Look at us. One is Norse, one Celtic, and another Saxon. It is not community of tongue. We have it not among ourselves, and we have it almost to perfection with English, Irish, or American. It is no tie of faith, for we detest each other's errors. And yet somewhere, deep down in the

heart of each one of us, something yearns for the old land, and the old kindly people.[5]

How could a Scotsman be no more than American? As one born in Canada shouted on being called a Canadian, "If a cat had kittens in the oven, would they be buskits?" [6]

"Here's tae us; wha's like us?" Proud of their peculiarities, Scots fostered their own culture in America through the Caledonian clubs. A few Boston Scotsmen who for several summers had met for their traditional games organized the first in 1853.[7] Within the next twenty or thirty years others, generally composed of workingmen, sprang up in Scottish-American communities all across the country. By 1918 they had held games in more than 125 towns and cities. Although their year climaxed in the Highland field day, Caledonian societies were more than athletic clubs. They sponsored balls — dancing quadrilles, reels, and the Lancers until the "wee hours" — and concerts of piping and broad-Scots songs; on Bannockburn Day they picnicked on the Yankee heath.[8]

Nor were the Highland games merely imprecise track meets. Besides the caber tossing and the tug o' war, there were contests for the bagpipers' best pibrochs and strathspeys, the most meticulous Highland costumes, and the most flawless sword dance and Highland fling. All could join in reels and quadrilles, and, at least in the earlier years, Highland dew flowed freely at the "chief's tent." [9] Whether managed by a Caledonian club or some other group, the games gave Scots in many an American city their year's best holiday and "let a body see a body." Young and old — "bankers, railway magnates, tradesmen, and mechanics" — turned out, the women in tartan dress, the men — if they had nerve enough — in kilt and sporran, plaid, and eagle-plumed bonnet.[10] A New York Scot remarked in 1896 that he had seen "more wearers of the Highland costume . . . at the annual games of the New York Caledonian Club than at most similar gatherings in the Land o' Cakes." [11] What did it matter if Irishmen and Negroes carried off a few athletic medals or if a dancer interpolated a hornpipe step into the Highland fling

— or even performed *seann triubhas* in kilt instead of trews — so long as Jock Tamson's bairns could meet for a friendly crack? [12]

In 1867 the Caledonian clubs of both the United States and Canada held their first international games; three years later they federated as the North American Caledonian Association. During the next thirty years more than a hundred local clubs throughout the country followed the Association's rules at their annual games.[13]

The Caledonians were less assiduous about their other mission of fostering Scottish literature, but other British-American societies did celebrate the homeland's men of letters.[14] During the 1830's English, Scottish, and Irish New Yorkers annually banqueted on Byron's birthday.[15] In 1871 most Scottish-American communities marked the centenary of Scott's birth; in New York his countrymen raised a fund for a Central Park replica of his Edinburgh statue.[16] Lowlanders commemorated the birthday of James Hogg, the "Ettrick Shepherd." [17] In 1912 all the British societies of Boston observed the Dickens centenary.[18]

The cult of Burns surpassed all others. Hardly a Scottish concert or banquet ended without a dozen songs or recitations from their ain darlin' bard. He who wrote

> The rank is but the guinea's stamp;
> The man's the gowd for a' that,

exactly suited his countrymen seeking their fortunes in America. As early as 1820 they held a banquet in New York on his birthday, and everywhere thereafter the twenty-fifth of January was the one day which all Scottish-Americans were sure to celebrate.[19] Wherever they lived, in 1859 they marked the hundredth anniversary of his birth and in 1896 that of his death.[20] If there were several Waverley societies dedicated to the aristocratic Sir Walter, Burns clubs sprang up by scores, modeled on those in Scotland. The first in America began at New York in 1847.[21] Unlike other Scottish groups, most of these clubs were open to all; some probably included very few Scots. But most members were Scotsmen who knew no better way to demonstrate their love of the homeland than by proclaiming that they were "a' prood o' Robin." In a dozen cities after years of money raising they placed statues of Burns in the public parks.[22]

Amateur recitations were well enough, but Scottish-Americans welcomed professional entertainers who toured their communities year after year. "Concert companies" presented ballads, piping, and dances.[23] The kiltie bands of Canadian Highlander military units made the American circuit.[24] Harry Lauder was not the first Scottish comedian for whom all his countrymen would turn out.[25] Professional actors played up and down the country, while the immigrants themselves essayed such plays as "Rob Roy Macgregor, or, Auld Lang Syne," "Cramond Brig," and "The Relief of Lucknow."[26]

Town and shire patriotisms also flourished. In Fall River, East Liverpool, or upper Michigan any British organization was inevitably straight Lancashire, Staffordshire, or Cornwall, but in more mixed city populations most parochialism was among the Scots. In Boston, New York, and Chicago the natives of Caithness, Lewis and Skye, the Orkneys and Shetlands, Aberdeen, Dundee, Glasgow, and many another Highland district or Lowland town belonged to their own societies as well as the broader ones. In Scottish Border Clubs in Boston and Philadelphia, for instance, men from the counties of Roxburgh, Selkirk, Peebles, Dumfries, and Berwick annually observed the Hawick Color Bussing and Common Riding, singing "I Like Auld Hawick the Best" and that town's interminable war-song with its booming refrain,

> Teribus, ye Teri Odin,
> Sons of heroes slain at Flodden,
> Imitating Border bowmen,
> Aye defend your rights and Common![27]

The Shetland Benevolent Association of Chicago each year reproduced the Lerwick Up-Helly-A festival with "guizers" in Viking garb.[28] Nor were antique clan loyalties wholly dead; MacLeans, Sinclairs, and MacKinlays foregathered in Chicago in 1893.[29]

A few societies of Highlanders, many of them Maritime Provincialists, fostered the Gaelic language in New York and Chicago.

Besides Highland games, some held an annual *ceilidh* with contests in piping and Gaelic singing or staged a waulking (cloth fulling) ceremony.[30] But since Gaelic-speaking Scottish-Americans were too few to maintain their language and its sparse literature, they usually had to resort to some Irish *feis* to hear their mother tongue.[31] Members of most "Highland" societies actually were Lowlanders who, having adopted the kilt as a national badge only after immigrating, were a bit "fasht" when American women and children stared at its skirtiness above their pallid knees.[32]

Although the Welsh were not athletes like the English or Scots and frowned on dancing and whisky, of all the British-Americans they were the most anxious to preserve the culture — particularly the language — of their fatherland.[33] To many industrial workers from South Wales as well as to farmers and slate quarrymen from the North, English was nearly as foreign as it was to continental Europeans. One later recalled that in Pittsburgh during the 1850's Welsh was "the only tongue spoken in those quarters of the city where our ancestors resided . . . Their children were likewise as 'Welshy' as their parents, and the different dialects that were used enabled one almost instantly to discern from what section of Wales a man came."[34]

In America as in Wales, language was the prime mover of Welsh institutions. "*Oes y byd i'r iaith Gymraeg*" (the world's lifetime to the Welsh language) was their oftest-repeated motto. Many dreamed, between the 1850's and the 1880's, of founding a purely Welsh settlement — *Trefedigaeth Gymreig* — where, remote from their usual Irish, German, and Yankee neighbors, they could live under the ancient laws of Hywel Dda. One such colony which a Llanbrynmair group under Samuel Roberts, an Independent minister, started in eastern Tennessee in 1856 soon foundered because of poor soil and the Civil War. In 1865 another party, fearing that in the United States their vernacular would be lost within a few generations, emigrated from Wales to a remote part of the Argentine. A few Welsh North Americans sailed south to this Patagonian *Wladfa Gymreig*.[35]

Even immigrants who had only a smattering of Welsh clung to it proudly. A Milwaukee Welshwoman wrote in 1891 to a relative in the homeland:

> I must ask pardon first for one thing & that is I am not able to write a correct Welsh Letter in return so I will take the liberty of writing it in English but now I don't wish you to carry the wrong idea & think I have forgotten my *Dear* Native *Language* as I can speak that as good as ever & I am proud of it & I know I will never forget it & I like to read any Welsh Letter yet I cant spell the Words so I always write in English.[36]

In some isolated and generally North Walian farming communities the fourth generation, "keeping a good Welsh accent by saying their Bible verses," could still speak Welsh.[37] In 1894 a traveler found north of Utica that "many of the Welsh farmers in the district had little or no acquaintance with English." Cut off from Wales, however, the American-born spoke "a Welsh neither of the North nor of the South" but more like "the literary language than . . . colloquial Welsh in any part of Wales." [38]

Coming from the most Anglicized parts of South Wales, most immigrants to American industrial centers, where they were still more completely surrounded by English-speaking neighbors, shifted to English within a generation. Welsh-speaking children in Columbus lost their fluency after a few terms in the public schools.[39] Some farm families dropped the old language almost as quickly.[40] A few who mixed with the Pennsylvania Dutch even picked up their German dialect.[41] Welsh-Americans rapidly absorbed Saxon words into their *Cymraeg*—a more gradual process in the homeland. "O! mother, mother, dyna lots o oxens and bucots!" one of their children was heard to exclaim.[42] An old-country minister who preached in pure Welsh might be nearly unintelligible to a Welsh-American congregation.[43]

Whatever their tongue, Welsh-Americans shared a vigorous national culture. The Anglicization of the gentry of Wales had left the country's medieval bardic tradition in the hands of the working people; theirs was its nineteenth-century renaissance. Even more than the Scots, the Welsh immigrants burned to recreate their folkways in America. In their relatively compact settlements the dream was practicable.[44]

Thus religion was but one side—though the most important to most—of Welsh-American life. One who, when a youth, had worked in an Illinois coal mine recalled, years later,

> the gob-side meetings where comrades used to meet to eat their ten o'clock or noon lunch. How keen were the minds, how eager the discussions, how full the flow of spirit in these gob-side parliaments; in those underground rooms, where the feeble light of the miners' lamps shone dimly on props and pillars, the rough stone roof, and the heaps of slack and shale that formed our seats. . .
>
> Yes, they were days of education, days of culture. There were the long summers with half work, when the other half could be devoted to study. There were our study clubs, there were our singing societies, our mining institutions, our social meetings.[45]

Singing was the chief avocation, even at the "literary meeting" (*cyfarfod llenyddol*). The ancient art of *canu penillion gyda'r delyn* (singing poems in a descant to a harp melody) was nearly forgotten, but every settlement had its men's and women's choruses or choral societies. They put to shame the soloists at Scottish or English immigrants' "concerts." [46] Never limited to simple folk tunes or music-hall ditties, they performed classical cantatas and oratorios, few of which, of course, had Welsh themes. And no sooner did "Blodwen" appear in 1880—the first opera in Welsh, by Joseph Parry of Aberystwyth College and once of Danville, Pennsylvania—than Welsh-Americans produced it.[47] In whatever language, it was the excellence of the singing which evoked memories of Wales.

The choruses awed Americans ignorant of four-part harmony. In the 1830's people near Carbondale, hearing the strong minor chords of Welsh hymns on the frosty night air for the first time, got out of bed to listen in fear of some heavenly portent.[48] "One of the grandest rehearsals it was ever my good fortune to listen to," said an American, "was the singing of 'Coronation' by the miners a mile under ground." [49] Among Welsh colliers in Ohio in the 1870's, while waiting for a car to come so that they could load the coal they had "shot down," someone would produce a piece of chalk or pick up a fragment of slate and write a four-part tune on the broad face of the wall of coal still standing. Then those in the room gathered around and soon the deep caverns underground re-echoed with men's voices singing an old Welsh hymn . . . They sang while working, they sang when going to work, and they sang when coming from work.[50]

In Wales the ancient *eisteddfod* (literally, "session"), long defunct, was revived in the late eighteenth and early nineteenth centuries and gradually assumed its modern pattern of literary and singing competitions. It embodied the recrudescent Welsh national consciousness at the heart of which lay the old language.[51] A competitive meeting was held in New York City as early as 1841; the first regular *eisteddfodau* began in Utica, Racine, and several Pennsylvania coal and iron towns during the 1850's.[52] After the Civil War such sessions, most often held during the Christmas season, became the characteristic means by which Welsh-Americans fostered their culture. By 1876 they were holding a dozen large *eisteddfodau* each year, the greatest at Utica and Scranton.[53] As they grew more ambitious, state, regional, and eventually, with the Chicago World's Fair session of 1893 and its sporadic successors, national meetings attracted choruses from every locality which could support one. In 1913 the *Gorsedd* of the bards of Wales, which controlled the parent institution, sanctioned an American *Gorsedd*, and the Archdruid Dyfed himself crossed the Atlantic to preside over the Pittsburgh International Eisteddfod.[54]

Competition was the essence of an *eisteddfod*. Not only did choirs vie in singing Handel or Bach, but there were prizes for recitations, original essays and poems in Welsh and English, translations, and musical compositions.[55] The Welsh poetry usually had to follow one of the medieval meters peculiar to the language, of which the alliterative, epigrammatic *englyn* was the favorite.[56] Prizes at an ordinary local session usually amounted to several hundred dollars, and, at the Chicago fair, to over twelve thousand, including five thousand for the best choir. Such a national gathering drew contestants from Wales itself; Rhondda singers won the male choral competitions at Chicago and twenty years later at Pittsburgh.[57] Sometimes Irish or German groups were invited to sing, but outsiders could hardly dislodge the Welsh as, at Caledonian games, they often did the Scots.[58] The adjudicators might be well-known non-Welsh musicians, whom the musical performances seldom failed to satisfy. The literary judges, however, never hesitated to withhold prizes if *awdl* or *cywydd* fell below their standard.[59] But original poetry gradually lost its place. Having to draw bards from a small detached community and striving for broader popularity, the American *eisteddfod* became almost wholly musical.[60] The best Welsh-American choruses were competent to enter the great National Eisteddfod of Wales itself.[61]

The trappings of the larger of these sessions — the robes of the druids, bards, and ovates and the chief prize winner's ceremonial chair — followed religiously the old-country mock-pagan fashion. Poets adopted bardic pseudonyms, and plain John Evans, Edward Williams, or David Jones thenceforth was Gwawrfryn, Iolo Mynwy, or Dewi Gwyllt.[62] Though all this was as foreign to a Welshman in his everyday life as to anyone else, the singing and the eloquently declaimed *hen iaith* attracted all who could come. When the assembled thousands joined in the national anthem, "*Hen Wlad Fy Nhadau,*" the future of Welsh culture in America looked secure indeed. As one singer related upon returning to Wales in 1912 from an American concert tour — no uncommon venture for part of a good Welsh choir — the emigrants were "ten times more Welsh than they were at home. They are Welsh to the core and will travel hundreds of miles to hear anything Welsh."[63]

In the homeland after mid-century another type of musical festival developed — the *gymanfa ganu* (singing assembly). Instead of the variegated choral and solo competitions of an *eisteddfod*, a *cymanfa ganu* included only an occasional anthem by a trained choir; its chief purpose was to give the entire assemblage a chance to practice well-known hymns together and to learn new ones.[64] A Pennsylvania Welsh minister explained:

> The *gymanfa ganu* is not an *eisteddfod* and not a concert. It is a call for all the people to praise the Lord, not a choir or a select few, but all that have life and breath, to sing to the Lord. It is a service of solemn sound. The *gymanfa ganu* is not for the correction of mistakes in the performances . . . It is not for display of conductor nor singers, or speakers, but an avenue of solid outpouring in song and worship.[65]

Although the earlier *gymanfa bregethu* (preaching assembly) included hymn singing, the *gymanfa ganu*, which was known at first as the *gymanfa gerddorol* (musical assembly) or as *canu cynulleidfaol* (congregational singing), became a familiar institution in America only after 1880.[66] Beginning about 1900, annual "Welsh Day" outings, which also permitted everyone to take part, attracted thousands of visitors to such centers as Scranton, Wilkes-Barre, and Pittsburgh.[67]

As already existing immigrant institutions, the chapels, or their Sunday schools and Bible societies, often sponsored these musical and social festivals. Here and there secular societies also appeared, usually called simply *Y Gymdeithas Lenyddol* (literary society) but sometimes Ancient Britons, Cymrodorion, Cymreigyddion, Cambrian, or Druid society. But compared to the Scots, the Welsh had few such organizations. People who lived close together in mining villages, mill towns, or rural colonies, around their own chapels, hardly needed formal societies. And even in larger cities the Welsh were seldom so numerous that a single organization could not combine convivial, literary, and musical functions; their one patriotic holiday was their patron saint's — *Dydd Gŵyl Dewi Sant*.[68]

Two other Celtic peoples from Great Britain had their own societies. After 1900, Cornish clubs in Chicago, Boston, and New York held picnics — playing Kissing Ring, French Tig, and Jolly Miller — and in the winter banqueted on "kiddley broth, marinated pilchards, fermades, limpets, turmut, taatre, lickey, screeds, gurty-mait, hogs pudding, stanning pie, saffron cake, figgy hobbin, junket and cream."[69] The Manx of Cleveland in 1851 organized Mona's Relief Society.[70] Probably inspired by some antiquarian enthusiast, in Los Angeles "the six Celtic races — Scotch, Irish, Welsh, Cornish, Manx, and Breton" — in 1906 merged their separate traditions in a unique Celtic Club.[71]

English immigrants showed little of the Welsh or Scottish concern for old-country culture. Their festivals hardly approached in scale or fervor the Highland games or the *eisteddfod*. Yet in their way they too kept old memories aglow and old banners aloft wherever they settled. On the facade of the Philadelphia St. George's Society's hall in the 1880's "a magnificent bronze group" depicted the saint slaying his dragon, while "on all gala days the British standard float[ed] over the building." [72] In Boston in 1903 after a visiting Glasgow professor proposed to an Englishmen's club a broader patriotism of all mankind, one of the immigrants expostulated that this was "too sublimated for the ordinary man"; far better was "that peculiar love which a man bears to the country of his birth." [73]

In many industrial cities English-American workingmen frequented rough approximations of old-country public houses, perhaps with bowling alley or green, billiard tables, a hall for dances, and a reading room. There, some Americans thought, English mill hands met "to pass resolutions, get rum and oysters, and . . . go home drunk." [74] But these clubs were usually more sedate. In Fall River their signboards were everywhere: "Harmony Hall," "The Avon Arms," "St. George's Hall." In the second-floor hall of one, between the bar at one end and a low stage at the other, an American observed fifty men and women, mostly cotton-mill hands, soberly drinking their beer one evening in 1879:

> When most of the glasses had been emptied once or twice, some one said, quietly, "Mr. Lee will oblige," and there was a general clapping of hands. A young Englishman ascended the stage and sang, in tolerable accord with the weary, protesting piano, a melancholy song about a sailor lover who sailed away from his mistress and never returned . . . At the close there was more applause and more beer and for some time busy, chattering talk. There was nothing loud or boisterous.[75]

While such a place may have been English only in that most of its patrons were Lancashire operatives, after 1890 the latter also formed specifically English or British clubs on the same lines, such as the

Washington Social and Musical Club and the Workingmen's Mutual Improvement Society of New Bedford, the English Social and Mutual Improvement Club of Lawrence, and the British Club of Fall River.[76] During the 1920's seventeen such clubs belonged to a New England federation.[77]

Lacking "Publick houses . . . where we can meet and chat over public affairs," English farmers in Wisconsin in the 1840's assembled at each other's houses to read and sing.[78] Fall River operatives enjoyed tea parties, "at which," according to an American neighbor, "the guests sang unending ballads to monotonous music" and listened to broad-Lancashire recitations.[79] Such teas — elaborate suppers in American estimation — were a standby of Episcopal parishes.[80] Ashton-under-Lyne folk sometimes met for their traditional "Ashton wakes."[81] Some English societies held annual picnics or field days with races, cricket, and perhaps Maypole dancing.[82] But their enthusiasm was never quite as open as the *perfervidium ingenium Scotorum.*

Merchants and professional men among the British immigrants organized clubs like those to which they might have aspired at home, with well-upholstered reading rooms. After 1900 such societies as the Victorian Club of Boston, the British Empire Association of Chicago, and the British Empire Club of Providence banqueted on Empire Day or the anniversary of Trafalgar, heard lectures in praise of the Empire, and entertained visiting British dignitaries.[83] Some St. George's and St. Andrew's charitable societies incidentally filled a similar role, and in New York during the 1880's the Scottish Society took in none but "the Scottish elite."[84]

Canadians of English or Scottish descent who moved to the States often joined the British organizations for which they were eligible.[85] Yet, an Ottawa newspaper remarked in 1886, a Canadian-American might also be "a better Canadian than when he lived on Canadian soil."

Here men are very apt to be indifferent to the glory of our country; they are English, or Scotch, or Irish, or French . . . For Canada they have very little regard or love. But when they cross the line and settle in great centres of population, Canadians . . . become enthusiastic over the northland which they have left.[86]

So Canadian organizations sprang up alongside the others. A British Colonial Society existed in Boston before the Civil War, and later in the century Nova Scotians, Cape Bretonners, Prince Edward Islanders, and Newfoundlanders each banded together in Boston, Lawrence, and Worcester.[87]

During the 1880's business and professional men in cities both north and south of the border began to organize Canadian clubs. In the Dominion, where these embodied the new national spirit which followed confederation, they tended to be hostile to the United States; annexation no longer was inevitable. But clubs below the border circumspectly fostered harmony between the two countries. The earliest, at Chicago and New York in 1884 and 1885, in fact antedated by several years the first in Canada. Despite fear that Americans would misinterpret any dual loyalty, clubs took root in a score of American cities and federated in 1899 with those of the Dominion in a League of Canadian Clubs.[88]

Cape Breton and Prince Edward Island folk in Boston, some stemming from Presbyterian and others from Roman Catholic Highlanders, divided as they had about the Bras d'Or. To rival the predominantly Protestant Canadian Club, Catholics about 1903 organized the Intercolonial Club. Yet they cherished traditions of the Maritime Provinces and the Hebrides no less warmly than did their Protestant countrymen.[89]

Canadian and British students at half a dozen American colleges had their own societies.[90] Likewise immigrant university graduates banded together.[91] Ontarians formed "Old Boys'" clubs for annual reunions in London, Hamilton, Kingston, Stratford, and other home towns.[92] The small Australian colonies of San Francisco, Chicago, and New York held annual corroborees.[93] Most loyal to the Union Jack after they ran into the American color line, British West Indian Negroes in Boston formed a charitable association to celebrate the Queen's Jubilee.[94]

Military organizations, dear as they were to the hearts of other mid-nineteenth-century immigrants, attracted few British. Unlike the Irish, they had no need to march and countermarch against the day of their country's liberation. Nevertheless, a few Scots, unable to resist the panache of Highlanders' uniforms, mustered their own militia units. Before 1860 the Union Light Infantry of Charleston, South Carolina, wore Cameron trews; kilts of that tartan and scarlet tunics set off a New York artillery company, the Highland Guard. Chicago had its Highland Guard, and Mobile the Scotch Guards. During the Civil War each took the side of its section — the New Yorkers as the 79th Highland Regiment — and thereafter held yearly reunions.[95] In the early 1880's a battalion of kilted Scots were on the rolls of the Illinois National Guard; Highland companies paraded in Cleveland and Buffalo a decade later.[96] But martial clansmen, failing to recruit further militia units, later had to fall back on kilted corps within their convivial societies.[97]

No doubt a Fourth of July parade by any Englishmen's militia company would have ended in riot, but Americans tolerated uniformed veterans of the Crimea, the Sepoy mutiny, and the colonial frontiers. Such a society in Boston celebrated the anniversary of Inkerman and on each Memorial Day after 1909 decorated redcoat graves at Concord bridge.[98]

The friendly societies of the United Kingdom — both social clubs and life insurance companies to nineteenth-century workingmen — were models for dozens of fraternal benefit orders in the United States. Some British immigrants joined American lodges; a few had their own in American orders.[99] Sometimes Caledonian and similar clubs maintained incidental benefit funds; in the 1870's the English of Boston had four groups which did nothing else.[100] Immigrants who had belonged to orders in Great Britain established branches in the United States. Of course many American orders stemmed from British roots; a few Masonic lodges kept their Scottish flavor for as long as a century and a half.[101]

The first Odd Fellows in the country were Englishmen who got their charters from the old home chapters. Although the American order split off in 1843, immigrant members of the Manchester Unity, the chief British branch, continued to form their own loyal lodges. By 1889 the English and Scottish communities of Massachusetts and Rhode Island had 29 lodges and 1,600 members. Twenty-one years later the 134 Manchester Unity lodges in the country joined under their own Grand Lodge; by 1922 there were 22,168 men in 167 lodges and 4,390 women in 61 lodges.[102]

English, Scottish, and Welsh members of the second largest British friendly society, the Ancient Order of Foresters, planted it in America during the 1870's; in Fall River they outnumbered members of all other orders together.[103] The Alfredians, the Ancient Order of Shepherds, and the Order of Free Gardeners — a Scottish society — each had a few chapters among the immigrants.[104]

But since Americans could hardly be refused admission, such societies were too apt to get out of old-country hands. During the 1860's and 1870's Welsh, English, and Scottish immigrants launched more exclusive fraternal orders. The Welsh *Urdd y Gwir Iforiaid Americanaidd* (American Order of True Ivorites) copied the name and organization of the one wholly Welsh friendly society in Great Britain. Though a Pittsburgh lodge of 1848 did not survive the 1857 depression, in 1863 anthracite colliers at St. Clair began afresh. Seven years later the five lodges united as the American Order, which during the next two decades spread through the slate and coal fields, the steel towns, and other Welsh-American centers. The lodge names breathed Welsh tradition: "*Hywel Dda*," "*Tywysog Llewelyn*," "*Owain Glyndŵr*," "*Seren y Dyffryn*." But like other societies the Ivorites found that Welsh-American communities were already too closely knit to need many formal organizations. The order reached its peak in the 1870's with over 40 lodges; twenty years later there were 30 and 2,500 members.[105]

Both the English and the Scottish orders were pure inventions of the immigrants. The Sons of St. George began among Scranton miners in 1870 and soon spread among workingmen, and sometimes employers too, in English-American communities throughout the North and West. They set up a Grand Lodge in 1872 and a Supreme

Lodge, with state Grand Lodges under it, in 1889. A higher rank of "Uniformed Sir Knights" began within the order in 1888. The rituals of both sections followed chivalric forms; accoutrements included the badge of the Order of the Garter. Most lodges took the names of British statesmen or soldiers or such proud English titles as "Hearts of Oak," "Red Rose," "Balaklava," and "Magna Carta." The order grew steadily until 1914, when there were 292 lodges and 31,680 members. By 1918 more than 550 lodges had existed at some time.[106]

Scots, already linked in scores of local clubs, in 1878 founded at St. Louis the first lodge of their national fraternity, the Order of Scottish Clans. It soon centered in New England and the Middle Atlantic states. The "clans," actually local lodges unrelated to the Highland families whose names and tartans they adopted, sponsored their own annual games and other Scottish celebrations. In their ritual the clansmen commemorated epic battles like Largs and Bannockburn; their journal they called the *Fiery Cross.* Some of the order's embroidery on Scottish tradition, however, seemed bizarre even to the members. The national head in 1906 lamented, "The men who started the order were southern Scots and full of big titles, and the title Royal Chief was a burden."[107] By the time of the first World War about 250 "clans" had existed, of which 160, with over 16,000 members, still were active.[108]

There were several other benefit orders on the same lines. The American Order of Scottish Clans, which seceded in 1889, had a dozen lodges in Massachusetts.[109] In the 1890's a Texas society of five lodges assumed the name of Universal Order of Scottish Clans.[110] A Canadian fraternity, the Sons of Scotland, had a few branches in the States.[111]

Canadians in the United States maintained no orders of their own, though natives of Nova Scotia, New Brunswick, and Prince Edward Island in eastern Massachusetts during the early 1890's started the short-lived Sons and Daughters of the Maritime Provinces.[112] Ulstermen, as such, had no societies of this type.[113]

British-American societies were usually men's affairs. Members' wives, however, often formed auxiliaries, and Burns clubs and other literary groups might include both sexes. Eventually immigrant women struck out on their own. The auxiliaries of the Order of Scottish Clans federated in 1898; another organization, the Daughters of Scotia, which began about the same time, welcomed any Scotswoman even though her husband or brothers were not clansmen. By 1918 thirty-five auxiliaries had existed, while the Daughters then had seventy-five active lodges and more than 6,500 members.[114] Similarly related to the Sons of St. George, two rival groups of Englishwomen, the Daughters and the Independent Daughters of St. George, began during the 1880's. In 1913 there were nine thousand Daughters in 129 lodges; the Independents, though the stronger in New England and New York, were about a fourth as many.[115] After 1897, when the Ivorites organized their first women's lodge as an organic part of the order, Welshwomen assumed a steadily increasing share of its direction.[116]

The first British-American women's federation wholly independent of any male society appeared in 1909. The Imperial Order, Daughters of the British Empire, took root at New York, soon spread to Chicago, and by 1916 had sixty chapters in the country.[117] In 1915, women in Ohio originated the National Women's Welsh-American Clubs, of which there were a dozen within three years.[118]

Their womenfolk's novel forwardness distressed many British-Americans. Gone was the day when Welshwomen were content, while their husbands greeted travelers from the homeland, to remain "outside about the windows of the hotel nursing in shawls their rosy Cymric offspring in the true Cymric fashion." [119] In 1913 the Scots of Boston were shocked by a lady who wore a kilt — hardly a grown woman's garb in the Highlands — to the annual games.[120] America was altering women's place in the immigrants' scheme of things. Of course women in Great Britain too were assuming greater independence, but in America they had long been the patronesses of "culture." Not for their money-grubbing husbands did painters daub and novelists hack. In this atmosphere the preservation of imported folkways likewise fell ever more into women's hands. But they did not yet monopolize such interests. In the early twentieth century British-American men had by no means forgotten their old-country memories.

British-Americans evidently clung to their own cultural traditions. But few thought of these as primarily *British*; England, Wales, Scotland, Canada, or perhaps even some county or town held their loyalty. While most shared such sentiments as devotion to the Queen and pride in British economic and diplomatic prestige, the nationalities of the United Kingdom remained distinct in the United States. The Welsh were the most clannish and worked hardest to uphold their national customs — and language. Scots spoke English but were hardly less intent on maintaining their identity. Though far more numerous and likewise devoted to their homeland, English-Americans had relatively fewer formal institutions for preserving its culture. The Canadian-American community was even more rudimentary.

In these differences the Welsh, Scottish, and English immigrants did not reflect unlike experiences in the United States. Americans certainly regarded the Welsh and Scots no less warmly than they did the English. The cultural consciousness of Welshmen and Scots mirrored rather the position of their countries in the home island. With nationalism rampant in nineteenth-century Europe, they began in one way or another to resist England's dominance. While the Irish political urge was unique, the Scots and the Welsh turned to cultural self-determination. Defending their folkways was nothing new to those who emigrated to the United States. Their still more precarious position there only sharpened their efforts.

In their comparative indifference English-Americans in fact likewise carried over old-country attitudes; in the dominant nation of the United Kingdom they had felt no external threat to their national folkways, if indeed they ever reflected that there were such things. In America they were slow to respond to their new minority status. Could mere Yankees really undermine the *proper* way of living? English immigrant institutions were much less elaborate than those of the Scots or the Welsh. And less exclusive: of the British fraternal orders, only the Sons of St. George could even contemplate admitting men of other British nationalities.[121] As for British Canadian immigrants, distance detached them from old-world particularism. Resembling at many points their North American neighbors, they were only beginning to feel their own national identity.

Thus despite the political and economic unity of Great Britain, British immigrants in the United States were split by their cultural heritage into several groups. Some force from within or without still was necessary to bind the Canadian-Americans, the English-Americans, the Scottish-Americans, the Welsh-Americans, and lesser splinters together in a British-American community.

12

Welding the British-American Community

Through most of the nineteenth century the Welsh, Scottish, and English immigrants showed little sign that they would ever fuse into a truly British-American community. The stronger one of these people's cultural provincialism was, the weaker their feeling for the larger entity of Great Britain. The English, for their part, were content — when naming their societies or newspapers, for instance — to equate "England" and "English" with "Great Britain" and "British." Coming from the nation which dominated the United Kingdom, they did not harp on narrowly English elements in their culture.

The lesser partners under the crown, however, carefully distinguished the political whole from its cultural parts. While few Scots responded to agitation for Scottish self-government, they were sensitive about the legal equality of their country with England within the United Kingdom.[1] Woe to the English or American editor who said that Victoria was "Queen of England," that the sun never set on the "English" flag, or that "Anglo-Saxons" were a race superior to "Celts" — as even Lowlanders sometimes fancied themselves to be.[2] A Scottish-American grumbled in 1865 that all that distinguished the so-called Anglo-Saxons of "the South Province of Britain" was "tow-colored hair, dough faces, spindle shanks, and shovel-built feet." [3] No Scot was a mere "British"-American.

With their prior claim to the title "British," the Welsh warmly resented any suggestion that Wales was in fact as in law only a province of England; were not the English — and the Queen herself — largely Celtic in blood? [4] But of all British-Americans the Welsh were the least loyal to the United Kingdom.[5] Ever ready to recount the ancient tale of "English treachery," and now in Nonconformist revolt against the established Church of England, they inclined toward home rule for Wales.[6] Of course they felt culturally unique. If left to themselves, neither Welshmen nor Scots were likely to find common American ground with their English fellow immigrants.

Only pressure and heat could weld them together. It happened that both were at hand, with men to fan the flames — the Irish. Just as the English, Scots, and Welsh preserved old-country loyalties, so Irish-Americans had left home with an abiding grudge. Centuries of English overlordship had culminated in the Act of Union of 1801, which added the cross of St. Patrick to the Union Jack but took away from Ireland even the semblance of self-government. Throughout the next hundred and twenty years British ministries, usually preoccupied with other matters, conceded Irish agrarian, religious, and political demands only after violence on both sides had destroyed all good will. To many Irishmen it seemed that the Queen whose ministers resisted O'Connell or Parnell was somehow to blame for potato blight and the starvation which drove them overseas. The millions who fled destitute to America in the 1840's and 1850's did not forget the goal of Erin's redemption.[7]

Although the Irish sought vengeance against the British government rather than against the British immigrants, many of the latter rallied about Her Majesty's Government in any Irish crisis. When the Fenian "army" invaded Ontario from American soil in 1866, Canadians from all over the United States rushed home to take up arms. Only the Fenians' speedy collapse kept the volunteers out of the fight.[8] No other British immigrant went as far as Lucille Yseult Dudley — "handsome" and "highly educated" but not quite sane — who in 1885 tried to assassinate O'Donovan Rossa, the leader of the dynamite faction among the Irish-American revolutionaries.[9] But several gratuitously spied for the Foreign Office on the Home Rulers' movements in the United States.[10] "I myself am Scotch by birth consequently a *Briton*," one explained. "The Cradle that rocked me I can never forsake." [11] And all resented such Irish outrages as the murder of the Chief Secretary for Ireland in 1882.[12]

Among workingmen job rivalry sharpened this ill will. When Irishmen crossed the Irish Sea to find work, wages fell — or seemed to — in England and Scotland. English agricultural laborers and Scottish, English, Welsh, and Cornish miners often came to blows with the Paddies. Religious prejudice deepened the grudge; in Lancashire towns during the 1850's the cry of "No Popery" was good for a three-day riot.[13] In the United States the skilled and well-paid British and the unskilled and ill-paid Irishmen renewed this strife. During the early years of Michigan copper mining Cornish and Irish mobs — "Pasties" and "Codfish" — waged pitched battles.[14] The Fall River Irish accused the English of a secret pact to keep them out of the skilled trade of loom-fixing.[15]

In the anthracite valleys of Pennsylvania brawls began as soon as British and Irish mineworkers appeared in the late 1820's.[16] At Carbondale a few years later, Irish resentment over the Welsh and Scots' working the best chambers kept the two factions on the brink of riot. "Welsh miners carried ammunition, while others had to be kept on watch night and day," an old Welshman later recalled.[17] Matters were worst during the 1860's and 1870's, the era of the Molly Maguires. The history of this secret Irish band, linked in some way with the local lodges of the Ancient Order of Hibernians, is still vague; men tended to blame it for any mysterious murder. Since most of the victims were colliery foremen and superintendents, many were British. Thus national hatreds tinged the labor disorders along the Susquehanna.[18] The murder of a Scottish mine superintendent in western Maryland at once was ascribed to the Mollies.[19] Nor were mine bosses the only British to offend the Irish. As in the old country, Irish mine laborers resented the Welsh and English near monopoly of skilled jobs, while the Welsh blamed Irish *black-legiaeth* for the weakness of their unions.[20] Here, too, religious passions fed the fire; at Edwardsville in 1869 Irish Catholics broke up Welsh Congregationalist services.[21]

But Irishmen did not foment all the turmoil. At Scranton in 1871 a mob of two hundred striking Welsh miners and their wives stoned thirty Irish "blacklegs" returning from work under militia escort;

the soldiers shot two Welshmen dead.[22] After the death of three Irishmen in a similar affray, an Irish mineworkers' meeting denounced "the premeditated assassination of Irishmen" and abjured all "unity and fraternity with Welshmen in the future." [23] Some British victims of the Mollies may have richly deserved their fate. One, a Welshman named Gomer James, probably was himself a murderer. "Why, everybody knew James was to be killed for a year before he was," a convicted Molly said. "He killed an Irishman, and as long as time lasts the man who kills an Irishman will suffer." [24]

In Shenandoah in 1875 the British objected when the Irish police chief, who had just released one of his own countrymen involved in a shooting, incarcerated a Welshman merely for discharging a gun in the street.

> Embittered as they were already at the thought that the victims of the recent murders [had] all been English or Welsh, it was with great difficulty that they could be restrained from forcible rescue. This excitement had scarcely time to subside when it was found that a young Welshman named James Johns, a quiet and inoffensive man, had been shot and his throat cut right in the centre of town and left for dead. The fury of the Welsh and English could no longer be restrained, and a scene of great lawlessness ensued. Houses were fired into, and indiscriminate shooting went on all over town all night.[25]

Such bad blood greatly weakened John Siney's union. The British members, one of them wrote, were "foolish dupes, who are forced to be governed by the McGinnes' and McCarty's, the 'Macs and the O's,' and the devil knows what." [26] As late as 1891 it was said of the English and Irish in the Clearfield County soft coal field, "The same stores are not frequented by them; in fact, there is no intercourse between them." [27]

It was the murder of a compatriot which brought English miners at Scranton together in the first lodge of the Sons of St. George.[28] Although their defensive league soon turned into a fraternal benefit society, it always rallied round any member embroiled with the Irish. In Clearfield County in 1891 the state secretary of the order successfully defended a brother indicted for an Irishman's murder.[29]

Blaming a Montana revival of the Molly Maguires for the slaying of William Penrose, a Cornish miner who edited the Butte *Mining Journal*, the Sons of St. George spent two thousand dollars on a fruitless prosecution.[30] In 1885, fearing that the order was about to retaliate against them for home-rule terrorism, anonymous Irishmen in Columbus threatened to blow up the lodge hall and forced the Englishmen to cancel their annual banquet.[31]

All this was mild alongside the bitterness between Irish factions. Ireland of course was split between the Celtic Catholics and the Anglo-Irish and Ulster Scottish Protestants. So were nineteenth-century emigrants from Erin to the United States. Once both groups had considered themselves equally "Irish"; the Scotch-Irish in fact had come to colonial America grumbling against the mercantilist English government for wrecking their industries.[32] Even in the early nineteenth century an occasional Protestant champion of Irish liberty had to flee to America.[33] The Anglo-Irishman Edwin L. Godkin, an immigrant of 1856 who long edited the liberal New York *Nation*, was always a staunch home-ruler.[34]

But as Catholic Ireland was gripped by nationalism, Protestants closed ranks in loyalty to the crown. There had been terrorist bands on both sides in the eighteenth century. Now the Loyal Orange Institution, founded in Armagh in 1795, became the chief anti-Catholic organization in Scotland, England, and Canada as well as in Ulster. Its arrogant celebrations of the Twelfth of July, the anniversary of William of Orange's victory at the Boyne, were sure to provoke Catholics to riot somewhere in the Empire each year.[35] The Fenian intrigues of the 1860's and the likelihood in the 1880's that Gladstone would win for Ireland its own — popish — parliament set Irish Protestants on edge. "Ulster will fight, and Ulster will be right!" was the new battlecry.[36] Until partition of North and South in 1922, Unionist and Nationalist intransigence constantly vexed British politics.

As Catholic Irish immigration increased during the early nineteenth century, the feuds of the green isle took root in America. In 1824 New York experienced its first "Orange riot" when two hundred shillelagh-brandishing Protestants marching through Greenwich village on Boyne Day — "with drum and fife and flags and grog" — were attacked by half as many Catholics.[37] Eighteen years later the Orange "Faugh-a-ballaghs" started another Donnybrook after the Catholic "Spartans" upset ballot boxes during an aldermanic election in the Irish sixth ward.[38]

The American anti-Catholic movement of the 1840's and 1850's enlisted the Protestant Irish immigrants' enthusiasm. But most Know-Nothing groups were also antiforeigner. Nothing daunted, the Ulstermen flocked into two which welcomed any Protestants: the Benevolent Order of Bereans and the American Protestant Association.[39] The latter carried on even after the collapse of the Know-Nothings, strongest in such bastions of Ulstermen as Philadelphia and Pittsburgh. In 1874 the Grand Lodge claimed three hundred lodges and fifty thousand members; fifteen years later more than ninety lodges still were active.[40] Although the American Protestant Association included Americans, Germans, and British, it was known as an Ulstermen's order; the officers felt obliged to avow its independence of the Orangeism of Ireland.[41]

By the 1870's Protestant Irish immigrants were Unionists almost to a man. The Fenian Brotherhood bemoaned the lack of Protestant recruits.[42] It was not merely the prospect of popish massacres in Londonderry or Belfast which concerned old Ulstermen. Americans were apt to confuse them with the destitute Catholics who for twenty years had been crowding into the slums of Boston and New York. As an American anti-Catholic journal harangued the Irish Protestants,

> The name of Ireland has become a hissing and a by-word among the nations of the earth, that of Irishman a synonym for the lowest caste in the social scale — a badge of servitude as marked as was, for so many years, a black skin. Have you felt it? Have your eyes flashed and lips quivered as the stinging sarcasm has been hurled in your face? . . . Too long have you left to the Church of Rome the representation of your country . . . until now an Irish Protestant requires both patriotism and courage to avow his nationality. Let there be an end to this silence; let

the world know that the Church of Rome is not the exponent of Irish sentiment . . . Let every Irish Protestant unite with his fellows for this great object.[43]

The answer was an Orange order for America. Its first lodge began in 1867 in New York; others soon sprang up in Boston, Philadelphia, and Pittsburgh. In 1870 the Grand Lodge of England chartered an American Supreme Grand Lodge which in turn set up state Grand Lodges. Within three years more the order claimed nearly a hundred local chapters and ten thousand members.[44] During the 1870's it added a higher rank, the Royal Black Knights of the Camp of Israel, and an auxiliary, the Ladies' Loyal Orange Association.[45]

Although the Loyal Orange Institution welcomed any Protestants and was strong where Canadians had settled, in most places in the United States it was virtually the Protestant Irish immigrants' fraternal order. Typical lodge names came straight from the Ulster of 1690: "Enniskillen True Blues," "Apprentice Boys," "Walls of Derry," "Sons of William," "Donegal Guiding Star." [46] On the annual outing of the New York lodges in 1883, "the Orangemen were almost exclusively Scotch-Irish, and the excruciating accent of Belfast prevailed." [47] In 1874 all but two officers of the Supreme Grand Lodge — workingmen or shopkeepers by occupation — were Ulstermen.[48] A generation later most of the leaders again were natives of the North of Ireland, with a few from Scotland, England, and Canada.[49] From the outset they sent delegates to the triennial sessions of the parent order's Imperial Grand Council, usually held in the United Kingdom or Canada but in 1900 at New York.[50] Yet as enemies of alien Catholics they had to deny their own foreign origin.[51] And in fact while the English, Scottish, and Welsh fraternal orders busied themselves with whole complexes of old-country folkways, the Orangemen did reduce everything to the single custom — not exclusively their own — of defying the minions of the Pope.

Irish Catholics in America took up the Orange gage of battle as eagerly as on the old sod. As the Seventeenth of March was their day to parade under the green banner, so they tore down the orange on the Twelfth of July. The New York Orange lodges, setting out for their second annual picnic on Boyne Day in 1869,

> marched to the Courtland street Ferry to the music of "Croppies lie down," the "Boyne Water," the "Protestant Boys," to the intense delight and satisfaction of our Irish Celtic immigrants. They must have imagined themselves again in the north of their native isle, and proceeded to act as is there customary. The Orangemen got over to New Jersey, where their train left under a shower of stones, to which little attention was paid, but on their return, while marching down the Bowery, a more serious attack was made, and one man was severely injured, and many slightly.[52]

The next year the Orangemen and the American Protestant Association, escorted by police, paraded up Eighth Avenue in full regalia, their banners flaunting Aughrim, Derry, and the Boyne and their band again insulting the "croppies." A crowd of Catholics dogged their steps. Two or three thousand Orangemen and their families were in the midst of their Elm Park picnic when the Catholics, reinforced by pick-wielding street laborers, fell on them shouting, "Down with the Irish traitors." After a two-hour battle the Orangemen and the police repulsed this assault, but a running fight followed as their horse cars moved back down the avenue. Five persons were killed, and scores seriously hurt. A detail of six hundred policemen prevented a further riot over the funeral of an Orangeman slain in this melee.[53]

In 1871 men predicted even worse turmoil. During the week before the Glorious Twelfth the Catholic clergy exhorted their parishioners not to molest the Orange celebration. Ever alert to Irish sensibilities, the Tweed Ring's police superintendent forbade the Orange parade. But indignant native Protestants and the more respectable newspapers forced the mayor to revoke the ban; the governor ordered out eleven regiments of the National Guard to protect the marchers.

Dawn of Boyne Day found effigies of Orangemen hanging from lamp poles about the city. During the morning mobs of Irish quarrymen, street laborers, and longshoremen skirmished with the police. At half past two, Gideon and No Surrender lodges — a hundred and sixty-one Orange diehards — moved out with a militia regiment ahead, another behind, one to the right flank, and two to the left; Catholics crowded the sidewalks. Before the Orangemen had marched five blocks, a shot felled a militiaman. Without orders the citizen soldiery volleyed into the onlookers. Along the rest of the route only one shot was fired, and after the parade the Orangemen doffed their regalia and quietly dispersed. On the battlefield at Eighth Avenue and Twenty-fourth Street, however, about fifty persons lay dead, and more than a hundred others had been wounded.[54]

In Brooklyn, Jersey City, Boston, and elsewhere that same day only a few stones harassed the Orange marchers.[55] That no violence marred subsequent New York parades and excursions was due, however, to "the procession of police by which it is now customary to celebrate the 12th of July."[56] Catholic authorities also worked for peace. On Boyne Day in 1877 before the excursion boats sailed, a priest, "on behalf of many influential Catholics, presented a written address to the Orangemen and a song of reconciliation to the air of 'Boyne Water.'"[57] At Boston, Philadelphia, and Pittsburgh, where Loyal Orange and American Protestant lodges also demonstrated in force each year, only jeers and catcalls and an occasional stray pistol shot disturbed the Protestant Boys.[58] Yet in 1875 the first public celebration by the Orangemen of Lawrence ended in a two-hour riot.[59]

These battles between orange and green, like British and Irish differences over home rule or rivalry for jobs, were simply old-country squabbles in a new setting. But besides the fresh battleground America introduced a new element into Irish home-rule strategy. By enlisting American public opinion in their cause and by trading the "Irish vote" for political support, Irish Nationalists hoped to turn the United States itself against the British government. After the Civil War, therefore, the Catholic immigrants' growing political influence dismayed the Protestant Irish and British. Unless they could muster equal strength, their adopted country might someday be maneuvered into war with their homeland.

More immediately, if the "Irish vote" and Irish politicians swayed American city governments, all those evils which Unionists feared for a Catholic-dominated Ulster might likewise overwhelm Protestants in the United States. Already it was evident how Anglophobia might be exploited in municipal campaigns. In New York, Boston, and other Irish Catholic strongholds, politicians were likely to vilify an English candidate merely for his birthplace. Berwick-born Andrew Cameron, when running for the Illinois legislature as a labor candidate in 1866, lost Irish votes because of rumors that he was an Englishman, an Orangeman, and an anti-Fenian.[60] At Fall River on election night in 1887 a crowd of Democrats stoned the house of an English Republican leader, shouting, "Why don't you go back to your country?"[61] In a campaign speech at Milwaukee in 1888 even John Jarrett — then president of the Pittsburgh St. David's Society — felt it necessary to apologize "for having been born under the British flag."[62]

Effective resistance required a revolution in the British immigrants' outlook. Few had ever cared much for American politics. Many failing even to become voters, they were not a self-consciously British bloc for whom party leaders contended as for the "Irish vote." With good jobs, they seldom had to turn to politics for personal recognition nor barter ballots for ward heelers' favors. And not living in any "British section" of a city, they were hard for politicians to organize.[63]

British-born men who did run for office seldom solicited the votes of their countrymen as such. In fact the most successful, for instance Frederick Greenhalge — in turn mayor of Lowell, member of Congress, and in the 1890's governor of Massachusetts — had grown up in the United States.[64] Greenhalge, another British-American charged in 1893, was "a *mongrel Englishman.*"

> Greenhalge during all the past years has studiously kept clear of all organizations where his countrymen gathered and furthermore has made all manner of excuses when invited to attend social and non-political

meetings of his countrymen . . . Greenhalge was after votes and political influence and did not consider the British American voters as an important factor in the politics of this state, hence catered by all manner of means to our friends of the *Home Rule* agitation.[65]

The few British trade unionists who ran for the state legislatures likewise avoided dividing their motley followers by any appeal to purely British loyalties.[66]

Once again the Welsh were an exception. Wholeheartedly antislavery on religious grounds in the 1840's, their enthusiasm for the Liberty and Free Soil parties led them into the Republican fold. Every four years from 1856 onward many a coal or iron town had its "*Clwb Gwerinol Cymreig*" to get out the vote for Fremont, Grant, or Garfield. Individuals who attempted to swing the Welsh to the Democrats wasted their time.[67] Even in greeting President Cleveland a delegation of Chicago Welshmen felt honor-bound to caution him that they did not share his political faith.[68]

Recognizing that the Welsh, like other foreign-language groups, were likely to vote for any candidate of their own kind, politicians issued pamphlets in Welsh, advertised in the *Drych* and *Druid*, and between 1844 and 1862 even published campaign newspapers for them.[69] During the 1870's the annual messages of the governor of Pennsylvania appeared in Welsh translation under the familiar motto "*Y gwir yn erbyn y byd*" — "the truth against the world." [70] Welsh-American candidates for local office called on their compatriots to "be loyal to your own," and their newspapers urged, "*Pleidiwch y Cymro*" (support the Welshman).[71] Though the Welsh were less addicted than the Scots to the immigrant mania for filling American parks with statues of noted countrymen, they had enough political influence in Pennsylvania in 1911 to squeeze an appropriation from the legislature to cast Robert Morris — a questionable Welshman — in bronze.[72] But they were too few to command many loaves and fishes. Beyond the legislature, a customshouse job, or perhaps the Cardiff consulate, a Welsh-American politician could hope for little.[73] Nor were American politicians likely to defer to the Welsh when the Irish vote was at stake. Nevertheless, during the decade of the Molly Maguires and after, Welsh-Americans redoubled their efforts to defeat the "vindictive, papistical, and cruel" Irish at the polls.[74]

The English, Scots, and British Canadians — quite numerous enough to balance the Irish — lacked both unity and sufficient naturalization certificates. Yet most of the citizens among them were faithful Republicans, if only because of the long-standing Irish affinity for the Democrats. And as American city councils, boards of aldermen, and finally even mayors' chairs became the domain of Irish politicians in the 1870's and 1880's, the unnaturalized British began to regret having no defensive weapon.[75]

Their countermovement got under way slowly. In Jersey City in 1874 they organized a Republican campaign club called the British-American Association.[76] In 1876 several leaders of the Fall River Lancashire community started an English-American club "to secure a share in the management of city affairs."[77] "This time it is not the Irish," George Gunton wrote, "but the bigoted English who have raised the issue of nationality."[78] Urging operatives to become citizens, the club annually endorsed friendly candidates for local offices. In 1879 and 1880 they could exult; Fall River once more had a Republican mayor and even more Englishmen than Irishmen on the council.[79] The next year, however, the Democrats regained control, and the English club collapsed.[80]

In Worcester a British-American Society in 1883 set up ward committees and assisted British immigrants through naturalization.[81] "Goaded . . . by the pretensions and presumption of other nationalities and the insignificance of themselves in all political contests," Philadelphia Englishmen in 1886 undertook the same task.[82] Lawrence had its Albion Club, and a Maine woolen town, Sanford, its British-American Republican Association.[83]

Irish influence in the presidential campaign of 1884 especially alarmed Canadian-American voters. Though most were Republicans, they feared James G. Blaine as "a 'jingo' candidate" whose expectedly "vigorous and adventurous foreign policy" — probably in a northerly direction — was one of "the strongest arguments used to influence the Anglophobists and the Celtomaniacs in his favor."[84] Though standing pat on the local Republican ticket, mass meetings of Minneapolis Canadians bolted to Grover Cleveland. During the week before the election several hundred of them qualified as voters for the first time.[85]

The simmering British and Canadian discontent boiled over in 1887, the year when throughout the United States the immigrants — except the Welsh — celebrated Victoria's Golden Jubilee. In Boston the English and Scottish societies obtained the aldermen's routine consent to use Faneuil Hall for a grand banquet on June 21. At once an Irish priest denounced this impending desecration of the Cradle of Liberty by the countrymen of George III. As Irish protests mounted, the aldermen reconsidered; by an even division, five native Americans and one English immigrant against six Irishmen, their permission stood. On the evening before the banquet, however, leaders of the Irish community addressed a protest meeting in Faneuil Hall. When the four hundred banqueters arrived the next night, they found fifteen thousand indignant Irishmen milling about the building. Although several hundred policemen kept order, the mob kept up its patriotic uproar all through the speeches inside the hall praising the Queen, pledging loyalty to America, and refuting Irish charges against the British government. The absence from the banquet of all the invited city, state, and federal officials except the British-born alderman painfully demonstrated the relative political weight of the British and the Irish.[86]

This single incident struck the spark of common British feeling among English, Scottish, Protestant Irish, and Canadian immigrants. They all resented the Irish slurs on Queen and Empire. Thus, unlike immigrant groups who were united by social and economic pressure from the native Americans above them, the British linked hands when assailed by a poorer and, they felt, culturally inferior group.

Within three weeks the Jubilee banquet committee — solid middle-class men — resolved themselves into the British-American Association.[87] Urging their countrymen to become voters, they argued,

"If the national government was controlled by the same element as is the local government, then America and England would be at war within five years." [88] By November more than half the English, Scottish, and Canadian subjects of the crown in Boston were reported to have taken out their first papers, the weekly *British-American Citizen* was on the newsstands, and with a dozen branches in eastern Massachusetts the Association was arousing the British in other states.[89]

The movement spread rapidly. In New York, where the Irish National League had called a Jubilee day meeting "to commemorate the dead of the Irish race who have perished on the scaffold, in dungeon, by famine, or by eviction during Victoria's reign," and throughout the country, Englishmen, Scots, Canadians, and Protestant Irishmen fell into line. (Welshmen, most of them already American citizens and still wary of "paying homage to John Bull," formed only one branch, in Chicago.) [90] Before 1887 was out, state organizations appeared in New York, Pennsylvania, and Illinois.[91] Two more weekly papers, the *British-American* and the *Western British-American*, commenced in New York and Chicago.[92] By October 1888, when a convention in Chicago effected a national association, there were about sixty branches in Massachusetts, eleven in Rhode Island, six in Connecticut, seventeen in New York, fifteen in Pennsylvania, eighteen in Illinois — besides two of a Canadian League with the same ends — and others in New Hampshire, New Jersey, Ohio, Michigan, Iowa, and California.[93] George Gooch, Norwich-born member of the Chicago Board of Trade, was national president until 1890, when, the Massachusetts association finally having entered the federation with delegates in proportion to its large membership, James Wemyss, a Scottish furniture manufacturer of Boston, took his place.[94]

But American politicians were too busy battling for the Irish vote to heed these tyros. Though the British generally would have preferred to enlist the Republicans in a straight party fight against the Irish Democrats, Republican strategists saw more profit in seducing the Irish. Already in the vicious campaign of 1884 Blaine's supporters had whispered that Cleveland was an Orangeman — an Orange lodge in Rochester did publicly "bolt Blaine" — only to lose the Irish when a blundering spokesman called the Democrats the party of "rum, Romanism, and rebellion." [95]

Four years later both parties' platforms championed Irish home rule, but Republicans imagined in Cleveland's low-tariff policy the intrigues of British exporters and the long arm of the Foreign Office. The *Chicago Tribune* alleged that fifty thousand Leeds and Manchester workingmen had each contributed a dollar to the Democratic campaign chest.[96] Lord Sackville, the inept British minister to Washington, gave substance to such tales when he advised a self-styled English-American correspondent to vote for Cleveland.[97] An Irish Republican asserted that this stupid "Murchison letter" was actually the British government's marching orders to those treasonable banditti, the Sons of St. George.[98]

Republicans found further political ammunition in the horrendous new British-American Association. Though it was never able to control its members' votes or even to unite its state and local branches behind one party, in 1888 a few officers and the *British-American Citizen*, indignant over the Republican bid for the Irish, did at least equivocally endorse Cleveland.[99] To Harrison men the meaning of this was clear: "The 'British-American' party is organizing for the support of Mr. Cleveland in order to induce English residents (always exotic in whatever land away from home they sojourn) to become naturalized and vote here for British interests." [100] It was useless for even an Irish Catholic to point out that most B.A.A. members were "Republicans and staunch Protectionists." [101] This year the Republicans succeeded not only in holding the Welsh, to whom the Democrats were still the "English-worshiping, un-American party," but also in scaring enough of the Irish voters to defeat Cleveland.[102]

This fiasco only heightened the British-American Association's determination to end the Irish balance of power. Although its leaders denied any enmity toward Irishmen or Catholics, they vehemently denounced both Home Rulers and the Church as insidious foreign meddlers in American affairs. The *British-American Citizen* excoriated Irish politicians, condemned Catholic pleas for public money for parochial schools, printed lurid revelations of convent life and the confessional by sundry "escaped nuns" and "converted priests," and exposed what it considered a great papal conspiracy against the American government.[103]

In all this the British-American Association steadily gained allies. The American Protestant Association recovered some of its earlier strength, and the Loyal Orange Institution expanded rapidly.[104] Many native American Protestants, though not concerned with preserving intact the United Kingdom, did fear the supposed Catholic menace. Throughout the country anti-Catholic organizations and weekly propaganda sheets sprang up.[105] Old Know-Nothing groups like the United American Mechanics and newer ones like the Patriotic Order Sons of America between 1887 and 1892 quintupled their membership and lodges. British-Americans and Orangemen joined them in the abortive "American" parties of 1887–1888 and 1893.[106]

In Massachusetts and Illinois they raised the standard of the "little red schoolhouse." The chief election issues in Boston in 1888 and 1889 were the new parochial schools and Catholic domination of the elected public-school committee. Since on such matters the state permitted female suffrage, the united anti-Catholics mobilized Protestant women as well as British immigrants to vote and in 1889 succeeded in electing a sympathetic school committee. For good measure a Republican ousted the Irish Democratic mayor.[107] Lawrence, where regular party labels gave way to "Mick" and "Anti-Mick," elected a Scottish Republican mayor.[108]

As this broad anti-Catholic movement gathered force during the early 1890's, it swallowed up the British-American Association. A few Massachusetts branches survived until as late as 1899, but the national federation expired in 1892.[109] Like earlier local political groups, it had failed to weld British-born voters into a disciplined partisan unit; to maintain any sort of unity the officers had to abjure political commitments.[110] Yet it had probably accomplished its immediate mission of turning a large number of British subjects into American citizens and voters.[111]

Though the B.A.A. disappeared, its members merely shifted the crusade into a new channel. A more important anti-Catholic group, the American Protective Association, had been rising in the Midwest. Spreading east about 1892, the A.P.A. in effect absorbed the B.A.A. The *British-American Citizen* began to appear also as the *American Citizen*. Though edited by a Nova Scotian, Robert J. Long, the paper under either masthead was thenceforth wholly anti-Catholic rather than specifically pro-British; the only immigrant societies whose activities it reported were the Orange lodges.[112] Many A.P.A. leaders in the Middle West as well as the East were Orangemen.[113] The Supreme Grand Master of the Loyal Orange Institution in the United States, W. J. H. Traynor, a native of Ontario, became president of the A.P.A. in 1893.[114] Though in a few years Populism, free silver, William Jennings Bryan, and other diversions choked off the A.P.A. and its anti-Catholic crusade, Traynor "saved many a group to the cause by bringing them into the Orange Order." [115]

Thus the Loyal Orange Institution throve down to 1914, when it had 364 lodges and perhaps 30,000 members in the country.[116] Although Catholics only occasionally harassed the annual Boyne Day celebrations at Boston, New York, Philadelphia, Pittsburgh, and Chicago, the Sons of William kept up the propaganda fight against the Irish Nationalists and cheered on the forces of Sir Edward Carson. But after 1914 a factional struggle split and decimated the American order.[117]

As for the British, here and there local groups carried on the work of the defunct British-American Association. Complaining that they were ignored by city governments under German or Irish Catholic control and even by the Republican national leadership, Welsh Republican clubs campaigned in Utica, Columbus, and Cincinnati in the 1890's.[118] At Pittsburgh the Cambro-American League, the North Side Welsh-American League, and the Welsh Republican Club successively mobilized the party vote.[119] The Victoria Club of Chicago in 1896 encouraged hundreds of British subjects to become citizens and Republicans.[120] In Massachusetts after 1900 the Rose and Thistle Club of Adams and the Anglo-American Association of Boston kept up the naturalization drive in the interests of "good government" and the friendship of "all branches of the Anglo-Saxon race."[121] When the mayor of San Francisco blackguarded Great Britain as "the most avaricious empire in the world" and slighted a British admiral whose flagship visited the port, the *British Californian* called on immigrant voters to defeat him at the polls.[122]

If Catholic mayors could arouse British-Americans to all this wrath, the threat of an Irish-inspired war between America and Britain was far more alarming. In December 1895 President Cleveland's brusque demand that Britain arbitrate her Guiana boundary dispute with Venezuela appeared to them a reckless gambit for Irish votes. For a few days war trembled in the balance. To British immigrants this was unthinkable. The *British-American Citizen* thundered that it was all the work of "Jesuit ecclesiastics, Irish dynamiters, and truckling pseudo-Americans who bow and cringe to the papal vote.[123] Agreeing that Cleveland was merely electioneering, even the peaceable *Scottish-American* growled that war would place the United States at the mercy of the Royal Navy.[124] *Y Drych* likewise minimized the possibility of war, though still grumbling that the English had always "despoiled and oppressed" small countries like Venezuela and Wales.[125]

As usual in such a crisis, a number of British-Americans at once assured the Foreign Office of their sympathy.[126] Within a few weeks mutual good sense resolved the impasse, but not until it had made clear to British immigrants that war between their native and adopted lands hinged on an American public opinion swayed by Irish agitators and politicians alert to Irish prejudices.[127] When the Queen's Jubilee of 1897 came around, even the Welsh expressed their loyalty as they had not done ten years before.[128]

The next few years first reduced and then abruptly magnified the danger. During the Spanish-American war of 1898 Great Britain's unique sympathy for the United States silenced her enemies there. "The 'Union of Hearts' sentiments of today," the British ambassador reported, "bid fair to pass the bounds of moderation in as great a degree as the dislike and distrust of yesterday."[129] Tampa, the port of embarkation for Cuba, officially celebrated the Queen's birthday, and the Senate remembered Her Majesty in their prayers. In both countries many looked forward to an "Anglo-Saxon alliance" which would dominate and regenerate the earth.[130]

Reaction was swift. Late in 1898 Irish-American organizations protested against the suggested Anglo-American treaty.[131] In 1899 the Boer War reawakened American Anglophobia. Irish and now German immigrants, like the Kaiser himself, commiserated with the Transvaal farmers, and the American press rang all the old changes on Albion's perfidy. With Democrats appealing to Irish and German voters, the State Department felt compelled in 1899 to deny rumors of a secret alliance with Britain.[132] In 1901, only three years after the pro-British ceremonies at Tampa, the Foreign Office had to refuse the request of a Jacksonville British group that a gunboat visit their port in honor of the King's coronation.[133]

A few immigrants returned home to volunteer for service in South Africa.[134] British-Americans generally contributed to London and Edinburgh funds for survivors of British soldiers. Furthermore, fearing that Irish and German propaganda would force American intervention, the fund-raising committees and the British and Orange societies held "patriotic meetings" in Boston, Philadelphia, and other cities. Even in Milwaukee, Chicago, and St. Louis, where the press was uniformly anti-British — the Democratic papers because of the Irish and the Republican because of the Germans — the British case thus had a hearing.[135] In Chicago naturalized Britons in 1900 formed a new political organization to support whichever party would abstain from a pro-Boer plank.[136] Societies of affluent and influential immigrants, like the Victorian Club of Boston and the British-American Association of Columbus, published pamphlets defending their homeland and sent copies to every member of Congress. A correspondence committee of the Victorian Club also countered anti-British speeches and newspaper stories.[137]

Of course not all British immigrants were so sure of the justice of the cause; among the Welsh, still sympathetic toward anyone downtrodden by the English, the debate was as hot as in Parliament.[138] But they, too, were coming to share the common British sentiment. As anti-Irish and anti-Catholic as the others, they now no longer had the inspiration of the politically nationalist *Cymru Fydd* movement which had flickered in Wales in the 1880's and 1890's.[139] Thus the Queen's death in 1901 evoked from them stout expressions of devotion to her memory and of loyalty to the new king—"Iorwerth VII"—who had been "Prince of Wales (not of England, Scotland, or Ireland)"![140]

The roots of a possible Anglo-American war lay deeper than the Boer question or any other current issue. American national mythology, reflected in school textbooks, had distorted the whole perspective of Anglo-American relations. Amateur historians now leaped into the breach. James H. Stark, a prime mover of the Massachusetts British-American Association and the Victorian Club of Boston, set about to rehabilitate the reputation of the Loyalists of the American Revolution—and to convict the rebels of all the atrocities.[141] Since Americans were under the impression that Great Britain had supported the Confederacy during the Civil War, a Pasadena Englishman asked the Foreign Office for counterarguments on behalf of "a large number of English in this section—mostly retaining allegiance to the old Country"—who were "anxious to promote good feeling between the two countries & good fellowship between the respective citizens while remaining—as I do—loyal to my own Country (Dear Old England)."[142]

Canadian-Americans were acutely disturbed by any roiling of the waters along the North American boundary. The hyperprotective Payne-Aldrich tariff, which Congress passed in 1909, jeopardized Dominion trade and amity with the United States. Disgruntled British-born Republicans in Massachusetts broke with the party and formed a Republican Independent Association. Together with the Nova Scotian head of the Democratic state committee they persuaded Eugene N. Foss, whom Henry Cabot Lodge had just excommunicated for advocating tariff reciprocity, to run for lieutenant governor. The next year Foss won the governorship on a reciprocity platform. But no political group could risk appearing to have British support. The Democrats repudiated the editorial endorsement of the *British-American Citizen* as, they asserted, a Republican trick like the Murchison letter of 1888.[143]

Never strong enough to overcome politicians' solicitude for Irish sensibilities, since 1887 British immigrants had at least discovered common ground beneath their cultural differences. Thus in 1905 the Boston Victorian Club called itself "an Imperial British society" and celebrated Empire Day with the Canadian Club, the Scots' Charitable Society, and the British Charitable Society as the United British Societies of Boston.[144] A Welshman praised this "forging of a chain of good will among Britishers."[145] Between 1897 and 1914 the United British Societies of Lawrence, the British Club of Rhode Island, the British-American Society of New Haven, the British Empire Association of Chicago, the British Empire Society of St. Louis, the British and American Union of San Francisco, and temporary committees at other places held combined Empire Day dinners; at their annual outings English, Scottish, and Welsh customs were intermingled, and Sons of St. George met Scottish Clans on cricket pitch or baseball diamond.[146] By 1914, English, Scottish, Welsh, Protestant Irish, and Canadian immigrants had added a new dimension to their national pride.

War in Europe then posed the problem of the Boer conflict on a vaster scale. Immigrants at once organized branches of British war-relief agencies; in three months they contributed $75,000 in New York, and another three brought nearly as much from Chicago.[147] Though Scots, Welsh, and Canadians could subscribe to special funds to aid their own countrymen, usually all the British societies of a city banded together to raise money through concerts, balls, and field days.[148] New joint organizations sprang up: the American-British Federation in Boston, the United British Societies of Philadelphia, and the British Patriotic Society of San Francisco.[149] Under the stress of war they also coöperated with immigrants from allied countries; at a Chicago concert for the Canadian Red Cross in 1916 Scottish pipers and a Welsh chorus shared the stage with Croatian singers.[150]

Many immigrants returned home to enlist. On the outbreak of war British reservists reported to the consulates; five hundred left New York for Halifax early in September 1914.[151] Others volunteered during the early months; by mid-1915 word came of casualties among their ranks.[152] Apparently most men, however, did not rush to join the forces of the homeland. Since under existing law—even after the United States entered the war in April 1917—immigrant aliens could not be conscripted by either the British or the American governments, a British and Canadian Recruiting Mission arrived in June 1917 to set up stations throughout the North and West.[153] In Boston a kilted battalion of Canadians and Scots, the MacLean Highlanders, was raised for the Canadian Overseas Forces.[154] Before October 1918, when an Anglo-American convention on conscription finally went into effect, the mission accepted nearly fifty thousand volunteers and rejected fifteen thousand more (not, however, all British) for the Canadian and British services.[155] The immigrants' societies raised funds to assist the volunteers' families.[156] Thus despite legal exemption and low British army pay, tens of thousands offered to fight in the uniform of their native land.

Before 1917, while the United States was still struggling to remain neutral, British-Americans attempted to answer German propaganda. Though a Welsh minister of Chicago presided over a pacifist meeting which to his chagrin turned into a German-Irish rally, and though, surrounded by Germans, British businessmen in St. Louis concealed their sympathies, speakers at British fund-raising meetings generally "handled the Germans without gloves."[157] The Pittsburgh St. David's Society distributed pamphlets from Wales exposing German atrocities.[158] The British-American Leagues of Los Angeles and San Francisco refuted German arguments and expostulated with anti-British newspaper editors.[159] "An English ranchman in New Mexico" published a pamphlet outlining for skeptical Americans the magnitude of the British war effort.[160] The American branch of the Amalgamated Society of Carpenters and Joiners warned its members against German conspirators.[161] The London-born Chicago utilities magnate, Samuel Insull, from first to last was indefatigable in raising money for war relief and keeping the Union Jack aloft.[162]

Although it was U-boat tactics rather than immigrants' propaganda which ultimately drove American opinion into the Allied camp, at all events in 1916 British-born citizens could vote certain that the election either of Wilson, whom the German-Americans detested for his unneutrality, or of Hughes, that "anti-German Welshman," would not injure their native land.[163] A few months later America cast her lot with Great Britain and ended thirty years of anxiety for those whose loyalties lay in both countries. To be sure, after the war, when American mayors threatened to "poke King George in the snoot" or ferreted "English propaganda" out of school textbooks, the Irish problem still vexed British-Americans.[164] But the heartening fact remained that war between Britain and America had not occurred and that the virtual Anglo-American alliance — to them as natural as their own easy transition from one land to the other — had at least temporarily come to pass.

The years of resistance to Irish — and German — traducers of the United Kingdom had profoundly affected the British immigrants' outlook. While the Welsh, the Scots, the English, and the Canadians continued to carry on their different customs in their parallel societies, in all there had quickened a defensive pride in the "meteor flag" of the larger homeland. As one English immigrant remarked in 1918, "They used to call me John Bull, because I argued so much in favor of England, but they have all got to be John Bulls now."[165] As the single "British-American community" thus became more than a figure of speech, its members' place in American life also changed. Sharpening their British identity did not make their American assimilation any less easy than it had been. On the contrary, in order to counter the "Irish vote" they were obliged to enter into the public affairs of the country. In becoming more British they became more American.

Note: "English Gold" and the British-Americans

Attacked by anti-Catholic and anti-home-rule British immigrants, Irish-Americans were apt to charge "that English gold was at the bottom of the whole affair." [166] British diplomatic and consular officers did keep an eye on Irish revolutionaries in America; their reports fill forty-eight volumes of the Foreign Office's American correspondence between 1866 and 1902.[167] But their meager mention of Orange riots, the British-American Association, or the Murchison episode suggests that the British government did not inspire or subsidize the immigrants' pro-British activities and in fact first learned of them from the laconic consuls.[168] In view of American Anglophobia, any Whitehall scheme to make political use of the British-Americans would obviously have been highly dangerous. At the time of the 1887 Jubilee the Foreign Office feared even to illuminate the legation and consulates in the United States.[169] It never went further than in 1901, when at the request of a British society in Boston it curtly acknowledged the efforts of an English-American there to popularize the British side of the Boer War.[170] Although as a matter of course some British consuls belonged to societies of well-to-do immigrants, the British government hardly instructed them to do so.[171] A Foreign Office report of 1920 sums up the official attitude. While recommending that the government foster a "spirit of solidarity" among British subjects overseas, it observed, "The position of the British community in the United States of America differs so much from that of all others that our recommendations are not intended to extend to that country." [172] Anti-Irish sentiment among British-Americans was quite spontaneous.

13

Epilogue

By the early twentieth century, when the British-American community emerged, its English, Scottish, and Welsh components had already begun to shrink in size — though hardly in spirit. Emigrants leaving the United Kingdom no longer favored the United States. After the first World War, in fact, the British movement to industrial America was done. A brief revival in 1923 and 1924, years of American prosperity and old-country depression, did bring a swarm of Scots from Clydeside and the Highlands.[1] But by this time America could offer the British little. American industry seldom needed their skills, and even when they were out of work at home, the government dole now enabled them at least to survive there. Furthermore, the United States was putting up the bars against foreigners. True, the nationality quota acts of 1921 and 1924 were designed to keep out southern and eastern Europeans and Asiatics; Congress' racial notions permitted Great Britain a relatively high annual quota. But in 1923 and 1924 even this was too small for the number who suddenly wished to come.[2] Thereafter, though the British were the third largest group of new arrivals, fewer only than Canadians, who were exempt from quotas, and Germans, they did not fill a quarter of their quota. Even admissible foreigners such as they were discouraged by all the new red tape of the later 1920's; depression and war in the 1930's and early 1940's almost completely stopped them.[3] The subsequent postwar rush — mainly war brides — was soon over.[4]

Would the earlier immigrants' children fill the place left empty for lack of newcomers? British-American societies did their best to welcome the American-born generation; some even established juvenile sections from which young men would pass into the adult lodges.[5] Children of other immigrant nationalities carried on the parents' societies, but despite British pride in the culture of England, Wales, or Scotland and of Great Britain, the children usually abandoned the organizations founded to preserve it. A few might have the habit of referring to their parents' native land as "home." [6] But with no old-country memories of their own and, unlike many foreigners' children, finding that what they did retain of their foreign heritage was no bar to success among old-stock Americans, they easily cut loose from the British-American community. The second generation usually did not even follow their parents' skilled occupations, as they would have been likely to do in the old country.[7] Perhaps most of those who did were the less enterprising individuals. In many trades they earned wages lower than men trained in Britain itself. But the second generation was apt to take up the more promising pursuits that attracted the run of Americans.[8]

Thus in a sense the British-Americans had no "second generation," no ill-adjusted class, like the children of less fortunate foreigners, without firm roots in either the old or the new culture. In effect their children were simply Americans, neither better nor worse adapted to the normal life of the country than were the children of old-stock parents. They seldom thought of themselves as anything but Americans. To an Englishman who had lived in the United States it seemed in 1895, "The children born in America of English parents out-herod Herod and are the most decided partisans of the America for the Americans policy." [9] The young son of a Chicago Yorkshireman bragged to his father after a school lesson on the Revolution, "You had the king's army, and we were only a lot of farmers, but *we* thrashed you!" [10]

Reinforced from neither within nor without, the British-American community dwindled after the first World War. The Scottish and English newspapers soon expired; only *Y Drych* — reduced since 1940 to a monthly printed almost wholly in English — survives among the Welsh. To be sure, many societies which existed in 1918 have continued to the present or have been replaced by similar ones.

New lodges of the Sons of St. George, the Order of Scottish Clans, the Loyal Orange Institution, and their auxiliaries, and new Welsh, Manx, Canadian, and other groups have sprung up during the past thirty years. The Daughters of the British Empire, the Women's Welsh-American Clubs, and other women's organizations for a time did continue to expand.[11] But the period of innovation was all but over. Apart from Canadian or British Legion posts among immigrant veterans of the first World War, the immigrant institutions have merely resisted the general decline of their pre-1918 vigor. Of the fraternal societies only the Scottish Clans, probably still drawing on the Scots who came in the early 1920's, is not in imminent danger of disbanding. Even the new (1929) National Gymanfa Ganu Association has in effect replaced the elaborately planned *eisteddfod* with the simpler and impromptu hymn-singing meeting as the principal Welsh-American musical festival.[12] Thus the history of the British-American community since 1918 has been an epilogue to its vigorous nineteenth-century story. As it recedes into the past, its long perspectives should now be clear.

What, then, was the nature of the British immigrants' experience in industrial America? In two major respects it differed from that of most other foreigners. While Irish, Italian, or Polish peasants endured years of poorly paid rough labor, and while Germans or Scandinavians were more apt to go into farming, many of the British, trained in the mines and factories of the foremost industrial nation, moved directly into the best-paid American jobs. With the exception of the Welsh- and Gaelic-speakers, they were also more at home in American society and culture than were any other immigrants. Both their economic and their social adjustments were relatively so easy that they could enter into American affairs as equals of natives of the country.

Yet in another respect they did resemble other immigrants. In passing from the civilization of the homeland to that of the New World, no foreigners could at once throw off the old. Though old-country ways had inevitably to be modified, they were straws to which men and women adrift in an alien sea might cling. It was not only those immigrants whose economic and cultural adjustment was most difficult who needed such support. The British likewise, for all their advantages in America, clung to the distinctive in their own tradition. A steadfast belief in their old country's superiority set them apart just as Irishmen or Poles were set apart by that anxiety which American ridicule and discrimination could engender. Like the men and women who identified themselves with an Irish-American or a Polish-American community, the British felt that they belonged to an English-American, a Welsh-American, a Scottish-American, even a Canadian-American or, ultimately, when they all recoiled from the Irish challenge, a British-American community. But this "hyphenation" never lessened the welcome which their native American neighbors extended them. Accepting it, the British immigrants nevertheless chose also to stand with their own kind.

Notes

Special Periodical Sources

The sources of this book are so scattered that the full bibliography in the dissertation copy in the Harvard University Library is inordinately long. Any reader interested in such things will observe that the references here fall into these categories: records of the immigrants' societies and churches; manuscript British diplomatic and consular correspondence; manuscript letters from immigrants to friends in the old country; printed Parliamentary, Congressional, and state documents; immigrant guidebooks; descriptive books and articles by British travelers or immigrants and other contemporaries; general newspapers; miscellaneous secondary books and articles; and the author's correspondence and conversations with various immigrants.

The most fruitful sources of all are the immigrant press, trade-union newspapers, trade journals, and other special periodicals of the time. As most of these are long forgotten, the following list gives their places and inclusive dates of publication, the years consulted in detail, and libraries holding files.

Albion (New York, 1822–1876). 1822–1876. Boston Athenaeum.

Amalgamated Engineering Journal (London, 1895–). 1902–1918. Harvard University Library.

American Canadian (Boston, 1874–1876). 1874–1876. Boston Public Library.

American Federationist (Washington, 1894–). 1894–1918. Library of Congress; Harvard University Library.

American Journal of Fabrics and Knit Goods Manufacturer (Boston, 1881–1884). 1883–1884. Library of Congress.

American Manufacturer (Pittsburgh, 1862–1916). 1865–1900. Library of Congress.

American Protestant (New York, 1870–1874). 1871–1874. Library of Congress.

American Silk Journal (New York, 1882–1938). 1882–1892. Library of Congress.

Anglo-American (London, 1898– ?). 1898–1902. British Museum.

Anglo-American Magazine (New York, 1899–1902). 1899–1902. New York Public Library.

Anglo-American Times (London, 1865–1896). 1865–1896. Boston Public Library; British Museum.

Boston Scotsman (Boston, 1906–1914). 1906–1907. Order of Scottish Clans, Boston.

British-American (New York, Philadelphia, 1887–1919). 1887–1919. British Museum.

British-American Citizen (Boston, 1887–1913). 1887–1903. Massachusetts Historical Society; Huntington Library.

British Californian (San Francisco, 1897–1931). 1897, 1903–1905, 1913–1921. Library of Congress; British Museum.

Bulletin of the American Iron and Steel Association (Philadelphia, 1866–1912). 1866–1896. Library of Congress; Boston Public Library.

Cambrian (Cincinnati, Utica, 1880–1920). 1880–1920. Harvard University Library; Library of Congress; New York Public Library.

Canadian American (Chicago, 1883–1934). 1884–1888. University of Minnesota Library.

Cenhadwr Americanaidd (Utica, Remsen, 1840–1901). 1840–1866. National Library of Wales.

Church Militant (Boston, 1898–). 1898–1903. Library of the Episcopal Diocese of Massachusetts.

Cyfaill o'r Hen Wlad (New York, Utica, 1838–1933). 1838–1866. National Library of Wales.

Cymro America (New York, 1832). 1832. National Library of Wales.

Druid [*Welsh-American*] (Scranton, Pittsburgh, 1907–1939). 1907–1918. National Library of Wales; Welsh National Library of North America.

Drych (New York, Utica, 1851–). 1851–1952. National Library of Wales; University College of North Wales Library; Harvard University Library.

Emigrant (New York, 1833–1835). 1833–1835. Library of Congress.

Emigrant and Old Countryman (New York, 1835–1840). 1835–1840. Library of Congress; American Antiquarian Society.

English-American (New York, 1884–1885). 1884–1885. British Museum.

English-Speaking World [*British-American*] (New York, 1917–1922). 1917–1919. New York Public Library.

Fall River Churchman (Fall River, 1894– ?). 1894–1900. Church of the Ascension, Fall River.

Fall River Weekly News (Fall River, 1845–1926). 1865–1896. Boston Public Library.

Fiery Cross (Boston, 1894–). 1900–1950. Order of Scottish Clans, Boston.

Granite Cutters' Journal (Quincy, 1877–). 1881–1900. Johns Hopkins University Library; Harvard University Library; U.S. Department of Labor Library.

Gunton Institute Bulletin (New York, 1897–1903). 1897–1903. Boston Public Library; Harvard University Library.

Inter-Nation (Boston, 1905–1907). 1905–1907. Harvard University Library.

Iron Age (New York, 1859–). 1867–1873. Boston Public Library.

Iron Molders' [*International*] *Journal* (Cincinnati, 1863–), 1866–1888. Johns Hopkins University Library.

John Swinton's Paper (New York, 1883–1887). 1883–1887. Columbia University Library.

Journal of Commerce (St. Louis, c. 1870– ?). 1879–1883. Library of Congress.

Labor Journal (Fall River, 1874–1878). 1874. Fall River Public Library.

Labor Standard [*Socialist*] (New York, Fall River, 1876–1881). 1876–1881. New York Public Library.

Lawrence Journal [*and Citizen*] (Lawrence, 1868–1891). 1874–1888. Essex Institute.

Machinists' and Blacksmiths' International Journal (Cleveland, c. 1865–1875). 1871–1872. John Crerar Library.

Miners' Journal (Pottsville, 1825–1909). 1825–1882. Historical Society of Pennsylvania; University of Pennsylvania Library; Library of Congress.

Miners' National Record (Cleveland, 1874–1876). 1874–1876. New York Public Library.

National Labor Tribune (Pittsburgh, 1872–). 1874–1900. Harvard University Library; New York Public Library.

New York Anglo-American (New York, 1843–1847). 1843–1846. New York Public Library; Library of Congress.

Old Countryman (New York, c. 1842–1848). 1843. Library of Congress.

Paterson Labor Standard (Paterson, 1878–1898). 1878–1896. Wisconsin State Historical Society.

Protestant Standard (Philadelphia, 1878–1894). 1884–1893. Chicago Historical Society; New York Public Library.

Purple Bell (Saugus, 1902– ?). 1902–1907. Library of Congress.

Quarrymen's Journal (Quincy, 1891–1893). 1891–1893. Massachusetts Institute of Technology.

Scottish-American [*Journal*] (New York, 1857–1919). 1859–1919. Chicago Historical Society; New York Public Library; Boston Public Library; New York Historical Society.

Scottish Patriot [*Journal*] (New York, 1840–1842). 1840–1842. New York Historical Society.

Stone (Indianapolis, 1888–). 1888–1898. Library of Congress; Massachusetts Institute of Technology.

Stone Cutters' Journal (Indianapolis, 1887–). 1893–1902. Johns Hopkins University Library; Massachusetts Institute of Technology.

Textile America (New York, 1896–1900). 1897–1900. Library of Congress.

Textile Worker (New York, 1912–1935). 1912–1918. Harvard University Library.

Textile World [*Record, Journal*] (New York, 1888–). 1890–1915. New York Public Library; Harvard University Library.

United Mine Workers' Journal (Indianapolis, 1891–). 1900–1918. Harvard University Library.

Wade's Fibre and Fabric (Boston, 1885–). 1885–1887. Boston Public Library.

Western British-American (Chicago, 1888–1922). 1901, 1903, 1905–1907, 1911–1918. Chicago Historical Society; University of Illinois Library; Manitoba Provincial Library.

Workingman's Advocate (Chicago, 1864–1877). 1864–1877. Harvard University Library.

Notes

1. Great Britain: Immigrants and Emigrants

1. Josiah Strong, *Our Country* (New York, 1885), pp. 159, 161.

2. V. Gordon Childe, *Prehistoric Communities of the British Isles* (London, 1940), pp. 258–263; R. H. Hodgkin, *A History of the Anglo-Saxons* (Oxford, 1935), I, 154–183, II, 473–572; W. Cunningham, *Alien Immigrants to England* (London, 1897), *passim*.

3. J. H. Clapham, "Irish Immigration into Great Britain in the Nineteenth Century," *Bulletin of the International Committee of Historical Sciences*, V (1933), 596–604; Barbara M. Kerr, "Irish Seasonal Migration to Great Britain, 1800–1838," *Irish Historical Studies*, III (1943), 365–380.

4. "Report from the Select Committee on Emigration and Immigration (Foreigners)," *Parliamentary Papers*, 1889, X (311), vii–x.

5. James A. H. Murray, *The Dialect of the Southern Counties of Scotland* (London, 1873), p. 5. Cf. E. G. Ravenstein, "On the Celtic Languages in the British Isles," *Journal of the Statistical Society*, XLII (1879), 579–607.

6. Peter F. Anson, *The Catholic Church in Modern Scotland* (London, 1937), pp. 73–82.

7. D. F. Macdonald, *Scotland's Shifting Population* (Glasgow, 1937), pp. 125–137.

8. James Edmund Handley, *The Irish in Scotland* (Cork, 1945) and *The Irish in Modern Scotland* (Cork, 1947), *passim*.

9. David Williams, *A History of Modern Wales* (London, 1950), p 229.

10. A. H. John, *The Industrial Development of South Wales* (Cardiff, 1950), pp. 61–68; "Report from the Select Committee on Coal," *Parliamentary Papers*, 1873, X (313), Q. 1538–1540, 1557–1558, 1607–1610.

11. Ravenstein, pp. 608–623.

12. Henry Jenner, "The Cornish Language," *Transactions of the Philological Society*, 1873–1874, pp. 165–186.

13. Henry Jenner, "The Manx Language," *Transactions of the Philological Society*, 1875–1876, pp. 172–197.

14. Ravenstein, pp. 581–591.

15. Arthur Redford, *Labour Migration in England 1800–1850* (Manchester, 1925), *passim*; Macdonald, *passim*; E. G. Ravenstein, "The Laws of Migration," *Journal of the Statistical Society*, XLVIII (1885), 167–219.

16. Marcus Lee Hansen, *The Mingling of the Canadian and American Peoples* (New Haven, 1940), pp. 20–91.

17. Charles W. Dunn, *Highland Settler* (Toronto, 1953), *passim.*

18. *Census of Canada 1880–1881*, I, 300–301.

19. "Report of the Committee on Linguistic and National Stocks in the Population of the United States," *Annual Report of the American Historical Association*, 1931, I, 124–125.

20. Marcus Lee Hansen, *The Atlantic Migration* (Cambridge, 1941), 72–76.

21. *Ibid.*, pp. 134–135; W. F. Adams, *Ireland and Irish Immigration to the New World* (New Haven, 1932), pp. 64–65.

22. "Returns of the Number of Emigrants," *Parliamentary Papers*, 1868–69, L (397); "Miscellaneous Statistics of the United Kingdom," 1872, LXIV (C. 669), 186; 1875, LXXX (C. 1305), 211; 1879, LXXIV (C. 2332), 208; "Emigration and Immigration," 1877, LXXXV (5), 12, *et seq.* to 1913, LV (183), 4–5; U. S. Bureau of Statistics on Commerce and Navigation, *Annual Reports*, 1869–1891; U.S. Superintendent of Immigration, *Annual Reports*, 1892–1895; U.S. Commissioner-General of Immigration, *Annual Reports*, 1896–1918.

23. "Emigration Statistics of Ireland," *Parliamentary Papers*, 1877, LXXXV (C. 1700), *et seq.* to 1919, LI (Cmd. 77), 10; "Census of Ireland," *Parliamentary Papers*, 1873, LXXII (C. 873–1), 1071, and 1912–13, CXVIII (Cd. 6663), 210–211.

24. "Emigration and Immigration," *Parliamentary Papers*, 1897–1914; U.S. Commissioner-General of Immigration, *Annual Reports*, 1908–1918.

25. "Emigration and Immigration," *Parliamentary Papers*, 1877–1914.

26. U.S. Bureau of Statistics on Commerce and Navigation, *Annual Reports*, 1873–1885.

27. U.S. Commissioner-General of Immigration, *Annual Reports*, 1908–1918.

PART I. THE ECONOMIC ADJUSTMENT

2. "Pies and Puddings"

1. "Report on the Trade and Commerce of New Orleans," *Parliamentary Papers*, 1881, LXXXIX (C. 2843), 416.

2. *Druid*, October 7, 1909. Cf. *Drych*, May 17, 1851.

3. *Post*, pp. 104, 154, 158–159.

4. Edwin C. Guillet, *The Great Migration* (New York, 1937), pp. 233–248.

5. George A. Gordon, *My Education and Religion* (Boston, 1925), p. 133. Cf. John Wilson, *Memories of a Labour Leader* (London, 1910), pp. 148–150.

6. *Amalgamated Engineering Journal*, June 1903, pp. 25–26.

7. *Ante*, p. 6.

8. Robert Louis Stevenson, *The Amateur Emigrant* (New York, 1895), pp. 14–23.

9. *Post*, pp. 52, 80–83.

10. Fred H. Hitchins, *The Colonial Land and Emigration Commission*

(Philadelphia, 1931), pp. 203–234; Stanley C. Johnson, *A History of Emigration from the United Kingdom to North America* (London, 1913), pp. 85–100; W. A. Carrothers, *Emigration from the British Isles* (London, 1929), pp. 174–185, 208–222, 228–255; Monica Glory Page, "A Study of Emigration from Great Britain 1802–1860" (unpublished doctoral thesis, University of London, 1931), *passim*; Wilbur S. Shepperson, "British Views on Emigration to North America 1837–1860" (unpublished doctoral thesis, Western Reserve University, 1951), *passim.*

11. Johnson, pp. 69–80; Carrothers, pp. 228–236; John Wilson, *The Migrations of the English People* (Brighton, c. 1870), pp. 77–78.

12. West Virginia Commissioner of Immigration, *Seventh Annual Report* (1870), p. 8.

13. *Bulletin of the American Iron and Steel Association*, XVIII (1884), 33, 67; *Scottish-American Journal*, February 21, March 6, 13, 1884.

14. Roy L. Garis, *Immigration Restriction* (New York, 1927), pp. 88–89.

15. *Bulletin of the American Iron and Steel Association*, XXII (1888), 333.

16. "Correspondence Respecting the Admission into the United States of Destitute Aliens and State Aided Emigrants," *Parliamentary Papers*, 1887, LXXXI (C. 5109), 1–8, 18–29; "Reports from the Select Committee on Colonisation," *Parliamentary Papers*, 1889, X (274), Q. 2460–2463, 2846–2847, 3057–3058.

17. Garis, p. 95.

18. *Ibid.*, pp. 86–87.

19. "Enforcement of Alien Contract Labor Laws," *House Executive Document*, 52 Cong., 1 sess., no. 235, pt. 1 (February 22, 1892), pp. 189–191.

20. *Scottish-American Journal*, May 4, 1867, December 25, 1907, October 18, 1911; *Western British-American*, May 3, 1913.

21. "Third Report from the Select Committee on Emigration from the United Kingdom," *Parliamentary Papers*, 1826–7, V (550), Q. 2240; "Report from the Select Committee on Colonisation," Q. 1326–1329; "Diplomatic and Consular Reports on Emigration," *House Miscellaneous Document*, 50 Cong., 1 sess., no. 572, pt. 2 (1889), p. 6; Johnson, pp. 70–71.

22. *Anglo-American Times*, November 20, 1869.

23. *Ibid.*, 1865–1896, *passim.*

24. "Enforcement of Alien Contract Labor Laws," pp. 187–188; *The Emigrants' Guide for 1883* (London, 1882).

25. Stevenson, p. 80.

26. Harry Jerome, *Migration and Business Cycles* (New York, 1926), pp. 179–187; Willard Long Thorp, *Business Annals* (New York, 1926), pp. 24–25, 28–29, 94–95, 125–143, 163–177.

27. W. W. Rostow, *British Economy of the Nineteenth Century* (Oxford, 1948), pp. 90–97, 179ff.

28. *Drych*, February 11, 1875; *American Manufacturer*, September 7, 1876; *Anglo-American Times*, September 1, 1876, October 26, 1877; *Iron Molders' Journal*, October 10, 1877, July 1, 1878; John T. Robeson to Frederick W. Seward, August 13, 1879, in U.S. Consular Correspondence (MS), p. 151.

29. Marcus Lee Hansen, *The Mingling of the Canadian and American Peoples* (New Haven, 1940), p. 172.

30. "Report on the Commerce of the United States," *Parliamentary Papers*, 1877, LXXXI (C. 1802), 299; *Bulletin of the American Iron and Steel Association*, XI (1877), 139.

31. *Drych*, October 2–8, 1879, October 28, 1880; *Scottish-American Journal*, November 13, 1879.

32. Thorp, pp. 296–307; Lloyd G. Reynolds, *The British Immigrant* (Toronto, 1935), pp. 36–37, 46, 92–96.

33. Francis A. Walker, "Our Foreign Population," *Advance*, VIII (1874), 261.

34. U.S. Bureau of Statistics on Commerce and Navigation, *Annual Reports*, 1873–1891; U.S. Superintendent of Immigration, *Annual Reports*, 1892–1895; U.S. Commissioner-General of Immigration, *Annual Reports*, 1896–1918.

35. *Eleventh Census of the U.S.* (1890), II, 484–488.

36. "Reports of the Immigration Commission," *Senate Document*, 61 Cong., 2 sess., no. 633 (June 15, 1910), VI, 44; VIII, 41; XVI, 24, 227.

37. *Ibid.*, X, 73, 665; XI, 34.

38. *Ibid.*, XIX, 95.

39. *Ibid.*, VI, 50; VIII, 48; X, 83; XI, 37; XVI, 27–28, 230; XIX, 104, 111.

40. *Eleventh Census of the U.S.* (1890), II, 485–489.

41. "Reports of the Immigration Commission," XIX, 95.

42. *Scottish-American Journal*, November 5, 1864.

43. Charlotte Erickson, "The Encouragement of Emigration by British Trade Unions, 1850–1900," *Population Studies*, III (1949), 252–253, 260, 264.

3. Spindle and Shuttle

1. Isaac Holmes, *An Account of the United States of America* (London, 1823), p. 126.

2. Paul Mantoux, *The Industrial Revolution in the Eighteenth Century* (London, 1928), pp. 193–257; J. H. Clapham, *An Economic History of Modern Britain* (Cambridge, 1926–1930), I, 441–442, 551–553; II, 28–30; Laurance James Saunders, *Scottish Democracy 1815–1840* (Edinburgh, 1950), pp. 101–104, 125–126.

3. *Dictionary of American Biography* (New York, 1928–1937), XVII, 205–206.

4. Herbert Heaton, "The Industrial Immigrant in the United States," *Proceedings of the American Philosophical Society*, XCV (1951), 521–524.

5. Charles Cowley, "The Foreign Colonies of Lowell," *Contributions of the Old Residents' Historical Association*, II (1883), 168–169; H. C. Meserve, *Lowell, an Industrial Dream Come True* (Boston, 1923), pp. 71–72; Henry Ashworth, *A Tour in the United States, Cuba, and Canada* (London, 1861), p. 149; *Cotton and Its Manufacture: The Industries of Fall River* (n.p., n.d.,), p. 123; *Dictionary of American Biography*, XII, 305.

6. "Third Report from the Select Committee on Emigration from the United Kingdom," *Parliamentary Papers*, 1826–27, V (550), Q. 2174; Walter F. Willcox, ed., *International Migrations* (New York, 1931), II, 252.

7. Melvin Thomas Copeland, *The Cotton Manufacturing Industry of the United States* (Cambridge, 1912), pp. 3–8, 12–13.

8. *Ibid.*, p. 31; Arthur Redford, *Labour Migration in England 1800–1850* (Manchester, 1926), pp. 154–155; Massachusetts Bureau of Statistics of Labor, *Third Annual Report* (1872), pp. 395–397; "Third Report from the Select Committee on Emigration from the United Kingdom," pp. 301–302, Q. 2174, 2239; *Textile Record of America*, I (1880), 2.

9. Copeland, pp. 13, 118; "Reports of the Immigration Commission," *Senate Document*, 61 Cong., 2 sess., no. 633 (June 15, 1910), X, 30, 225–226.

10. "Report of the Industrial Commission," *House Document*, 57 Cong., 1 sess., no. 183 (December 5, 1901), XIV, 544.

11. Constance McLaughlin Green, *Holyoke, Massachusetts* (New Haven, 1939), pp. 48–49; *Scottish-American Journal*, February 4, 1875.

12. Green, p. 76; Sylvia Chace Lintner, "A Social History of Fall River 1859–1879" (unpublished doctoral thesis, Radcliffe College, 1945), pp. 64–67; Daniel Creamer, "Recruiting Labor for the Amoskeag Mills," *Journal of Economic History*, I (1941), 42–46; W. O. Henderson, *The Lancashire Cotton Famine 1861–1865* (Manchester, 1934), pp. 115–118; Charlotte Erickson, "Encouragement of Emigration by British Trade Unions 1850–1900," *Population Studies*, III (1949), 255–256; *Fall River Weekly News*, March 18, 1875.

13. Massachusetts Bureau of Statistics of Labor, *Tenth Annual Report* (1879), p. 135.

14. Erickson, pp. 256–258, 262.

15. Copeland, pp. 27–30; Lintner, pp. 1–53; "Reports of the Immigration Commission," X, 30, 38–47; "Study of a New England Factory Town," *Atlantic*, XLIII (1879), 690; Maine Bureau of Industrial Labor Statistics, *Second Annual Report* (1888), p. 121, and *Twenty-second Annual Report* (1908), p. 4; *Report of the Committee of the Senate upon the Relations between Labor and Capital* (Washington, 1885), III, 6, 28; Evelyn H. Knowlton, *Pepperell's Progress* (Cambridge, 1948), pp. 163–164; *Fall River Weekly News*, March 11, 1875; *New York Herald*, October 19, 1875.

16. Benjamin Brierley, *Ab-o'th'-Yate in Yankeeland* (Manchester, 1885), p. 19.

17. *Report of the Committee of the Senate upon the Relations between Labor and Capital*, I, 632; III, 496.

18. Brierley, p. 135.

19. *New York Herald*, October 13, 1875.

20. *John Swinton's Paper*, January 6, 1884. Cf. Erickson, pp. 265–267.

21. "Report from the Select Committee on Colonisation," *Parliamentary Papers*, 1889, X (274), 92.

22. "Diplomatic and Consular Reports on Emigration," *House Miscellaneous Document*, 50 Cong., 1 sess., no. 572, pt. 2 (1889), p. 15.

23. New York Bureau of Statistics of Labor, *Third Annual Report* (1885),

p. 480; Rhode Island Commissioner of Industrial Statistics, *First Annual Report* (1887), p. 41.

24. *New York Herald*, October 13, 1875; Meserve, p. 72; Copeland, p. 121.

25. Creamer, pp. 47–56.

26. *Fall River Weekly News*, April 26, 1883; Cf. *Textile Record*, IV (1883), 81.

27. *British-American*, April 23, 1882; *Report of the Committee of the Senate upon the Relations between Labor and Capital*, III, 150; "Report of the Industrial Commission," XIV, 479.

28. E.g., classified advertisements in *Wade's Fibre and Fabric*, September 5, 1885.

29. T. M. Young, *The American Cotton Industry* (London, 1902), pp. 16–17; *Textile World Record*, XXXIX (1910), 740, 745.

30. Young, p. 22.

31. Massachusetts Bureau of Statistics of Labor, *Thirteenth Annual Report* (1882), pp. 338, 349–350, 359.

32. *Ibid.*, *Second Annual Report* (1871), pp. 500–502; Young, pp. 10–11; Clapham, II, 449.

33. Massachusetts Bureau of Statistics of Labor, *Thirteenth Annual Report* (1882), p. 304.

34. Copeland, pp. 295–303.

35. Massachusetts Bureau of Statistics of Labor, *Thirteenth Annual Report* (1882), p. 306.

36. *Ibid.*, p. 338. Cf. *First Annual Report* (1870), pp. 114–115.

37. *Fall River Weekly News*, August 15, 1894.

38. Young, pp. 129–131.

39. *Ibid.*, p. 17.

40. *Ibid.*, p. 133.

41. *Report of the Committee of the Senate upon the Relations between Labor and Capital*, III, 496.

42. *Ibid.*, I, 55; "Consular Reports on Emigration and Immigration," *House Miscellaneous Document*, 49 Cong., 2 sess., no. 157 (February 11, 1887), p. 425; "Report of the Industrial Commission," XIV, 568; *Fall River Weekly News*, September 6, 1893.

43. Edward Porritt, "A Labor Conflict without Violence," *Outlook*, LXXVIII (1904), 976.

44. Young, p. 4.

45. *Massachusetts Labor Bulletin*, no. 37 (September, 1905), p. 186; "Reports of the Immigration Commission," X, 32–47.

46. "Report on the Trade and Commerce of the Consular District of Boston," *Parliamentary Papers*, 1910, CIII (Cd. 4962–85), 37–38.

47. Mantoux, pp. 47–56, 267–276; Clapham, I, 442–443; II, 82–83.

48. Arthur Harrison Cole, *The American Wool Manufacture* (Cambridge, 1926), I, 86–136.

49. Redford, pp. 37–43, 58, 87, 91, 112, 151.

50. G. Poulett Scrope, *Extracts of Letters from Poor Persons Who Emi-*

grated Last Year to Canada and the United States (London, 1832), p. 17; "Report of the Foreign Commerce of the United States," *Parliamentary Papers*, 1881, LXXXIX (C. 2916), 288.

51. Cowley, pp. 172–174.

52. Cole, I, 234–235, 368–369; "Reports of the Immigration Commission," X, 652.

53. Cole, II, 183–185.

54. "Diplomatic and Consular Reports on Emigration," 32.

55. Massachusetts Bureau of Statistics of Labor, *Second Annual Report* (1871), p. 291.

56. *American Manufacturer*, October 3, 1879, June 3, 1881.

57. "Diplomatic and Consular Reports on Emigration," p. 33.

58. *Ibid.*, pp. 18–19; "Enforcement of Alien Contract Labor Laws," *House Executive Document*, 52 Cong., 1 sess., no. 235, pt. 2 (February 22, 1892), p. 88.

59. Cole, II, 88–91, 95–98, 112–113; *Eleventh Census of the U.S.* (1890), II, 486–488.

60. Cole, I, 277–278; II, 81–83.

61. "Reports of the Immigration Commission," X, 745–746.

62. James Burnley, *Two Sides of the Atlantic* (London, 1880), pp. 62–66; William Smith, *A Yorkshireman's Trip to the United States and Canada* (London, 1892), pp. 130–132.

63. "Report of the Industrial Commission," XIV, 214–215.

64. *Ibid.*, XIV, 215, 521, 527; "Importation of Contract Laborers," *House Miscellaneous Document*, 50 Cong., 1 sess., no. 572, pt. 1 (1888), pp. 189–195, 201, 238, 586–591; *Textile Record*, IV (1883), 306.

65. Pennsylvania Bureau of Industrial Statistics, *Seventeenth Annual Report* (1889), pp. D3–D4.

66. Cowley, pp. 171–172.

67. *Scottish-American Journal*, November 2, 1882; Arthur H. Cole and Harold F. Williamson, *The American Carpet Manufacture* (Cambridge, 1941), p. 38.

68. *Ibid.*, pp. 57–58.

69. *Ibid.*, p. 36; Pennsylvania Bureau of Industrial Statistics, *Eighth Annual Report* (1879–1880), pp. 100–101.

70. *Textile Record of America*, I (1880), 2.

71. "Report on the Foreign Commerce of the United States," pp. 288–293; Pennsylvania Bureau of Industrial Statistics, *Tenth Annual Report* (1881–1882), p. 55; Cole and Williamson, p. 164.

72. *Eleventh Census of the U.S.* (1890), II, 486–488.

73. *British Californian*, November 1903, p. 9.

74. Cole and Williamson, p. 84.

75. Gladys L. Palmer, *Union Tactics and Economic Change* (Philadelphia, 1932), p. 29.

76. Gladys L. Palmer, *et al.*, *The Philadelphia Upholstery Industry* (Phila-

delphia, 1932), pp. 6, 15; Pennsylvania Bureau of Industrial Statistics, *Thirty-Fourth Annual Report* (1906), p. 256.

77. F. A. Wells, *The British Hosiery Trade* (London, 1935), pp. 54–85, 128–159.

78. *Textile Record*, I (1880), 2; III (1882), 195; "Report on the Foreign Commerce of the United States," pp. 294–296.

79. *American Wool and Cotton Reporter*, January 5, 1911; Massachusetts Bureau of Statistics of Labor, *Second Annual Report* (1871), p. 274.

80. *Textile Record*, VI (1885), 28, 235.

81. "Importation of Contract Laborers," pp. 234–235.

82. *Eleventh Census of the U.S.* (1890), II, 486–488.

83. Copeland, p. 122; Pennsylvania Bureau of Industrial Statistics, *Thirty-Second Annual Report* (1904), pp. 433–434; *Thirty-Fourth Annual Report* (1906), pp. 157, 245, 249.

84. Mantoux, pp. 197–201; Ratan C. Rawlley, *Economics of the Silk Industry* (London, 1919), pp. 271–273.

85. L. R. Trumbull, *A History of Industrial Paterson* (Paterson, 1882), pp. 164–191; Agnes Hannay, *A Chronicle of Industry on the Mill River* (Northampton, 1936), pp. 89, 93.

86. Rawlley, p. 308.

87. William Nelson and Charles A. Shriner, *History of Paterson* (New York, 1920), I, 342–357; Trumbull, pp. 198–260.

88. "Third Report of the Royal Commission Appointed to Inquire into the Depression of Trade and Industry," *Parliamentary Papers*, 1886, XXIII (C. 4797), Q. 14,055.

89. Silk Association of America, *Fourth Annual Report* (1876), p. 19; *New York Herald*, March 8, 1880.

90. *American Silk Journal*, XI (1892), 140; Herbert S. Swan, *The Plain Goods Silk Industry* (Paterson, 1937), pp. 4–28.

91. *American Manufacturer*, September 12, December 26, 1879; *Paterson Labor Standard*, March 27, 1880.

92. *New York Herald*, March 8, 1880; "Third Report of the Royal Commission Appointed to Inquire into the Depression of Trade and Industry," Q. 14,067.

93. Thomas Greenwood, *A Tour in the States and Canada* (London, 1883), p. 139. Cf. *American Silk Journal*, I (1882), 136.

94. *American Silk Journal*, I (1882), 67–68.

95. "Reports of the Immigration Commission," XI, 17–18.

96. Brierley, pp. 43, 198.

97. *American Silk Journal*, XX (1901), 50; cf. IV (1885), 31.

98. *Ibid.*, XI (1892), 216.

99. *Ibid.*, II (1883), 96, 213; XI (1892), 216.

100. *Ibid.*, XI (1892), 145.

101. *Ibid.*, X (1891), 142, 166, 190, 217; *Scottish-American*, May 20, 1891; Rawlley, p. 311.

102. *Textile World Record*, XXIX (1905), 70–71.

103. *Paterson Labor Standard*, March 20, 1880.

104. Frank R. Mason, *The American Silk Industry and the Tariff* (Cambridge, 1910), pp. 50–52, 110–114, 130–133.

105. *Eleventh Census of the U.S.* (1890), II, 488.

106. "Reports of the Immigration Commission," XI, 18–19.

107. *Scottish-American Journal*, September 9, 1880; Clapham, II, 87, 513.

108. New York Bureau of Statistics of Labor, *Third Annual Report* (1885), p. 507.

109. *British-American*, June 18, 1892; Pennsylvania Bureau of Industrial Statistics, *Twenty-Seventh Annual Report* (1899), pp. 56–57; Gladys L. Palmer, "Labor Relations in the Lace and Lace-Curtain Industries in the United States," *Bulletin of the U.S. Bureau of Labor Statistics*, no. 399 (November 1925), p. 12.

110. *Ibid.*, pp. 19, 22, 25; Pennsylvania Bureau of Industrial Statistics, *Twenty-Seventh Annual Report* (1899), pp. 61, 70; *Thirty-Seventh Annual Report* (1909), p. 211.

111. *British Californian*, November 1903, p. 9.

112. *Scottish-American*, August 19, November 11, 1903, July 1, 1908; Pennsylvania Bureau of Industrial Statistics, *Thirty-Fourth Annual Report* (1906), p. 252 .

113. *Ibid.*, *Twenty-Seventh Annual Report* (1899), pp. 58, 61, 70; Palmer, "Lace and Lace-Curtain Industries," pp. 11–12.

114. *Ibid.*, pp. 19, 25.

115. *Scottish-American*, September 13, 1893.

116. *Fall River Weekly News*, July 19, 1888.

117. *Scottish-American Journal*, October 5, 1867; "Report of the Industrial Commission," XIV, 724–725.

118. *Scottish-American*, May 11, 1887; *Fall River Weekly News*, November 9, 1892.

119. *Chicago Journal of Commerce*, April 12, 1882.

120. *Scottish-American*, August 24, 1898, January 4, 1899.

121. Clapham, II, 28; III, 127.

122. *American Manufacturer*, September 28, 1876; *Scottish-American*, May 31, 1893, August 19, 1908.

123. John Leng, *America in 1876* (Dundee, 1877), p. 240; *Boston Scotsman*, May 11, 1907.

124. California Bureau of Labor Statistics, *Fourth Biennial Report* (1889–1890), p. 28; Trumbull, pp. 268–270.

125. William Lane Booker to Marquis of Salisbury, June 26, 1885, in C.O. 384/157; "Enforcement of Alien Contract Labor Laws," pt. 1, p. 210.

126. Cf. obituaries and other biographical articles in *Textile World* [*Record*], 1890–1915; *American Silk Journal*, 1882–1892; Trumbull, pp. 198–260; Nelson and Shriner, *passim*; London *Times*, December 28, 1876.

4. Pick and Powder Charge

1. "Report from the Select Committee on Coal," *Parliamentary Papers*, 1873, X (313), Q. 3557, 3745, 3792–3794, 5877, 6858, 1538; Maryland Bureau of Industrial Statistics, *First Annual Report* (1892), p. 212.

2. J. H. Clapham, *An Economic History of Modern Britain* (Cambridge, 1926–1930), I, 430–436; II, 103; III, 167; Wilfred Smith, *An Economic Geography of Great Britain* (London, 1949), pp. 124–128.

3. U.S. Bureau of the Census, *Historical Statistics of the United States 1789–1945* (Washington, 1949), p. 142.

4. *Miners' Journal*, June 16, 1827; cf. July 11, 1829.

5. Ohio Chief Inspector of Mines, *Thirty-Second Annual Report* (1906), pp. 30–31.

6. Eli Bowen, ed., *The Coal Regions of Pennsylvania* (Pottsville, 1848), p. 48.

7. *Post*, p. 111.

8. *Cymro America*, January 15, February 15, 1832; *Druid*, July 24, 1907, December 17, 1908, December 11, 1913.

9. "Report from the Select Committee on Coal," Q. 1539.

10. *Miners' Journal*, April 11, 1857; cf. April 5, May 24, 1856.

11. David Williams, *A History of Modern Wales* (London, 1950), p. 229.

12. *Miners' Journal*, July 10, 1830.

13. *Scottish-American Journal*, July 29, 1875; Peter Ross, *The Scot in America* (New York, 1896), p. 271.

14. Clapham, I, 558–559; II, 575–576.

15. G. O. Virtue, "The Anthracite Mine Laborer," *Bulletin of the Department of Labor*, no. 13 (November 1897), pp. 729–730; "Report from the Select Committee on Coal," Q. 4766; *Druid*, July 24, 1907.

16. Bowen, p. 48. Cf. *Miners' Journal*, June 4, 1853.

17. "Reports of the Immigration Commission," *Senate Document*, 61 Cong., 2 sess., no. 633 (June 15, 1910), XVI, 591–593, 659; *Cambrian*, IV (1884), 136; John Wilson, *Memories of a Labour Leader* (London, 1910), pp. 148ff.

18. Marcus Lee Hansen, *The Mingling of the Canadian and American Peoples* (New Haven, 1940), p. 162.

19. Andrew Roy, *A History of the Coal Miners of the United States* (Columbus, 1907), p. 69; Ross, p. 270; Ohio State Inspector of Mines, *Sixth Annual Report* (1880), p. 1408; Maryland Bureau of Industrial Statistics and Information, *First Biennial Report* (1884–1885), pp. 75–76; "Report on the Trade of the Consular District of Baltimore," *Parliamentary Papers*, 1911, XCVII (Cd. 5465–27), 6; *Fall River Weekly News*, June 23, 1870; *American Manufacturer*, September 12, 1884; *Cambrian*, IV (1884), 157; *Druid*, October 29, 1908; "Reports of the Immigration Commission," VI, 614–617.

20. "Report from the Select Committee on Coal," Q. 5832–5833, 5875.

21. Wilson, p. 194.

22. *Workingman's Advocate*, November 2, 16, 30, 1867, November 20, 1869, November 4, 1876.

23. Robert D. Thomas, *Hanes Cymry America* (Utica, 1872), pt. II, 17–18; Illinois Bureau of Labor Statistics, *Third Biennial Report* (1883–1884), p. 436; "Reports of the Immigration Commission," VI, 592–610; *Scottish-American Journal*, March 1, 1883; *British-American Citizen*, June 29, 1889.

24. William D. Davies, *America a Gweledigaethau Bywyd* (Merthyr Tydfil, 1899), pp. 142–143, 259; Thomas, pt. II, 96–100.

25. Jacob Van der Zee, *The British in Iowa* (Iowa City, 1922), p. 48; Thomas, pt. II, 74–76; Davies, pp. 134–135; *Druid*, October 12, 1911.

26. Trefnyddion Calfinaidd, "Cofnodion o Weithrediadau y Gymanfa Gyffredinol," 1869–1920 (MS), I, 86–93; W. H. Carruth, "Foreign Settlements in Kansas," *Kansas University Quarterly*, I (1892), 79; Frederick Lynn Ryan, *The Rehabilitation of Oklahoma Coal Mining Communities* (Norman, 1935), pp. 27–28; Union Pacific Coal Company, *History of the Union Pacific Coal Mines* (Omaha, 1940), *passim*; Thomas, pt. II, 126; Davies, pp. 153–156, 183–197; "Reports of the Immigration Commission," VII, 16, 25–29; *Miners' Journal*, January 10, 1852; *Drych*, June 8, 1876, March 28, 1878, March 20, 1879.

27. *Druid*, March 30, 1911.

28. George Jacob Holyoake, *Among the Americans* (Chicago, 1881), p. 177; *Cambrian*, V (1885), 132, 164; "Reports of the Immigration Commission," VI, 583–584; VII, 136, 140–144.

29. Arthur Redford, *Labour Migration in England 1800–1850* (Manchester, 1926), p. 133; E. Welbourne, *The Miners' Union of Northumberland and Durham* (Cambridge, 1923), p. 200; James E. Handley, *The Irish in Scotland* (Cork, 1945), pp. 118–120; Williams, p. 229.

30. *Philadelphia Evening Journal*, June 8, 1857; "Report from the Select Committee on Coal," Q. 1557.

31. Pennsylvania Bureau of Industrial Statistics, *Thirteenth Annual Report* (1885), pp. 28a–42a, 94a–101a.

32. Ohio State Inspector of Mines, *Sixth Annual Report* (1880), pp. 1423–1424.

33. Pennsylvania Inspectors of Mines of the Anthracite and Bituminous Coal Regions, *Reports*, 1888, pp. 98–99; Maryland Bureau of Industrial Statistics, *First Annual Report* (1892), p. 212.

34. "Report from the Select Committee on Coal," Q. 4634.

35. *Workingman's Advocate*, November 2, 1867, November 4, 1868; *Anglo-American Times*, March 7, 1868, December 11, 1869; *Miners' Journal*, February 12, 1870. Cf. Charlotte Erickson, "Encouragement of Emigration by British Trade Unions, 1850–1900," *Population Studies*, III (1949), 261.

36. *American Manufacturer*, January 24, 1879.

37. *Scottish-American Journal*, August 21, 1879.

38. Welbourne, p. 181.

39. *Workingman's Advocate*, February 20, 1875.

40. "Report from the Select Committee on Coal," Q. 4637, 6648.

41. London *Mining Journal*, May 14, 1870.

42. "Report from the Select Committee on Coal," Q. 4637.

43. "Diplomatic and Consular Reports on Emigration," *House Miscellaneous Document,* 50 Cong., 1 sess., no. 572, pt. 2 (1889), p. 22.

44. Bowen, p. 48. Cf. "Report from the Select Committee on Coal," Q. 4639.

45. Ohio Bureau of Labor Statistics, *Third Annual Report* (1879), p. 94; Pennsylvania Bureau of Industrial Statistics, *Thirteenth Annual Report* (1885), pp. 124, 129–131, 136, 145, 170, 171, 173, 177, 186.

46. "Report from the Select Committee on Coal," Q. 4788.

47. Pennsylvania Bureau of Industrial Statistics, *Thirteenth Annual Report* (1885), p. 174.

48. "Report from the Select Committee on Coal," Q. 4804, 4895–4900, 6650.

49. Pennsylvania Bureau of Industrial Statistics, *Thirteenth Annual Report* (1885), p. 131.

50. *Ibid.*, p. 176.

51. Vyrnwy Morgan, *The Cambro-American Pulpit* (New York, 1898), p. 52.

52. Pennsylvania Bureau of Industrial Statistics, *Thirteenth Annual Report* (1885), p. 178.

53. Welbourne, p. 213.

54. Ohio State Mine Inspector, *Fourth Annual Report* (1877), p. 120.

55. Joseph F. Patterson, "Reminiscences of John Maguire after Fifty Years of Mining," *Publications of the Historical Society of Schuylkill County,* IV (1912–1914), 315.

56. Pennsylvania Bureau of Industrial Statistics, *Fifth Annual Report* (1876–1877), pp. 598–599; Ohio Bureau of Labor Statistics, *Third Annual Report* (1879), 88.

57. Pennsylvania Inspectors of Mines of the Anthracite Coal Regions, *Reports,* 1887 *et seq.*

58. *Scottish-American Journal,* October 9, 1884.

59. Ohio State Mine Inspector, *Annual Reports,* 1876 *et seq.*

60. W. P. Morgan, "The Welsh in the United States," *Wales,* III (1896), 22.

61. *Idem*; Roy, p. 422; *Iron Molders' Journal,* August 10, 1878; *Druid,* December 26, 1912.

62. Illinois Bureau of Labor Statistics, *Twenty-Second Annual Coal Report* (1903), pp. 134–140; *Thirty-Second Annual Coal Report* (1913), p. 73.

63. *Druid,* December 17, 1908.

64. Illinois Bureau of Labor Statistics, *Twenty-Fourth Annual Coal Report* (1905), pp. 138–151; Ohio Chief Inspector of Mines, *Eighteenth Annual Report* (1892), p. 48, and *Thirty-Second Annual Report* (1906), pp. 30–31.

65. Illinois Bureau of Labor Statistics, *Tenth Annual Coal Report* (1891), pp. 24, 27; *Twenty-Ninth Annual Coal Report* (1910), p. 151; *Thirty-Sixth Annual Coal Report* (1917), p. 73.

66. *American Manufacturer,* December 3, 1874, March 11, 1875, March 25,

1881, December 7, 1883, July 18, October 31, 1884; Virtue, pp. 750–753; "Reports of the Immigration Commission," VI, 254–255, 423–424, 534–535; XVI, 591–593, 659–661.

67. *Philadelphia Press*, December 27, 1882.

68. "Report of the Select Committee on Immigration and Naturalization," *House Report*, 51 Cong., 2 sess., no. 3472 (January 15, 1891), II, 235. Cf. *Wilkes-Barre Record*, September 22, 1897; *Bulletin of the American Iron and Steel Association*, XXIV (1890), 92.

69. C. P. Scott to Foreign Office, September 20, 1902, in F.O. 5/2506.

70. Pennsylvania Department of Mines, *Report*, 1915, I, 65; 1918, II, 73.

71. Pennsylvania Bureau of Mines, *Report*, 1900, pp. 19–288.

72. Stephen Graham, *With Poor Immigrants to America* (New York, 1914), pp. 133–134.

73. "Reports of the Immigration Commission," XVI, 593.

74. *Ibid.*, VI, 481.

75. *Ibid.*, VI, 582–583.

76. Illinois Bureau of Labor Statistics, *Thirteenth Biennial Report* (1904), pp. 156–165.

77. Joseph Husband, *A Year in a Coal Mine* (Boston, 1911), pp. 35, 38, 148–151, 158. Cf. J. E. George, "The Coal Miners' Strike of 1897," *Quarterly Journal of Economics*, XII (1898), 191; "Report of the Industrial Commission," *House Document*, 57 Cong., 1 sess., no. 184 (December 5, 1901), XV, 189; "Reports of the Immigration Commission," VI, 581–589; VII, 9–31.

78. *Druid*, June 2, 1910.

79. *Ibid.*, April 1, 1909.

80. *Ibid.*, April 24, 1913. Cf. Rosamond D. Rhone, "Anthracite Coal Mines and Mining," *American Monthly Review of Reviews*, XXVI (1902), 60–61.

81. A. K. Hamilton Jenkin, *The Cornish Miner* (London, 1927), pp. 172ff, 302–303.

82. Clapham, II, 47–50.

83. Jenkin, pp. 303–305, 321–331.

84. *American Manufacturer*, December 16, 1881.

85. James M. Swank, *Progressive Pennsylvania* (Philadelphia, 1908), p. 217.

86. Louis Albert Copeland, "The Cornish in Southwest Wisconsin," *Collections of the State Historical Society of Wisconsin*, XIV (1898), 301–334; Joseph Schafer, *The Wisconsin Lead Region* (Madison, 1932), pp. 45, 55, 189–208.

87. *Miners' Journal*, May 29, 1847; *American Manufacturer*, September 20, 1878; Massachusetts Bureau of Statistics of Labor, *Second Annual Report* (1871), p. 309; Pennsylvania Bureau of Statistics of Labor and Agriculture, *First Annual Report* (1872–1873), pp. 266–267.

88. Ohio State Mine Inspector, *Sixth Annual Report* (1880), pp. 1443–1444; *Eighth Annual Report* (1882), pp. 18–21.

89. G. A. Lawrence, *Silverland* (London, 1873), p. 88; Evan Williams,

Hanes Cymry Colorado (Denver, 1889), *passim*; David Hughes, *Welsh People of California 1849–1906* (San Francisco, 1923), pp. 4–14, 23–40; Lynn I. Perrigo, "The Cornish Miners of Early Gilpin County," *Colorado Magazine*, XIV (1937), 92–101; Caroline Bancroft, "Cousin Jack Stories from Central City," *ibid.*, XXI (1944), 51–56; Copeland, p. 329; Jenkin, pp. 326–327.

90. Victor I. Noxon, "Hard Rock Drilling Contests in Colorado," *Colorado Magazine*, XI (1934), 81–82.

91. *Anglo-American Times*, October 27, 1865; *Scottish-American Journal*, February 12, 1885.

92. *Bulletin of the American Iron and Steel Association*, XXIV (1890), 249; XXV (1891), 325.

93. Orrin W. Robinson, *Early Days of the Lake Superior Copper Country* (Houghton, 1938), p. 5.

94. James Fisher, "Michigan's Cornish People," *Michigan History Magazine*, XXIX (1945), 379; *Bulletin of the American Iron and Steel Association*, XVII (1883), 181, 188; "Reports of the Immigration Commission," XVI, 81, 292ff, 391ff.

95. Michigan Commissioner of Mineral Statistics, *Report*, 1886, p. 6.

96. *Bulletin of the American Iron and Steel Association*, XIV (1880), 125.

97. T. A. Rickard, *The Copper Mines of Lake Superior* (New York, 1905), pp. 19–20, 152, 154–158; John Bartlow Martin, *Call It North Country* (New York, 1944), pp. 92–93.

98. E. A. Bond, *History of the Hoosac Tunnel* (n.p., 1880); *Miners' Journal*, February 20, 1869.

99. John Sirjamaki, "The People of the Mesabi Range," *Minnesota History*, XXVII (1946), 206–211; "Reports of the Immigration Commission," XVI, 292ff.

100. C. B. Glasscock, *The War of the Copper Kings* (New York, 1935), pp. 74, 114.

101. T. A. Rickard, *The Utah Copper Enterprise* (San Francisco, 1919), pp. 36, 41; "Report of the Industrial Commission," XII, 572, 611; *British Californian*, April 1918.

102. "Reports of the Immigration Commission," XVI, 88, 301, 313–314, 339, 393–394, 397, 403, 414.

5. Furnace and Anvil

1. Paul Mantoux, *The Industrial Revolution in the Eighteenth Century* (London, 1928), pp. 287–317; J. H. Clapham, *An Economic History of Modern Britain* (Cambridge, 1926–1930), I, 148–150, 426–427.

2. James M. Swank, *History of the Manufacture of Iron in All Ages* (Philadelphia, 1884), p. 265.

3. Pennsylvania Bureau of Industrial Statistics, *Tenth Annual Report* (1881–1882), pp. 24, 28.

4. Frank H. Rowe, *History of the Iron and Steel Industry in Scioto County*

(Columbus, 1938), p. 16; *Bulletin of the American Iron and Steel Association*, XXIII (1889), 283.

5. *American Manufacturer*, June 26, 1873.

6. *Dictionary of American Biography* (New York, 1928–1937), XVIII, 427–428.

7. *Bulletin of the American Iron and Steel Association*, XI (1877), 252.

8. *Ibid.*, XXIII (1889), 283; Muriel Earley Sheppard, *Cloud by Day* (Chapel Hill, 1947), pp. 31–33.

9. *Bulletin of the American Iron and Steel Association*, XI (1877), 252; *Dictionary of American Biography*, XVIII, 428. Cf. *Miners' Journal*, October 26, 1839.

10. Swank, p. 373.

11. *Ibid.*, pp. 434, 441; *Bulletin of the American Iron and Steel Association*, XII (1878), 164.

12. *American Manufacturer*, October 5, 1876.

13. Swank, p. 453.

14. *Ibid.*, pp. 385–389. Cf. Rowe, pp. 32–34.

15. Swank, p. 455.

16. *Dictionary of American Biography*, III, 272.

17. *Ibid.*, XV, 465–467.

18. London *Mining Journal*, September 23, 1871.

19. Clapham, I, 149; Pennsylvania Commissioner of Labor and Industry, *First Annual Report* (1913), p. 246.

20. J. L. Abrams, "The Welsh People of Ironton," *Cambrian*, I (1880–1881), 86–87; William Harvey Jones, "Welsh Settlements in Ohio," *Ohio Archaeological and Historical Quarterly*, XVI (1907), 218; Vernon David Keeler, "An Economic History of the Jackson County Iron Industry," *ibid.*, XLII (1933), 169–171.

21. "Reports of the Immigration Commission," *Senate Document*, 61 Cong., 2 sess., no. 633 (June 15, 1910), VIII, 389.

22. *Emigrant and Old Countryman*, March 22, 1837.

23. *Miners' Journal*, April 11, 1857.

24. Owen Bromley and J. William Jones, *Hyfforddwr yr Ymfudwr* (Denbigh, 1866), p. 97; *Cenhadwr Americanaidd*, XIII (1852), p. 170.

25. Allan Nevins, *Abram S. Hewitt* (New York, 1935), pp. 88, 114; "Reports of the Immigration Commission," VIII, 497.

26. Charlotte Erickson, "Encouragement of Emigration by British Trade Unions, 1850–1900," *Population Studies*, III (1949), 258–261, 269–272; *Iron Age*, June 13, 1867; *Workingman's Advocate*, November 2, 1867.

27. "Reports of the Immigration Commission," VIII, 591.

28. Ethel Armes, *The Story of Coal and Iron in Alabama* (Birmingham, 1910), p. 262.

29. *Druid*, August 19, 1909.

30. Daniel Jenkins Williams, *The Welsh of Columbus, Ohio* (Oshkosh, 1913), pp. 49–50.

31. *Scottish-American Journal,* March 14, 1868; *Bulletin of the American Iron and Steel Association,* VII (1872), 106.

32. Ohio State Mine Inspector, *Third Annual Report* (1876), pp. 26–27, and *Eighth Annual Report* (1882), pp. 18–21; Armes, pp. 377–391.

33. "Report on the Foreign Commerce of the United States of America," *Parliamentary Papers,* 1880, LXXII (C. 2570), 176–178.

34. *American Manufacturer,* September 19, 26, October 10, 31, 1879.

35. Jesse S. Robinson, *The Amalgamated Association of Iron, Steel, and Tin Workers* (Baltimore, 1920), p. 44.

36. *Idem.*

37. Clapham, II, 54–61.

38. R. W. Hunt, "A History of the Bessemer Manufacture in America," *Engineering,* XXII (1876), 509, 532–533.

39. Swank, pp. 416–417.

40. William R. Jones, "On the Manufacture of Bessemer Steel and Steel Rails in the United States," *Journal of the Iron and Steel Institute,* XIX (1881), 131.

41. J. Stephen Jeans, ed., *American Industrial Conditions and Competition* (London, 1902), pp. 510–511, 521, 525ff; Clapham, III, 149–156.

42. James Howard Bridge, *The Inside History of the Carnegie Steel Company* (New York, 1903), p. 81.

43. *Druid,* December 23, 1909.

44. James Kitson, "The Iron and Steel Industries of America," *Contemporary Review,* LIX (1891), 629.

45. *Post,* p. 95.

46. *Eleventh Census of the U.S.* (1890), II, 304–305, 486–489.

47. "Consular Reports on Emigration and Immigration," *House Miscellaneous Document,* 49 Cong., 2 sess., no. 157 (February 11, 1887), p. 423; "Enforcement of Alien Contract Labor Laws," *House Executive Document,* 52 Cong., 1 sess., no. 235, pt. 1 (February 22, 1892), p. 187.

48. *Druid,* March 17, 1910, February 2, 1911.

49. Jeans, pp. 577–580; Armes, p. 430.

50. "Reports of the Immigration Commission," VIII, 338, 497, 591–594, 741; IX, 43–45.

51. Pennsylvania Bureau of Industrial Statistics, *Fifteenth Annual Report* (1887), pp. F3–F5; *Thirty-Third Annual Report* (1905), pp. 471–472.

52. *British Californian,* November 1903, p. 9.

53. Margaret F. Byington, *Homestead: The Households of a Mill Town* (New York, 1910), p. 214.

54. Jeans, p. 82.

55. *American Manufacturer,* January 23, 1880, December 22, 1882, October 12, 1883, October 10, 1884, July 10, September 25, 1885, October 4, 1900; *Bulletin of the American Iron and Steel Association,* XVI (1882), 235; XX (1886), 189, 309; XXIII (1889), 236, 276–277; XXV (1891), 27; XXVII (1893), 43–45; XV (1881), 123; *Iron,* XII (1888), 61; *Cambrian,* V (1885), 293–295;

Swank, p. 373; Armes, pp. 173–177, 230, 429; *Dictionary of American Biography*, XV, 467–468.

56. David Williams, *A History of Modern Wales* (London, 1950), p. 223.

57. *National Labor Tribune*, April 24, 1875; Pennsylvania Bureau of Industrial Statistics, *Twenty-Third Annual Report* (1895), pp. 17–18.

58. *American Manufacturer*, November 26, 1880; *Bulletin of the American Iron and Steel Association*, XVIII (1883), 52; XXI (1887), 115, 133.

59. *Ibid.*, XXV (1891), 2.

60. *Ibid.*, XXV (1891), 241; XXVI (1892), 157, 269; Henry Dickerson Scott, *Iron and Steel in Wheeling* (Toledo, 1929), pp. 115–117; David Williams, p. 224; "Enforcement of Alien Contract Labor Laws," pp. 182, 203–208; Pennsylvania Bureau of Industrial Statistics, *Twenty-Third Annual Report* (1895), p. 49.

61. "Report on the American Tin Plate Industry and the Welsh Tin-Plate Export Trade to the United States," *Parliamentary Papers*, 1897, LXXXVIII (C. 8278–25), 4.

62. Ebenezer Edwards, *Welshmen as Factors* (Utica, 1899), pp. 332–333.

63. "Report on the Effect of the McKinley Tariff on the Tin Plate Industry of the United States," *Parliamentary Papers*, 1893, XCI (C. 6856–28), 20–22; *Bulletin of the American Iron and Steel Association*, XXVI (1892), 121, 325.

64. D. E. Dunbar, *The Tin-Plate Industry* (Boston, 1915), pp. 31–53.

65. London *Ironmonger*, April 23, 1892.

66. "Report of the Industrial Commission," *House Document*, 56 Cong., 2 sess., no. 495 (March 1, 1901), VII, 388–393.

67. Pennsylvania Bureau of Industrial Statistics, *Thirty-Fourth Annual Report* (1906), p. 38.

68. *Druid*, March 9, 1911.

69. *Ibid.*, November 2, 1908, May 27, 1909, January 5, 1911.

70. "Report of the Industrial Commission," *House Document*, 57 Cong., 1 sess., no. 184 (December 5, 1901), XV, 424.

71. *Scottish-American Journal*, August 8, 1872.

72. *Bulletin of the American Iron and Steel Association*, IV (1870), 290.

73. *Ibid.*, VII (1873), 426.

74. "Report on the Trade, Commerce, &c., of the States of California, Nevada, and Utah and the Territory of Arizona," *Parliamentary Papers*, 1906, CXXIX (Cd. 2682–89), 13.

75. *Dictionary of American Biography*, V, 291–292.

76. *The British Mechanic's and Labourer's Hand Book and True Guide to the United States* (London, 1840), p. 233.

77. James Roberts to John Loxley, September 30, 1849, in Cornell Collection of Regional History; Agnes Hannay, *A Chronicle of Industry on the Mill River* (Northampton, 1935), p. 94; Constance McL. Green, *History of Naugatuck* (New Haven, 1948), pp. 136, 171; Massachusetts Bureau of Statistics of Labor, *Second Annual Report* (1871), p. 385; "Reports of the Immigration Commission," XVII, 131–133.

78. *British Mechanic's and Labourer's Hand Book*, p. 234.

79. Thomas J. Bradley to James Roberts, July 23, 1867, November 26, 1869, in Cornell Collection of Regional History.

80. London *Times*, December 28, 1876; London *Ironmonger*, August 2, 1879; *American Manufacturer*, September 26, 1879.

81. *New York Times*, August 7, 1879.

82. "Second Report of the Royal Commission Appointed to Inquire into the Depression of Trade and Industry," *Parliamentary Papers*, 1886, XXI (C. 4715), Q. 1274–1277.

83. "Consular Reports on Emigration and Immigration," p. 522 [slightly rearranged].

84. *Eleventh Census of the U.S.* (1890), II, 488.

85. Theodore W. Glocker, *The Government of American Trade Unions* (Baltimore, 1913), p. 86; Lyman Horace Weeks, *A History of Paper Making in the United States* (New York, 1916), pp. 182–184.

86. *Dictionary of American Biography*, V, 506–507.

87. *American Manufacturer*, April 11, 1879.

88. *Iron Age*, February 20, 1873.

89. *American Manufacturer*, September 18, 1873.

90. Clapham, I, 152.

91. John L. Hayes, *American Textile Machinery* (Cambridge, 1879), *passim*; *Textile Record*, III (1882), 144.

92. "First Report from the Select Committee Appointed to Inquire into the Operation of the Existing Laws Affecting the Exportation of Machinery," *Parliamentary Papers*, 1841, VII (201), Q. 1691.

93. David Laing to sister, February 15, 1873, July 12, 1874, in Cornell Collection of Regional History.

94. "First Report from the Select Committee Appointed to Inquire into the Operation of the Existing Laws Affecting the Exportation of Machinery," Q. 3034; *Scottish-American Journal*, May 7, 1874; *Textile Record*, IV (1883), 307; VIII (1895), no. 5, pp. 19–20; XVI (1899), no. 6, p. 127; XXI (1901), 345; XXVIII (1904), 174; XXXIX (1910), 541; *American Journal of Fabrics and Knit-Goods Manufacturer*, III (1883), 99; *Western British-American*, February 14, March 28, 1914.

95. "First Report from the Select Committee Appointed to Inquire into the Operation of the Existing Laws Affecting the Exportation of Machinery," Q. 1758, 1761.

96. Jonathan Thayer Lincoln, "The Cotton Textile Machine Industry," *Harvard Business Review*, XI (1932), 94; *Bulletin of the American Iron and Steel Association*, XXII (1888), 27, 257; XXIII (1889), 209; XXVI (1892), 28; *American Manufacturer*, L (1892), 721; Armes, pp. 142–145.

97. *Amalgamated Engineers' Journal*, December 1902, p. 23.

98. *Scottish-American Journal*, July 15, 1865.

99. *American Manufacturer*, May 21, 1874.

100. *Scientific American*, XII (1865), 392.

101. Henry Ashworth, *A Tour in the United States, Cuba, and Canada* (London, 1861), p. 136.

102. "Report from the Select Committee on Colonisation," *Parliamentary Papers*, 1889, X (274), Q. 1775.

103. Amalgamated Society of Engineers, *Nineteenth Annual Report* (1869), p. 8.

104. *Amalgamated Engineers' Journal*, November 1904, p. 23. Cf. Kansas Bureau of Labor and Industrial Statistics, *Third Annual Report* (1887), p. 183.

105. "Report by Mr. Harriss-Gastrell on the Iron and Steel Industries of the United States," *Parliamentary Papers*, 1874, LXV (C. 1050), 769; *Iron Molders' International Journal*, May 1866.

106. "Final Report of the Royal Commission Appointed to Inquire into the Depression of Trade and Industry," *Parliamentary Papers*, 1886, XXIII (C. 4893), Q. 14,756–14,758; *Iron Molders' International Journal*, November 1873; Ohio Bureau of Labor Statistics, *First Annual Report* (1877), p. 115; *Scottish-American Journal*, February 17, 1881; *American Manufacturer*, June 4, 1884.

107. Frank T. Stockton, "Agreements between American and European Molders' Unions," *Journal of Political Economy*, XXIV (1916), 287–298; Glocker, p. 92; *Workingman's Advocate*, January 24, 1874.

108. *American Manufacturer*, August 27, 1879.

109. London *Ironmonger*, August 2, 1879.

110. Amalgamated Society of Engineers, *Thirtieth Annual Report* (1880), xi.

111. "Report from the Select Committee on Colonisation," Q. 1777.

112. *Eleventh Census of the U.S.* (1890), II, 488.

113. *Amalgamated Engineers' Journal*, November 1902, p. 88.

114. *Ibid.*, April 1904, p. 74; December 1904, p. 76; April 1915, p. 58; *Scottish-American*, January 14, 1903.

115. "First Report from the Select Committee Appointed to Inquire into the Operation of the Existing Laws Affecting the Exportation of Machinery," Q. 1788.

116. *American Manufacturer*, December 5, 1879. Cf. *Cyfaill o'r Hen Wlad*, IV (1841), p. 42.

6. A Chest of Tools

1. Paul Mantoux, *The Industrial Revolution in the Eighteenth Century* (London, 1928), pp. 395–397.

2. Heinrich Ries and Henry Leighton, *History of the Clay-Working Industry in the United States* (New York, 1909), pp. 88, 202–203.

3. Harold Owen, *The Staffordshire Potter* (London, 1901), pp. 63–101; Grant Foreman, "English Settlers in Illinois," *Journal of the Illinois State Historical Society*, XXXIV (1941), 304–310.

4. *Potter's Herald*, June 18, 1908.

5. New Jersey Bureau of Statistics of Labor and Industry, *First Annual Report* (1878), p. 229.

6. *Ibid.*, *Twenty-Eighth Annual Report* (1905), p. 184; U.S. Bureau of Foreign and Domestic Commerce, *The Pottery Industry* (Miscellaneous Series, no. 21, 1915), pp. 312–314.

7. Ohio Bureau of Labor Statistics, *First Annual Report* (1877), p. 231.

8. *Ibid.*, p. 235.

9. *Ibid.*, *Third Annual Report* (1879), p. 142; "Report of the Industrial Commission," *House Document*, 57 Cong., 1 sess., no. 183 (December 5, 1901), XIV, 631; John Spargo, *The Potters and Potteries of Bennington* (Boston, 1924), pp. 78, 237.

10. "Consular Reports on Emigration and Immigration," *House Miscellaneous Document*, 49 Cong., 2 sess., no. 157 (February 11, 1887), p. 537.

11. *Eleventh Census of the U.S.* (1890), II, 488.

12. *The Pottery Industry*, p. 67.

13. United States Potters' Association, *Proceedings of the Annual Conventions*, 1909–1945, *passim.*

14. *Ibid.*, *Proceedings of the Thirty-Fifth Annual Convention* (1913), p. 87.

15. Pennsylvania Bureau of Industrial Statistics, *Thirteenth Annual Report* (1885), p. 49; Frederick T. Irwin, *The Story of Sandwich Glass* (Manchester, N. H., 1926), p. 16.

16. *Scottish-American Journal*, March 4, 1865.

17. *Workingman's Advocate*, January 2, 1869; *American Manufacturer*, July 24, 1873, August 1, December 26, 1879; "Report of the Select Committee on Immigration and Naturalization," *House Report*, 51 Cong., 2 sess., no. 3472 (January 15, 1891), II, 344; "Reports of the Immigration Commission," *Senate Document*, 61 Cong., 2 sess., no. 633 (June 15, 1910), XIV, 27–40.

18. "Diplomatic and Consular Reports on Emigration," *House Miscellaneous Document*, 50 Cong., 1 sess., no. 572, pt. 2 (1889), p. 21.

19. *Anglo-American Times*, August 23–30, November 15, 1889.

20. *Eleventh Census of the U.S.* (1890), II, 488.

21. Pennsylvania Bureau of Industrial Statistics, *Thirty-Fourth Annual Report* (1906), pp. 191, 219; "Reports of the Immigration Commission," XIV, 27–40.

22. Lyman Horace Weeks, *A History of Paper Manufacturing in the United States* (New York, 1916), pp. 183–184.

23. *Dictionary of American Biography* (New York, 1928–1937), XX, 10.

24. *Scottish-American*, October 10, 1894; "Reports of the Immigration Commission," XII, 216–217, 225–227, 361–365.

25. *Ibid.*, XII, 777–790; *Eleventh Census of the U.S.* (1890), II, 488; private information.

26. Emigrants' Information Office, *General Information Relating to North, Central, and South America* (London, 1910), p. 33; "Reports of the Immigration Commission," XV, 467–479.

27. *The British Mechanic's and Labourer's Hand Book and True Guide to the United States* (London, 1840), pp. 236, 239.

28. *Report of the Committee of the Senate upon the Relation between Labor and Capital* (Washington, 1885), I, 41; "Report from the Select Committee on Colonisation," *Parliamentary Papers*, 1889, X (274), Q. 1863.

29. *British-American*, December 24, 1887.

30. "Reports of the Immigration Commission," XI–XX, *passim*.

31. Bob Owen, "Y Barque Hindoo, Caernarfon," *Caernarvonshire Historical Society Transactions*, V (1944), 60–70.

32. *Maryland Geological Survey*, II (1898), 215–221.

33. William John Parry, *Chwareli a Chwarelwyr* (Caernarvon, 1897), pp. 18–33; Pennsylvania Bureau of Industrial Statistics, *Eleventh Annual Report* (1882–1883), pp. 67–69.

34. *Drych*, November 15, 1851; Maine Bureau of Industrial and Labor Statistics, *Third Annual Report* (1889), pp. 72–75.

35. Andrew N. Adams, *A History of the Town of Fair Haven* (Fair Haven, 1870), pp. 207–218; *American Manufacturer*, April 24, 1882; *Stone*, VI (1893), 189–190; Evan R. Jones to William F. Wharton, June 11, 1891, in U.S. Consular Correspondence, p. 229.

36. *Druid*, June 10, 1909.

37. George F. Harris, *Granites and Our Granite Industries* (London, 1888), pp. 34–97; "Enforcement of Alien Contract Labor Laws," *House Executive Document*, 52 Cong., 1 sess., no. 235, pt. 1 (February 22, 1892), p. 184; *Drych*, December 16, 1873.

38. *Scottish-American*, September 7, 1887; *Stone*, II (1889), 42; Maine Bureau of Industrial and Labor Statistics, *Third Annual Report* (1889), pp. 11–28.

39. *Boston Scotsman*, April 21–28, 1906.

40. *Granite Cutters' Journal*, XVIII (1893), 200; *Stone*, V (1892), 670; Vermont State Geologist, *Report on the Marble, Slate, and Granite Industries* (1898), p. 55.

41. *Scottish-American Journal*, February 11, 1875, August 13, 1890; *Drych*, April 26, 1888; *Stone*, II (1889), 74; *Druid*, February 29, 1912; Wisconsin Bureau of Labor and Industrial Statistics, *Second Biennial Report* (1885–1886), p. 424.

42. Arthur W. Brayley, *History of the Granite Industry of New England* (Boston, 1913), I, 95–107, 144–166; II, 38–119; *Granite Cutters' Journal*, August 1888.

43. Brayley, I, 84.

44. Howard Thomas, "The Welsh Came to Remsen," *New York History*, XXX (1949), 34.

45. *American Manufacturer*, August 28, 1873.

46. *Stone*, X (1895), 140.

47. *Granite Cutters' Journal*, May–July 1880, July 1881, August 1887, June–July 1888; *Scottish-American Journal*, April 28, 1886; "Importation of Con-

tract Laborers," *House Miscellaneous Document*, 50 Cong., 1 sess., no. 572, pt. 1 (1888), pp. 138–148; "Report of the Select Committee on Immigration and Naturalization," II, 271–272, 280–281.

48. *Scottish-American*, September 7, 1910.

49. *Ibid.*, March 27, 1889, August 30, 1893; Rhode Island Commissioner of Industrial Statistics, *Second Annual Report* (1888), p. 73.

50. *Scottish-American*, September 14, 1887.

51. Illinois Bureau of Labor Statistics, *Third Biennial Report* (1883–1884), p. 412.

52. Maine Bureau of Industrial and Labor Statistics, *Third Annual Report* (1889), p. 21.

53. Rhode Island Commissioner of Industrial Statistics, *Sixth Annual Report* (1892), p. 137; *Stone Cutters' Journal*, September-October 1901, January 1903.

54. *Eleventh Census of the U.S.* (1890), II, 488.

55. *John Swinton's Paper*, May 10, 1885; *Quarryman's Journal*, April 1893; Maine Bureau of Industrial and Labor Statistics, *Third Annual Report* (1889), pp. 11–28; Brayley, I, 144–148; II, 79–122.

56. George E. Barnett, *Chapters on Machinery and Labor* (Cambridge, 1926), pp. 30–31; Brayley, I, 84–89.

57. *Fall River Weekly News*, July 2, 1885.

58. *Workingman's Advocate*, September 28, 1867, February 27, 1869.

59. *Ibid.*, October 20, 1869; "Report of the Industrial Commission," XV, 448.

60. *Workingman's Advocate*, June 23, 1866.

61. *British-American*, December 24, 1887.

62. New York Bureau of Statistics of Labor, *Third Annual Report* (1885), pp. 488–489.

63. *British-American*, December 24, 1887.

64. Rhode Island Commissioner of Industrial Statistics, *Second Annual Report* (1888), pp. 77, 82; *Scottish-American*, June 10, 1891, November 30, 1892; "Diplomatic and Consular Reports on Emigration," pp. 12, 18, 24; "Enforcement of Alien Contract Labor Laws," p. 183.

65. *Scottish-American*, May 25, 1887.

66. "Enforcement of Alien Contract Labor Laws," p. 187.

67. New York Bureau of Statistics of Labor, *Third Annual Report* (1885), p. 488; "Report of the Industrial Commission," XV, 428.

68. *Ibid.*, VII, 160; "Enforcement of Alien Contract Labor Laws," p. 184.

69. *Eleventh Census of the U.S.* (1890), II, 486–489.

70. "Report of the Industrial Commission," XV, 428, 448; *Scottish-American*, January 14, 1903.

71. Amalgamated Society of Carpenters and Joiners, *Forty-Seventh* and *Forty-Eighth Annual Reports* (1905–1906, 1906–1907).

72. Marcus Lee Hansen, *The Mingling of the Canadian and American Peoples* (New Haven, 1940), pp. 161, 208; "Importation of Contract Laborers," pp. 571–575; "Report of the Select Committee on Immigration and Naturalization," II, 364–369.

73. "Further Reports from H.M. Diplomatic and Consular Agents Abroad Respecting the Condition of the Industrial Classes," *Parliamentary Papers*, 1871, LXVII (C. 414), 858; "Enforcement of Alien Contract Labor Laws," p. 234.

74. "Report on the Trade and Commerce of New Orleans," *Parliamentary Papers*, 1878, LXXIII (C. 1993), 549–550.

75. *Ibid.*, 1882, LXX (C. 3191), 397, 474, 506; correspondence in F.O. 5/2511.

76. "Report on the Trade of Pensacola," *Parliamentary Papers*, 1880, LXXIII (C. 2632), 1466; "Report of the Select Committee on Immigration and Naturalization," pp. 566–571.

77. Isaac Stephenson, *Recollections of a Long Life* (Chicago, 1915), pp. 48, 79, 104.

78. "Report on the Trade and Commerce of New Orleans," *Parliamentary Papers*, 1875, LXXV, pt. 2 (C. 1167), p. 451.

79. *Scottish-American*, December 17, 1902.

80. *Ibid.*, March 9, 1867, March 20, 1884.

81. *Ibid.*, September 26–October 17, 1900; U. P. Hedrick, *A History of Horticulture in America to 1860* (New York, 1950), pp. 258–259.

82. *Dictionary of American Biography*, V, 88.

83. *Canadian-American*, March 26, 1885.

84. *British Californian*, November 1903, pp. 9–10.

85. Peter A. Demens, quoted by Oscar Handlin, ed., *This Was America* (Cambridge, 1949), p. 362.

86. London *Times*, December 28, 1876.

87. Roland Gibson, *Cotton Textile Wages in the United States and Great Britain* (New York, 1948), pp. 1–4, 15–27.

88. J. H. Clapham, *An Economic History of Modern Britain* (Cambridge, 1936), III, 466–468, 474.

89. Paul H. Douglas, *Real Wages in the United States 1890–1926* (Boston, 1930), pp. 137, 231–232, 257–263, 272, 299, 353, 557ff.

90. *British Californian*, November 1903, p. 10.

91. *Anglo-American Times*, October 28, November 4, 1887, August 9–30, November 15, 1889, May 23, 1890; *American Silk Journal*, VI (1887), 157; XI (1892), 213.

92. *Amalgamated Engineering Journal*, June 1903, pp. 25–26.

93. C. P. Scott to Foreign Office, September 20, 1902, in F.O. 5/2506.

94. "Emigration and Immigration," *Parliamentary Papers*, 1904, CVI (145), to 1914, LXIX (295).

7. The Rights of Craftsmen

1. *Boston Herald*, March 8, 1877.

2. *New York Herald*, October 13, 1875.

3. *Miners' Journal*, July 4, 1829. Cf. Theodore F. Marburg, "Aspects of

Labor Administration in the Early Nineteenth Century," *Bulletin of the Business Historical Society*, XV (1941), 5–6.

4. Sidney and Beatrice Webb, *The History of Trade Unionism* (London, 1926), pp. 64–232; Selig Perlman, *History of Trade Unionism in the United States* (New York, 1922), pp. 3–41.

5. William Z. Ripley, "Race Factors in Labor Unions," *Atlantic*, XCII (1904), 301.

6. Charlotte Erickson, "Encouragement of Emigration by British Trade Unions, 1850–1900," *Population Studies*, III (1949), 248–273; *Iron Molders' International Journal*, January 1867, April 30, 1873.

7. Amalgamated Society of Engineers, *Eleventh Annual Report* (1861), pp. 7–8; *Workingman's Advocate*, February 1, 1868, August 14, 1869.

8. Steam Engine Makers' Society, *Annual Reports*, 1881–1909, *passim*; *Monthly Report*, November 1917.

9. Amalgamated Society of Engineers, *Annual Reports*, 1861–1919; Amalgamated Society of Carpenters and Joiners, *Annual Reports*, 1864/5–1914/5, *passim*.

10. *Amalgamated Engineers' Journal*, January 1903, p. 71.

11. Theodore W. Glocker, *The Government of American Trade Unions* (Baltimore, 1913), p. 89.

12. *Ibid.*, pp. 90–91; James B. Jefferys, *The Story of the Engineers* (n.p., 1945), pp. 127–129, 172–173; S. Higinbotham, *Our Society's History* (Manchester, 1939), pp. 286–290.

13. "Report of the Industrial Commission," *House Document*, 57 Cong., 1 sess., no. 184 (December 5, 1901), XV, 425. Cf. New Jersey Bureau of Statistics of Labor and Industry, *Tenth Annual Report* (1887), p. 37.

14. *American Federationist*, XI (1904), 230.

15. "Report of the Industrial Commission," XV, 428, 448.

16. R. Page Arnot, *The Miners* (London, 1949), pp. 34–116; Ness Edwards, *The History of the South Wales Miners* (London, 1926), pp. 4–37.

17. "Report from the Select Committee on Coal," *Parliamentary Papers*, 1873, X (313), Q. 5445–5447; Webb, pp. 284, 291; Erickson, p. 263.

18. *Miners' Journal*, May 5–July 14, 1849.

19. *United Mine Workers' Journal*, August 20, 1908.

20. Edward A. Wieck, *The American Miners' Association* (New York, 1940), pp. 190–195.

21. Missouri Bureau of Labor Statistics, *Tenth Annual Report* (1888), pp. 129–138.

22. *Workingman's Advocate*, November 22, 1873.

23. *Mauch Chunk Coal Gazette*, quoted in *Miners' Journal*, February 6, 1874; *American Manufacturer*, October 14, 1875.

24. *Miners' Journal Coal Statistical Register*, 1871, p. 10.

25. *Miners' Journal*, April 16, 1870.

26. *Ibid.*, July 16, 1870, March 11, 1871; Chris Evans, *History of the United Mine Workers of America* (Indianapolis, 1919), I, 22–23.

27. *Miners' Journal*, March 4–11, 1871, May 21, 1875.

28. Evans, I, 43.

29. *Ibid.*, I, 27–83; Andrew Roy, *A History of the Coal Miners of the United States* (Columbus, 1907), pp. 125–127, 153, 229, 241–242; *Workingman's Advocate*, October 25, November 29, 1873.

30. Evans, I, 137ff, 394ff.

31. *Cambrian*, May 15, 1909.

32. Roy, pp. 262, 273.

33. *Ibid.*, pp. 260–261; *Scottish-American*, March 6, 1901.

34. Roy, p. 294.

35. *United Mine Workers' Journal*, July 9, 1908.

36. Ohio Chief Inspector of Mines, *Thirty-Fourth Annual Report* (1908), pp. 207–208; Roy, pp. 318–320.

37. Elsie Glück, *John Mitchell, Miner* (New York, 1929), pp. 4–5.

38. *Druid*, February 20, 1913.

39. A. K. Hamilton Jenkin, *The Cornish Miner* (London, 1927), pp. 197–199.

40. James Fisher, "Michigan's Cornish People," *Michigan History Magazine*, XXIX (1945), 381–382.

41. *Iron Molders' Journal*, July 1874.

42. "Reports of the Immigration Commission," *Senate Document*, 62 Cong., 2 sess., no. 633 (June 15, 1910), XVI, 393–394, 397–398.

43. *American Federationist*, VII (1900), 35.

44. U.S. Bureau of Labor Statistics, *Bulletin*, no. 139 (1914), pp. 40, 55, 99–100.

45. *National Labor Tribune*, July 3, 1875. Cf. *Drych*, April 5, 1856, October 3, 1857.

46. J. H. Clapham, *An Economic History of Modern Britain* (Cambridge, 1932), II, 162–163.

47. *Workingman's Advocate*, August 16, 1873; *National Labor Tribune*, August 14, 1875; *Iron Molders' Journal*, 1866–1890, *passim.*

48. George E. McNeill, *The Labor Movement* (Boston, 1887), p. 609; Carroll D. Wright, "The Amalgamated Association of Iron and Steel Workers," *Quarterly Journal of Economics*, VII (1893), 402–410; *Workingman's Advocate*, August 5, 1871.

49. *Workingman's Advocate*, February 14, 1874.

50. *British-American Citizen*, December 14, 1889; Wright, pp. 413, 418.

51. Wright, pp. 416–418.

52. *Labor Standard*, July 7, 1877.

53. John A. Fitch, *The Steel Workers* (New York, 1910), pp. 75–136; D. E. Dunbar, *The Tin-Plate Industry* (Boston, 1915), pp. 53–54; Perlman, pp. 130, 133, 196–198; "Report of the Industrial Commission," XV, 425.

54. Gladys L. Palmer, *Union Tactics and Economic Change* (Philadelphia, 1932), pp. 15, 22–30, 138–139, 142–144; Edgar Barclay Cole, *The Organization of Labor in Philadelphia 1850–1870* (Philadelphia, 1940), pp. 26–30; Arthur

H. Cole and Harold F. Williamson, *The American Carpet Manufacture* (Chicago, 1941), pp. 38–39, 58, 178–193.

55. *Textile Record*, V (1884), 23.

56. *Wade's Fibre and Fabric*, I (1885), 53.

57. Gladys L. Palmer, *Labor Relations in the Lace and Lace-Curtain Industries in the United States*, U.S. Bureau of Labor Statistics, *Bulletin*, no. 399 (November 1925), pp. 27–35.

58. *American Silk Journal*, VI (1887), 140; *Textile America*, October 30, 1897.

59. *American Silk Journal*, XX (1901), 43.

60. Massachusetts Bureau of Statistics of Labor, *Thirteenth Annual Report* (1882), p. 340. Cf. Webb, pp. 434–436; Clapham, II, 166–168.

61. McNeill, pp. 216–219.

62. *Fall River Weekly News*, March 25, 1880. Cf. *Paterson Guardian*, November 30, 1886.

63. *Fall River Weekly News*, October 28, 1875.

64. *Ibid.*, January 21, 1875.

65. James Macaulay, *Across the Ferry* (London, 1872), p. 354.

66. Massachusetts Bureau of Statistics of Labor, *Thirteenth Annual Report* (1882), p. 361.

67. *Labor Standard*, February 26, 1881.

68. *Fall River Weekly News*, January 14–September 30, 1875.

69. *Ibid.*, February 25–March 18, 1875; *Socialist* [*Labor Standard*], July 15, 1876. Cf. *Lawrence Journal and Citizen*, April 17, 1875.

70. *Labor Standard*, March 3, 1877; *Fall River Weekly News*, March 8, 1877.

71. *Labor Standard*, August 26, December 30, 1877, April 14, May 19–26, June 14, August 25, October 19, 1878, February 7, March 13–April 10, 1880; *Fall River Weekly News*, May 29, 1879, December 15, 1881.

72. *Fall River Weekly News*, May 1–September 4, 1879, March 26, May 14, 1885; *Wade's Fibre and Fabric*, January 23, 1886.

73. *Fall River Weekly News*, June 10, 1886, August 15, 1894.

74. Statement of James Tansey to author, November 18, 1949.

75. *Idem.*

76. Charles B. Spahr, "The Old Factory Towns of New England," *Outlook*, LXI (1899), 292.

77. "People of a New England Factory Village," *Atlantic*, XLVI (1880), 462.

78. *New York Herald*, October 19, 1875.

79. *Report of the Committee of the Senate upon the Relations between Labor and Capital* (Washington, 1885), III, 9, 61–62.

80. *Lawrence Journal*, October 31, 1874, May 8, 1875; *Workingman's Advocate*, July 20, 1870.

81. Massachusetts Bureau of Statistics of Labor, *Thirteenth Annual Report* (1882), pp. 362–363.

82. "Report of the Industrial Commission," XV, 421.

83. London *Times*, April 17, 1834; *Fall River Weekly News*, September 25, 1879, April 17, 1884; Massachusetts Bureau of Statistics of Labor, *Thirteenth Annual Report* (1882), p. 407.

84. United Textile Workers of America, *Proceedings of the Second Annual Convention* (1902), pp. 30, 49; statement of James Tansey to author, November 18, 1949.

85. *Textile Worker*, November 1913, December 1916.

86. Robert R. R. Brooks, "The United Textile Workers of America" (unpublished doctoral thesis, Yale University, 1935), pp. 75–76.

87. McNeill, p. 607; *Dictionary of American Biography* (New York, 1928–1937), V, 510.

88. *Labor Standard*, April 7, 1878; *Granite Cutters' Journal*, 1881–1895, *passim*.

89. *Quarrymen's Journal*, 1891–1893, *passim; Stone Cutters' Journal*, 1893–1902, *passim*; *Scottish-American*, May 18, 1892.

90. *Drych*, April 12, 1851, January 9, 1868, March 10, 1870, January 14, April 15, 1875; William John Parry, *Chwareli a Chwarelwyr* (Caernarvon, 1897), pp. 220–239; International Union of Slate Workers, *Proceedings*, 1904–1909, *passim*.

91. *Iron Molders' Journal*, February 10, 1877.

92. Philip S. Foner, *History of the Labor Movement in the United States* (New York, 1947), pp. 241–242; George Rogers Taylor, *The Transportation Revolution* (New York, 1951), p. 284.

93. *Dictionary of American Biography*, III, 433–434; XVIII, 640–641; *Iron Molders' International Journal*, September 1866.

94. *Labor Standard*, January 6, April 7, August 25, 1878; *Fall River Weekly News*, March 28, December 26, 1878, May 8, 1879.

95. Illinois Bureau of Labor Statistics, *Fourth Biennial Report* (1886), pp. 224–226; New Jersey Bureau of Statistics of Labor and Industries, *Tenth Annual Report* (1887), pp. 26–31.

96. *Dictionary of American Biography*, VII, 369.

97. American Federation of Labor, *History, Encyclopedia, Reference Book* (Washington, 1919), pp. 427–429.

98. New Jersey Bureau of Statistics of Labor and Industries, *Tenth Annual Report* (1887), pp. 42–46.

99. William English Walling, "British and American Trade Unionism," *United Mine Workers' Journal*, December 28, 1905; Evans, I, 6–7, 14, 21, 38, 109, 141, 404; II, 18ff; Wieck, pp. 85–86, 93–94.

100. Webb, pp. 180ff.

101. Glocker, pp. 137–141.

102. *Workingman's Advocate*, March 23, 1872.

103. Glocker, p. 114.

104. Edward W. Bemis, "Benefit Features of American Trade Unions," *Department of Labor Bulletin*, no. 22 (1899), pp. 363–400.

105. Webb, pp. 388–389, 401–407, 420–421.

106. *Textile Worker*, August 1915.

107. Robert W. Dunn and Jack Hardy, *Labor and Textiles* (New York, 1931), pp. 183–184, 201–202.

108. *Textile Worker*, June-July 1912.

109. Commonwealth *v.* Caruso *et al.* (MS transcript, 1912), 2227–2383; *Lawrence Sun*, January 18, 1912.

110. Paul Frederick Brissenden, *The I.W.W.* (New York, 1919), pp. 121–122; Jefferys, p. 173.

111. *Amalgamated Engineers' Monthly Journal*, January 1906, p. 36; July 1906, p. 31; Amalgamated Society of Carpenters and Joiners, *Monthly Report*, February 1910, p. 109.

112. Wieck, p. 192.

113. *American Federationist*, January 1901, p. 26; Roy, pp. 157–158, 174–175.

114. Evans, I, 144–187, 212–223, 279–356, 417–460.

115. *Bulletin of the American Iron and Steel Association*, XVII (1883), 228.

116. *Fall River Weekly News*, January 14, September 2–23, 1875.

117. *Ibid.*, October 9, 1895; *Wade's Fibre and Fabric*, March 7, 1885, January 23, 1886; *Fall River Herald News*, March 18, 1943; *Report of the Committee of the Senate upon the Relations between Labor and Capital*, I, 632; III, 499.

118. Edward W. Bemis, *Cooperation in New England* (Baltimore, 1886), pp. 48–96; Wisconsin Bureau of Labor and Industrial Statistics, *Twelfth Biennial Report* (1905–1906), pp. 56–65.

119. George Jacob Holyoake, *Among the Americans* (Chicago, 1881), p. 140; *Fall River Weekly News*, January 6, 1870, January 25, 1893.

120. *Workingman's Advocate*, April 3, 1869; Massachusetts Bureau of Statistics of Labor, *Second Annual Report* (1871), p. 482.

121. *Fall River Weekly News*, September 21, 1871; *Labor Standard*, October 14, 1877, February 23, 1880.

122. *Labor Standard*, August 27, 1881.

123. Carroll D. Wright, *A Manual of Distributive Cooperation* (Boston, 1885), p. 103; James Ford, *Cooperation in New England* (New York, 1913), pp. 29–33, 69–70; "Reports by H.M. Representatives Abroad on the System of Cooperation in Foreign Countries," *Parliamentary Papers*, 1886, LXVII (C. 4783), 139.

124. G. O. Virtue, "The Anthracite Mine Laborer," *Bulletin of the Department of Labor*, II (1897), 759.

125. James Roberts to John Loxley, February 6, 1852, in Cornell Collection of Regional History.

126. *Fall River Weekly News*, June 4, 1874, February 28, 1884.

127. *Textile Record*, VI (1885), 201; VII (1886), 48, 306; VIII (1887), 133; *Journal of United Labor*, VII (1886), 2183.

128. *Dictionary of American Biography*, III, 434.

129. *Ibid.*, XVIII, 641; *Workingman's Advocate*, March 20, 1875, May 20, 1876.

130. Susan M. Kingsbury, ed., *Labor Laws and Their Enforcement* (New York, 1911), pp. 106–107; *Fall River Weekly News*, January 29, 1874; *Lawrence Journal*, September 12, 1874; *Labor Standard*, April 17, 1880.

131. *Socialist* [*Labor Standard*], June 17, 1876, June 16, December 23, 1877, January 13, June 9, 1878, May 29, 1880.

132. *Boston Globe*, November 9, 1879; *Fall River Weekly News*, November 23–30, 1876, August 15, October 3, November 7, 1878, November 6, 1879.

133. *Labor Standard*, August 14, October 30, November 8, 1880.

134. *Fall River Weekly News*, 1885–1894, *passim*.

135. *Ibid.*, October 11, 1883, July 17–24, August 21, November 13, 1884.

136. *Ibid.*, October 1, 1885; Spahr, p. 292.

137. *Lawrence Journal*, September 12, 1874.

138. *Workingman's Advocate*, March 4, 1874; *United Mine Workers' Journal*, October 1, 1908.

139. Roy, pp. 256, 261.

140. Joseph F. Patterson, "Reminiscences of John Maguire after Fifty Years of Mining," *Publications of the Historical Society of Schuylkill County*, IV (1912–1914), 313.

141. *United Mine Workers' Journal*, September 24, 1908.

142. Paul Warburton Pritchard, "William B. Wilson" (unpublished doctoral thesis, University of Pennsylvania, 1942), *passim*.

143. London *Times*, October 4, 1839.

144. Frederick J. Gould, *Chats with Pioneers of Modern Thought* (London, 1898), pp. 22–25; *John Swinton's Paper*, August 24, 1884; *Fall River Weekly News*, July 23, 1885; *Gunton Institute Bulletin*, II (1899), 431–432.

145. David Johnston, *Reminiscences of an Octogenarian Scotsman* (Chicago, 1885), *passim*; S. J. Harvey to author, December 11, 1952; *Scottish-American Journal*, April 21, 1886.

146. Matthew Mark Trumbull, *Wheelbarrow: Articles and Discussions on the Labor Question* (Chicago, 1894), pp. 19–40; Henry David, *The History of the Haymarket Affair* (New York, 1936), pp. 404, 431, 440–441.

147. H. J. Carr, "John Francis Bray," *Economica*, VII (1940), 397–415; Joseph Dorfman, *The Economic Mind in American Civilization* (New York, 1949), III, 46–47, 232.

148. William Dealtry, *The Laborer: A Remedy for His Wrongs* (Cincinnati, 1869); cf. *Money, Its History, Evils and Remedy* (Albany, 1858).

149. H. G. Wells, *The Future in America* (New York, 1906), pp. 169–178; *New York Tribune*, June 19, 1902, April 11, 1904.

150. *Workingman's Advocate*, May 21, 1870.

151. John Spargo, *Americanism and Social Democracy* (New York, 1918), p. 165.

152. John Spargo to author, April 24, 1950; John Spargo, "Why Socialism Is Pro-Ally," *Independent*, XCV (1918), 90.

153. Morris Hillquit, *History of Socialism in the United States* (New York, 1903), pp. 299–300; *Western British-American*, June 16, 1906; *Druid*, June 29, 1911.

154. *New York Herald*, March 8, 1880; *Paterson Labor Standard*, March 20, 1880. Cf. *American Silk Journal*, V (1886), 48.

155. "Cost of Living in American Towns," *Parliamentary Papers*, 1911, LXXXVIII (Cd. 5609), 338.

156. "Report of the Industrial Commission," XV, 406–407.

157. Charles B. Spahr, *America's Working People* (New York, 1900), pp. 167–169.

158. *John Swinton's Paper*, July 13, 27, 1884; *Bulletin of the American Iron and Steel Association*, XXIII (1889), 165; Fitch, pp. 106–107.

159. *Labor Standard*, April 17, 1880; *Fall River Weekly News*, March 25, 1891; *Dictionary of American Biography*, VIII, 55–56.

160. *Paterson Labor Standard*, March 20, 1880.

161. "Report of the Industrial Commission," XIV, 415.

8. Countrymen and Fortune Seekers

1. Arthur Redford, *Labour Migration in England 1800–1850* (Manchester, 1926), pp. 152–156; Marcus Lee Hansen, *The Atlantic Migration* (Cambridge, 1941), p. 144.

2. W. Hasbach, *A History of the English Agricultural Labourer* (London, 1908), pp. 178–268; Laurance James Saunders, *Scottish Democracy 1815–1840* (Edinburgh, 1950), pp. 7–63; John Waugh Paterson, *Analysis of the Causes and Consequences of Rural Depopulation in Scotland* (Leipzig, 1896), pp. 41–55; A. H. Dodd, *The Industrial Revolution in North Wales* (Cardiff, 1933), 31–88, 379–386; Hansen, pp. 80, 89–90, 131, 134, 265–266.

3. J. H. Clapham, *An Economic History of Modern Britain* (Cambridge, 1926–1930), II, 279–284; III, 72–83, 94–95.

4. *Ibid.*, I, 98–108; II, 252–253, 284–286, 292, 295–296; III, 96–102; Hasbach, pp. 339–347.

5. Marcus Lee Hansen, *The Mingling of the Canadian and American Peoples* (New Haven, 1940), pp. 115, 135, 172–174, 182–201, 219ff.

6. Fred A. Shannon, *The Farmer's Last Frontier* (New York, 1945), pp. 26–50.

7. New Jersey Bureau of Statistics of Labor and Industry, *Second Annual Report* (1879), p. 19.

8. J. F. C. Grayston to sister, January 26, 1879, in Cornell Collection of Regional History.

9. Finlay Dun, *American Farming and Food* (London, 1881), *passim.*

10. Catherine Grayston Bond to sister, 1888[?], in Cornell Collection of Regional History.

11. Francis Jameson Rowbotham, *A Trip to Prairie-Land* (London, 1885), pp. 67, 160ff.

12. Maurice Farrar, *Five Years in Minnesota* (London, 1880), pp. 221–222.

13. *Eleventh Census of the U.S.* (1890), II, 530–627.

14. George Flower, *History of the English Settlement in Edwards County, Illinois* (Chicago, 1882), *passim.*

15. William Vipond Pooley, *The Settlement of Illinois from 1830 to 1850* (Madison, 1908), p. 503.

16. Joseph Schafer, *The Wisconsin Lead Region* (Madison, 1932), p. 209.

17. Grant Foreman, "English Emigrants in Iowa," *Iowa Journal of History and Politics,* XLIV (1946), 385–420.

18. *Scottish-American,* December 27, 1916.

19. Daniel G. Harvey, *The Argyle Settlement in History and Story* (Rockford, 1924), *passim.*

20. Thomas C. MacMillan, "The Scots and Their Descendants in Illinois," *Transactions of the Illinois State Historical Society,* 1919, pp. 61–64; Pooley, p. 504.

21. *Scottish-American Journal,* October 17, 1861, October 21, 1869.

22. Janette Stevenson Murray, "Lairds of North Tama," *Iowa Journal of History and Politics,* XL (1942), 227–260.

23. David Macrae, *America Revisited* (Glasgow, 1908), p. 94; *Scottish-American Journal,* April 10, 1884.

24. Paul Wallace Gates, *The Illinois Central Railroad and Its Colonization Work* (Cambridge, 1934), p. 234; John Poole *et al., Canada Settlement* (Polo, 1939).

25. Pomroy Jones, *Annals and Recollections of Oneida County* (Rome, 1851), p. 307; William Harvey Jones, "Welsh Settlements in Ohio," *Ohio Archaeological and Historical Quarterly,* XVI (1907), 194–227; Paul DeMund Evans, "The Welsh in Oneida County" (unpublished master's thesis, Cornell University, 1914), pp. 10–16, 34–42.

26. Benjamin W. Chidlaw, *Yr American* (Llanrwst, 1839); *Cambrian,* X (1890), 99.

27. Daniel Jenkins Williams, *The Welsh Community of Waukesha County* (Columbus, 1926), *passim*; Howell D. Davies, *History of the Oshkosh Welsh Settlement* (Amarillo, 1947), *passim*; Thomas E. Hughes *et al., History of the Welsh in Minnesota* (Mankato, 1895), *passim*; David Williams, *A History of Modern Wales* (London, 1950), pp. 259–260; *Cambrian,* V (1885), 73–78, 109–112, 137–141, 260; *Druid,* May 19, 1910; February 29, 1912.

28. William Harvey Jones, p. 217; *Drych,* May 3, 1877, June 27, 1878; *Cambrian,* V (1885), 74.

29. James B. Hedges, "The Colonization Work of the Northern Pacific Railroad," *Mississippi Valley Historical Review,* XIII (1926), 311–342, and "Promotion of Immigration to the Pacific Northwest by the Railroads," *ibid.,* XV (1928), 183–203.

30. *Anglo-American Times,* February 26, 1870.

31. *Ibid.,* March 25, 1881.

32. Hedges, "Promotion of Immigration," p. 198.

33. *Anglo-American Times*, January 14, 1876; "Report on the Foreign Commerce of the United States of America," *Parliamentary Papers*, 1880, LXXII (C. 2570), 207.

34. *Arweinydd i Diroedd yr Union Pacific Railway* (Carmarthen, 1872); *Anglo-American Times*, January 29, 1870; *Scottish-American Journal*, March 11, 1875, August 31, 1882.

35. *Anglo-American Times*, August 21, 1869, July 23, 1870, September 30, 1871.

36. W. H. Carruth, "Foreign Settlements in Kansas," *Kansas University Quarterly*, I (1892), 76.

37. *Workingman's Advocate*, April 27, 1872.

38. *Anglo-American Times*, December 9, 1871.

39. *New York Daily Tribune*, April 10, 1873; Harold F. Peterson, "Some Colonization Projects of the Northern Pacific Railroad," *Minnesota History*, X (1929), 138–140.

40. *Ibid.*, pp. 140–142.

41. Robert D. Thomas, *Hanes Cymry America* (Utica, 1872), pt. II, pp. 87–94, 103–107, 123–124, 128–134; William D. Davies, *America a Gweledigaethau Bywyd* (Merthyr Tydfil, 1899), pp. 65–261; *Arvonia, sef Sefydliad Cymreig yn Sir Osage* (Arvonia, 1869); "Report on the Trade and Commerce of the Puget Sound District and Washington Territory," *Parliamentary Papers*, 1886, LXVI (C. 4761), 745; *Cambrian*, X (1890), 99–100; *Druid*, March 11–18, November 18, 1909.

42. *Anglo-American Times*, January 26, 1883.

43. *Ibid.*, August 10, November 16, 1877; *Scottish-American Journal*, September 5, 1878; *Journal of Commerce*, XLVI (1879), 263.

44. *Anglo-American Times*, August 29, September 26, November 7, 1879.

45. C.O. 384/121.

46. "Report on the Foreign Commerce of the United States of America," p. 178.

47. "Report on the Trade and Commerce of Texas," *Parliamentary Papers*, 1888, CIII (C. 5252), 2–6.

48. "Report on the Trade and Commerce of Los Angeles," *Parliamentary Papers*, 1885, LXVI (C. 4737), 620.

49. "Report on the Trade of the Consular District of San Francisco," *Parliamentary Papers*, 1895, CI (C. 7581–116), 112–113; "Report on the Trade, Commerce, &c., of the States of California, Nevada, Utah, and Oregon," 1904, CI (Cd. 1766–119), 36.

50. *Ibid.*, 1897, XCIV (C. 8277–140), 39.

51. *Ibid.*, 1890, LXXVII (C. 5895–121), 45.

52. "Report on the Distress Caused to British Emigrants to California by Fraudulent Land Syndicates and Emigration Agencies," *Parliamentary Papers*, 1897, LXXXVIII (C. 8278–3), 2–9, 16–17; *British Californian*, November 1904, p. 12.

53. Marquis of Lorne, *A Trip to the Tropics and Home Through America*

(London, 1867), p. 300; *Scottish-American Journal*, April 4, 1872, October 22, 1874, February 25, 1875; *Anglo-American Times*, October 20, 1882.

54. "Report on the Trade of the Consular District of Baltimore," *Parliamentary Papers*, 1910, CIII (Cd. 4962–38), 51.

55. "Report on the Trade, Commerce, and Navigation of the Port of Pensacola," *Parliamentary Papers*, 1884, LXXX (C. 3964), 603; *Anglo-American Times*, January 29, February 5, 26, April 9, 1886.

56. "Report on the Trade and Commerce of New Orleans," *Parliamentary Papers*, 1886, LXV (C. 4654), 181.

57. W. Stamer, *The Gentleman Emigrant* (London, 1874), I, 22–53; H. Harcourt Horn, *An English Colony in Iowa* (Boston, 1931), p. 28.

58. Marjorie Gamet Raish, *Victoria* (Topeka, 1947), *passim.*

59. Archibald Sutter, *American Notes, 1881* (Edinburgh, 1882), p. 70.

60. *Ibid.*, pp. 69–70.

61. Thomas Hughes, *Rugby, Tennessee* (London, 1881), *passim*; *Anglo-American Times*, September 17, October 22–November 19, 1880, February 4, 25, July 15, September 2–16, 1881, February 10, December 15, 1882, January 5, 1883, June 6, 1884, April 23, 1886; *Scottish-American*, October 2, 1895.

62. William A. Baillie-Grohman, *Camps in the Rockies* (New York, 1882), pp. 321–322.

63. Jacob Van der Zee, *The British in Iowa* (Iowa City, 1922), *passim.*

64. Arthur Reginald Moro, "The English Colony at Fairmont," *Minnesota History*, VIII (1927), 140–149; Farrar, pp. 80–90; Horn, pp. 24–91.

65. "Report on the Trade, Commerce, &c., of the States of California, Nevada, Utah, and Arizona," *Parliamentary Papers*, 1904, CI (Cd. 1766–119), 25.

66. Benjamin Brierley, *Ab-o'th'-Yate in Yankeeland* (Manchester, 1885), pp. 299–305; A. G. Vansittart to Sir Julian Pauncefote, October 16, 1895, December 19, 1896, in F.O. 5/2263, 2291; Victor M. Hollinsworth to Marquis of Salisbury, August 11, 1897, in F.O. 5/2341; "Report on the Trade of the Consular District of Chicago," *Parliamentary Papers*, 1897, XCIV (C. 8277–71), 37; "Report on the Consular District of San Francisco," 1894, LXXXVIII (C. 7293–122), 18; *Scottish-American Journal*, December 15, 1881.

67. F. W. Grey, *Seeking Fortune in America* (London, 1912), pp. 1, 46.

68. *Scottish-American*, February 1, 1899, June 2, 1910; *New York Daily Tribune*, December 14, 1903; London *Times*, June 3, 1914; *New York Times*, July 20, 1914.

69. Joseph Nimmo, *Report in Regard to the Range and Ranch Cattle Business of the United States* (Washington, 1885), pp. 44–45; Walter von Richthofen, *Cattle-Raising on the Plains of North America* (New York, 1885), pp. 47–55.

70. Mrs. Irene Addison to author, April 13, 1951.

71. Nimmo, p. 75.

72. Wallis Nash, *Oregon: There and Back in 1877* (London, 1878), pp. 80–83.

73. *Scottish-American*, May 18, 1898.

74. Reginald Aldridge, *Ranch Notes in Kansas, Colorado, the Indian Territory and Northern Texas* (London, 1884), *passim;* "Bunny," *Two Years a Cow Boy* (London, 1887), *passim*; Mary J. Jaques, *Texan Ranch Life* (London, 1894), *passim*; William French, *Some Recollections of a Western Ranchman* (London, 1927), *passim*; *Eleventh Census of the U.S.* (1890), II, 530–627.

75. Milo M. Quaife, ed., *An English Settler in Pioneer Wisconsin* (Madison, 1918), p. 185.

76. *Manchester Examiner and Times*, July 29, November 22, 1851, quoted in Grant Foreman, "English Settlers in Illinois," *Journal of the Illinois State Historical Society*, XXXIV (1941), 329, 333.

77. William Ogle, "The Alleged Depopulation of the Rural Districts of England," *Journal of the Royal Statistical Society*, LII (1889), 231; Redford, pp. 54–58.

78. Stanley C. Johnson, *A History of Emigration from the United Kingdom to North America* (London, 1913), pp. 221–226; W. A. Carrothers, *Emigration from the British Isles* (London, 1929), pp. 228–255; "Consular Reports on Emigration and Immigration," *House Miscellaneous Document*, 49 Cong., 2 sess., no. 157 (February 11, 1887), pp. 462–464; "Report on the Decline in the Agricultural Population of Great Britain, 1881–1906," *Parliamentary Papers*, 1906, XCVI (Cd. 3273), 34, 44, 49, 54, 57.

79. "Report from the Select Committee on Colonisation," *Parliamentary Papers*, 1889, X (274), Q. 1792; *Anglo-American Times*, November 22, 1873.

80. Rowland Hill Macdonald, *The Emigration of Highland Crofters* (Edinburgh, 1885), pp. 30–31.

81. U.S. Bureau of Statistics on Commerce and Navigation, *Annual Reports*, 1873–1891; U.S. Superintendent of Immigration, *Annual Reports*, 1892–1895; U.S. Commissioner-General of Immigration, *Annual Reports*, 1896–1918.

82. *Eleventh Census of the U.S.* (1890), II, 484.

83. Hansen, *Mingling of Canadian and American Peoples*, p. 163.

84. "Reports of the Industrial Commission," *House Document*, 57 Cong., 1 sess., no. 184 (December 5, 1901), XV, 447–448.

85. Hansen, *Mingling of Canadian and American Peoples*, pp. 162–164, 205–206, 209–210.

86. *Eleventh Census of the U.S.* (1890), II, 485.

87. Thomas Greenwood, *A Tour in the States and Canada* (London, 1883), p. 158.

88. Peter Ross, *The Scot in America* (New York, 1896), pp. 221–281; D. MacDougall, ed., *Scots and Scots' Descendants in America* (New York, 1917), *passim*; George Fraser Black, *Scotland's Mark on America* (New York, 1921), pp. 101–114; Ebenezer Edwards, *Welshmen as Factors* (Utica, 1899), *passim*; Herbert N. Casson, "The Sons of Old Scotland in America," "The English in America," "The Canadians in the United States," "The Welsh in

America," *Munsey's*, XXXIV (1906), 599–611; XXXV (1906), 202–219, 473–487, 748–754; *Dictionary of American Biography* (New York, 1928–1937), Index, pp. 298–309.

89. *Eleventh Census of the U.S.* (1890), II, 484–487.

90. Herbert Heaton, "Yorkshire Cloth Traders in the United States, 1770–1840," *Publications of the Thoresby Society*, XXXVII (1941), 225–287.

91. Emigrants' Information Office, *General Information Relating to North, Central, and South America* (London, 1910), pp. 39, 90; *Canadian-American*, May 8, 1884.

92. Hamil Grant, *Two Sides of the Atlantic* (London, 1917), pp. 68–69; "Report on the Trade, Commerce, and Agriculture of the Consular District of Chicago," *Parliamentary Papers*, 1904, CI (Cd. 1766–136), 5–7.

93. *New York Daily Tribune*, January 24, 1901.

94. Macrae, pp. 12–13; *Scottish-American Journal*, March 22, 1877, August 3, 1882, May 10, 1883, March 20, October 16, 1895, April 29, September 23, 1896, April 13, 1898, April 6, 1904, October 14–21, 1908, April 21, September 22, 1909, December 17, 1913, March 3, 1915.

95. *New York Times*, July 17, 1938; London *Times*, July 18, 1938.

96. *Canadian-American*, October 30, 1885; *Who Was Who in America* (Chicago, 1942), I, 1364.

97. *Dictionary of American Biography*, III, 499–506.

98. *Lloyd's Clerical Directory for 1898* (Hamilton, Ohio, 1898), *passim*. Cf. Henry Caswall, *America and the American Church* (London, 1839), p. 347.

99. Edgar Sutton Robinson, *The Ministerial Directory* (Oxford, Ohio, 1898), I, 141–559.

100. U.S. Bureau of Statistics on Commerce and Navigation, *Annual Reports*, 1871–1891; U.S. Superintendent of Immigration, *Annual Reports*, 1892–1895; U.S. Commissioner-General of Immigration, *Annual Reports*, 1896–1918.

101. Matthew Mark Trumbull, *Wheelbarrow: Articles and Discussions on the Labor Question* (Chicago, 1894), pp. 13–40; *Workingman's Advocate*, May 19–26, 1866.

PART II. THE CULTURAL ADJUSTMENT

9. "In a Foreign Land Amongst Strangers"

1. Massachusetts Bureau of Statistics of Labor, *First Annual Report* (1870), pp. 111–118, 322–323; *Second Annual Report* (1871), pp. 476–485; *ante*, pp. 34–35, 53–54.

2. *Report of the Committee of the Senate upon the Relations between Labor and Capital* (Washington, 1885), III, 490. Cf. *New York Herald*, October 13, 1875.

3. *Miners' Journal*, June 30, 1855.

4. *New York Herald*, March 8, 1880.

5. "Report of the Industrial Commission," *House Document*, 57 Cong., 1 sess., no. 183 (December 5, 1901), XIV, 612.

6. "Report on the Foreign Commerce of the United States," *Parliamentary Papers*, 1881, LXXXIX (C. 2916), 297.

7. *New York Times*, August 21, 1892.

8. Massachusetts Bureau of Statistics of Labor, *First Annual Report* (1870), pp. 164–185; *Twenty-Third Annual Report* (1892), pp. 170–211, 303; "Report of the Industrial Commission," XV, 449–492.

9. *Miners' Journal*, August 13, 1859; *Drych*, March 10, 1881; *Druid*, February 10, 1910; William J. Heller, *History of Northampton County* (New York, 1920), II, 519.

10. William Charlton, *Four Months in North America* (Hexham, 1873), p. 24; *Cenhadwr Americanaidd*, XIII (1852), p. 170.

11. *Scottish-American*, May 7, 1902.

12. *American Manufacturer*, April 3, 1885; John Lewis, January 20, 1876, in Cornell Collection of Regional History .

13. Robert K. Webb, "Working Class Readers in Early Victorian England," *English Historical Review*, LXV (1950), pp. 333–351; Laurance James Saunders, *Scottish Democracy 1815–1840* (Edinburgh, 1950), pp. 241–251; "Reports of the Commissioners of Inquiry into the State of Education in Wales," *Parliamentary Papers*, 1847, XXVII, pt. 1 (870), pp. 3–10; pt. 2 (871), pp. 48–55; pt. 3 (872), pp. 55–59.

14. Denis Gwynn, *A Hundred Years of Catholic Emancipation* (London, 1929), pp. xiii–xxviii, 1–124, 276–287.

15. *Ante*, pp. 102–103.

16. Samuel Smiles, *Self-Help, with Illustrations of Character and Conduct* (London, 1859).

17. Harris E. Starr, *William Graham Sumner* (New York, 1925), pp. 3–18.

18. C. Reginald Enock, *Farthest West* (London, 1910), p. 298. Cf. J. Denley Spencer, "Young Welshmen Abroad," *Wales*, IV (1897), 200.

19. Percy G. Ebbutt, *Emigrant Life in Kansas* (London, 1886), p. 232.

20. *Fall River Weekly News*, October 19, 1882.

21. George Jacob Holyoake, *Among the Americans* (Chicago, 1881), pp. 219–220.

22. *British-American Citizen*, May 30, 1891.

23. Hamil Grant, *Two Sides of the Atlantic* (London, 1917), p. 67; *Labor Standard*, February 26, 1881; *New York Daily Tribune*, July 6, 1884.

24. Herbert N. Casson, "The English in America," "The Canadians in the United States," *Munsey's*, XXXV (1906), 207, 483; *Dictionary of American Biography* (New York, 1928–1937), *passim*.

25. F. W. Grey, *Seeking Fortune in America* (London, 1912), pp. 136–137.

26. *Drych*, January 27, 1870.

27. George Burton Adams, *Why Americans Dislike England* (Philadelphia, 1896), pp. 7–24; Oscar Handlin, "American Views of the Jew at the Opening

of the Twentieth Century," *Publications of the American Jewish Historical Society*, XL (1951), 332–334; *Anglo-American Times*, March 8, 1893.

28. James Dawson Burn, *Three Years Among the Working Classes in the United States during the War* (London, 1865), pp. 299–300.

29. Goldwin Smith, "The Hatred of England," *North American Review*, CL (1890), 548; *Anglo-American Times*, May 8, 1869.

30. London *Times*, December 21, 1895.

31. *British-American*, June 7, 1890.

32. *Fall River Weekly News*, February 3, 1892.

33. *The British Mechanic's and Labourer's Hand Book and True Guide to the United States* (London, 1840), pp. 157ff.

34. *Machinists' and Blacksmiths' International Journal*, VIII (1871), 141–143, 176–182.

35. Dixon Wecter, *The Saga of American Society* (New York, 1937), pp. 387ff.

36. *Canadian American*, December 31, 1885.

37. *Bulletin of the American Iron and Steel Association*, XVII (1883), 5.

38. Alan Dale, *Jonathan's Home* (Bristol, 1885), pp. 50–53.

39. "Gallynipper," *The Gallynipper in Yankeeland* (London, 1882), p. 79.

40. William Gordon Blaikie, *Summer Suns in the Far West* (London, 1890), p. 78; Earl of Birkenhead, *America Revisited* (London, 1924), p. 26.

41. *Scottish-American*, February 15, 1893.

42. David W. Mitchell, *Ten Years in the United States* (London, 1862), p. 59; Edward Young, *Special Report on Immigration* (Philadelphia, 1871), p. vi; Massachusetts Commission on Immigration, *The Problem of Immigration in Massachusetts* (Boston, 1914), *passim; Miners' Journal*, May 26, August 18, 1855.

43. Frank Dilnot, *The New America* (London, 1919), pp. 63–64.

44. Harold E. Adams, "Minority Caricatures on the American Stage," in George Peter Murdock, ed., *Studies in the Science of Society Presented to Albert Galloway Keller* (New Haven, 1937), pp. 6, 20–21.

45. Sir Frederick Smith, *My American Visit* (London, 1918), p. 64.

46. T. A. Rickard, *The Copper Mines of Lake Superior* (New York, 1905), p. 18; Eric Partridge, *A Dictionary of Slang and Unconventional English* (London, 1949), p. 184.

47. *Druid*, March 30, September 21, 1911, March 28, 1912.

48. *Partridge*, p. 484. Cf. *ante*, p. 83.

49. H. L. Mencken, *The American Language* (New York, 1946), p. 216; private information.

50. Order Sons of St. George, Grand Lodge, *Proceedings of the Sixteenth Annual Meeting* (1887), p. 90.

51. "Report from the Select Committee on Colonisation," *Parliamentary Papers*, 1889, X (274), Q. 1938–1939, 1944–1946.

52. James Fullarton Muirhead, *The Land of Contrasts* (Boston, 1898), p. 86.

53. Milo M. Quaife, ed., *An English Settler in Pioneer Wisconsin* (Madison, 1918), p. 166.

54. *Granite Cutters' Journal*, August 1885.

55. *Scottish-American Journal*, January 5, 1882, October 3, 1888; *British Californian*, June 1903; *Western British-American*, March 5, 1905.

56. *Labor Standard*, August 9, 1879, May 1, 1880, September 24, 1881.

57. *Fall River Weekly News*, October 24, 1878. Cf. *American Silk Journal*, II (1883), 141; VI (1887), 140.

58. *Drych*, April 10, 1873.

59. United Textile Workers of America, *Proceedings of the Sixth Annual Convention* (1906), p. 28. Cf. *ante*, p. 58.

60. "Reports of the Immigration Commission," *Senate Document*, 61 Cong., 2 sess., no. 633 (June 15, 1910), VI, 426.

61. Stephen Graham, *With Poor Immigrants to America* (New York, 1914), pp. 133–134.

62. Robert A. Woods, ed., *Americans in Process* (Boston, 1902), p. 66; Julius Drachsler, *Intermarriage in New York City* (New York, 1921), pp. 132–133, 182–184; Niles Carpenter, *Immigrants and Their Children* (Washington, 1927), pp. 234–235; Joseph Schafer, *The Wisconsin Lead Region* (Madison, 1932), pp. 299–310; Daniel Jenkins Williams, *The Welsh of Columbus, Ohio* (Oshkosh, 1913), pp. 81–83.

63. "Cost of Living in American Towns," *Parliamentary Papers*, 1911, LXXXVIII (Cd. 5609), XL.

64. *American Canadian*, July 31, 1875; *Canadian American*, March 5, 1886.

65. *Ante*, pp. 110–112.

66. Williams, pp. 58, 69; *Druid*, July 24, 1907.

67. Robert Ernst, *Immigrant Life in New York City* (New York, 1949), p. 44; *Scottish-American Journal*, February 21, 1884, June 27, 1888.

68. State of New York, *Census*, 1875, *passim; Thirteenth Census of the U.S.* (1910), II, III, *passim*.

69. *Fall River Churchman*, October 1896.

70. "Report on Immigration into the United States," *Parliamentary Papers*, 1906, LXXII, (Cd. 2683–19), 9.

71. Quaife, p. 184.

72. *Cymro America*, June 1, 1832; *Paterson Labor Standard*, March 20, 1880.

73. "Further Reports from H.M. Diplomatic and Consular Agents Abroad Respecting the Condition of the Industrial Classes," *Parliamentary Papers*, 1871, LXVII (C. 414), 855.

74. Quaife, p. 63.

75. *Scottish-American Journal*, August 18, 1881.

76. *Ibid.*, September 15, 1866.

77. Burn, p. 187.

78. *Scottish-American*, September 5, 1888. Cf. James Boardman, *America and the Americans* (London, 1833), p. 37.

79. *Canadian American*, April 17, 1884.
80. Benjamin W. Chidlaw, *Yr American* (Llanrwst, 1839), p. 39.
81. William A. Baillie-Grohman, *Camps in the Rockies* (New York, 1882), p. 363.
82. Enock, p. 299.
83. Benjamin W. Chidlaw, *The Story of My Life* (Philadelphia, 1890), p. 97.
84. Henry Ashworth, *A Tour in the United States, Cuba, and Canada* (London, 1861), pp. 171–172.
85. Wisconsin Commissioner of Labor and Industrial Statistics, *Fourth Biennial Report* (1888–1889), p. 33.
86. *Workingman's Advocate*, April 19, 1873.
87. Wisconsin Commissioner of Labor and Industrial Statistics, *Fourth Biennial Report* (1888–1889), p. 49.
88. *English-American*, April 25, 1885.
89. David Laing to sister, July 11, 1875, in Cornell Collection of Regional History.
90. Quaife, pp. 41, 52.
91. Catherine Grayston Bond to brother, August 21, 1881[?] in Cornell Collection of Regional History. Cf. London *Times*, January 1, 1877.
92. Burn, pp. 300–301.
93. Thomas Greenwood, *A Tour in the States and Canada* (London, 1883), p. 139.
94. T. M. Young, *The American Cotton Industry* (London, 1902), pp. 17–18.
95. *New York Herald*, March 8, 1880.
96. Harold Spender, *A Briton in America* (London, 1921), p. 84. Cf. John Edward Hilary Skinner, *After the Storm* (London, 1866), I, 285–293.
97. John Hogben, *First Impressions of America* (Leith, 1904), p. 82.
98. Owen Morgan, *A Souvenir: The Visit of the Iron and Steel Institutes of Great Britain and Germany to America* (Cardiff, 1890), pp. 66–67.
99. *A True Picture of Emigration* (London, 1848), pp. 45, 61–62; *Fall River Weekly News*, April 29, 1886, May 30, 1889; *New York Observer*, July 14, 1887; *Druid*, September 19, 1907, August 24, 1911.
100. David Macrae, *America Revisited* (Glasgow, 1908), p. 123.
101. *Albion*, January 13, 1855; *Scottish-American Journal*, December 11, 1862, April 13, 1887, February 6, 1924; *Fall River Weekly News*, February 14, 1889; *Druid*, March 16, 1914.
102. London *Times*, September 20, 1842.
103. Thomas L. Nichols, *Forty Years of American Life* (London, 1864), II, 79.
104. Rising Lake Morrow, "The Negotiation of the Anglo-American Treaty of 1870," *American Historical Review*, XXXIX (1934), 663–681.
105. *Twelfth Census of the U.S.* (1900), I, 914–921.
106. *Fourteenth Census of the U.S.* (1920), II, 826. Cf. *Rhode Island State*

Census, 1885, pp. 356–357; *Eleventh Census of the U.S.* (1890), II, 284ff; Carpenter, pp. 262–263; *post*, pp. 196–201.

107. *Post*, pp. 144, 185–186.

108. Frederick C. deSumichrast, *Americans and the Britons* (New York, 1914), p. 82.

109. *Western British-American*, June 5, 1915.

110. Alphaeus P. and Margaret Ward Cole, *Timothy Cole, Wood-Engraver* (New York, 1935), p. xv; *British Mechanic's and Labourer's Hand Book*, pp. 126–130; *British-American*, April 11, 1891.

111. *American Silk Journal*, III (1884), 140.

112. Benjamin Brierley, *Ab-o'th'-Yate in Yankeeland* (Manchester, 1885), pp. 313–317; deSumichrast, pp. 85–86.

113. John Spargo, "On Becoming an American Citizen," *Independent*, LXV (1908), 995, 997, 999.

10. Old Ways and New Ties

1. *Canadian American*, May 20, 1887; *Scottish-American*, June 24, 1896, June 27, 1900.

2. F. Cunliffe-Owen, "Englishmen in the United States," *Forum*, XXIX (1900), 41.

3. *Anglo-American Times*, January 3, 1874.

4. *Scottish Patriot*, March 28, 1840.

5. *Anglo-American Times*, 1865–1896, *passim*; *Scottish-American Journal*, 1861–1919, *passim*; *Canadian American*, 1883–1918, *passim*; *Western British-American*, 1888–1918, *passim*.

6. *Scottish-American*, June 22–29, 1887, June 16–July 7, 1897; *British-American Citizen*, June 26, 1897; *British Californian*, May-August 1897.

7. *British-American Citizen*, January 26–February 2, 1901; *Scottish-American*, January 30–February 6, 1901.

8. *Scottish-American*, July 2–9, 1902, November 15, 1905, May 11–25, 1910, June 28, 1911.

9. *Ibid.*, January 9, 1862, March 30, 1871, January 20, 1892.

10. *Anglo-American Times*, February 19, 1870.

11. *Scottish-American Journal*, July 17–24, 1879; *Boston Scotsman*, April 7, 1906.

12. *Drych*, February 3–April 21, 1881.

13. *Druid*, July–August 1911. Cf. *post*, p. 204.

14. *Anglo-American Times*, August 9, December 13, 1878.

15. *Druid*, October 16, 1913.

16. *Ibid.*, August 19, 1909; *Scottish-American*, October 13, 1909.

17. *Anglo-American Times*, July 20, 1872; *British-American Citizen*, October 10, 1903.

18. *Emigrant*, April 15, 1835; *Emigrant and Old Countryman*, October 28,

1835, July 19, 1837; *Old Countryman*, January 18, 1842; *Drych*, January 18, 1851.

19. *The British Mechanic's and Labourer's Hand Book and True Guide to the United States* (London, 1840), pp. 69–71.

20. *Workingman's Advocate*, May 21, 1870.

21. *Ibid.*, March 31, 1877; *Western British-American*, January 4, 1913.

22. *Scottish-American Journal*, December 28, 1882.

23. James Henderson, *Thistledown* (Boston, 1915), p. 66.

24. *Scottish-American*, May 18, 1892, April 5, 1893.

25. *Ibid.*, February 23, 1861, February 2, 1871.

26. Kenneth Mathieson, *How We Saw the United States of America* (Dunfermline, 1883), pp. 37–38.

27. "Report on the Trade, Commerce, &c., of the Consular District of San Francisco," *Parliamentary Papers*, 1902, CXI (Cd. 786–129), 8.

28. Henry Ashworth, *A Tour of the United States, Cuba, and Canada* (London, 1861), p. 140.

29. Isaac Fidler, *Observations on Professions, Literature, Manners, and Emigration in the United States and Canada* (New York, 1833), p. 97.

30. New Jersey Bureau of Statistics of Labor and Industries, *Sixth Annual Report* (1883), p. 262.

31. *Fall River Weekly News*, March 21, 1878.

32. John L. Hayes, *American Textile Machinery* (Cambridge, 1879), pp. 31–32. Cf. Kansas Bureau of Labor and Industrial Statistics, *Second Annual Report* (1886), p. 180.

33. *Drych*, September 7, 1871.

34. Massachusetts Bureau of Statistics of Labor, *Tenth Annual Report* (1879), p. 136; David Jones, *Welsh Congregationalists in Pennsylvania* (Utica, 1934), pp. 346–347.

35. Milo M. Quaife, ed., *An English Settler in Pioneer Wisconsin* (Madison, 1918), pp. 161–162.

36. *Report of the Committee of the Senate upon the Relations between Labor and Capital* (Washington, 1885), III, 631.

37. *Bulletin of the American Iron and Steel Association*, XIV (1880), 186.

38. *New York Times*, December 25, 1867.

39. Quaife, p. 64.

40. *Fall River Weekly News*, December 31, 1874; *Labor Standard*, December 18–25, 1880.

41. Jonathan Thayer Lincoln, *The City of the Dinner Pail* (Boston, 1909), pp. 15–16.

42. *Church Militant*, October 1908, p. 10.

43. *Scottish-American*, December 24, 1890, December 23, 1891.

44. *Ibid.*, December 28, 1887, December 30, 1891, January 17, 1894.

45. *Fall River Weekly News*, January 6, 1892.

46. *Scottish-American Journal*, January 23, 1869.

47. *Ibid.*, October 28, 1891; cf. October 28, 1880, November 3, 1881, October 25, 1893, October 30, 1895; *Miners' Journal*, November 3, 1855.

48. *British-American Citizen*, June 22, 1889, June 7, 1890, May 30, 1891, June 3, 1893.

49. James Roberts to John Loxley, February 14, 1850, in Cornell Collection of Regional History.

50. G. M. Young, ed., *Early Victorian England* (London, 1934), I, 265–296; Foster Rhea Dulles, *America Learns to Play* (New York, 1940), pp. 3–21, 84–91.

51. *British Mechanic's and Labourer's Hand Book*, p. 62.

52. Charles A. Peverelly, *The Book of American Pastimes* (New York, 1866), pp. 529–547; William Rotch Wister, *Some Reminiscences of Cricket in Philadelphia before 1861* (Philadelphia, 1904), pp. 5–30; New York *Anglo-American*, 1843–1846, *passim*; *Textile World*, June 1899, p. 25.

53. *Anglo-American Times*, May 11, 1867.

54. *Ibid.*, October 9, 1869; *Miners' Journal*, 1859–1874, *passim*; *Fall River Weekly News*, 1870–1895, *passim*.

55. *Scottish-American Journal*, 1865–1919, *passim*; *Anglo-American Times*, 1869–1879, *passim*; *Canadian American*, 1884–1888, *passim*; *British-American Citizen*, 1890–1892, *passim*; *British Californian*, 1903–1905, *passim*; *Western British-American*, 1901–1916, *passim*.

56. New York *Anglo-American*, September 28, 1844; *Anglo-American Times*, September 25, 1868, September 21, 1872; *Scottish-American Journal*, September 12, 1878, September 11, October 9–16, 1879, September 30, 1885, September 29, 1886, October 10, 1894, September 30, 1896, September 28, 1898, July 10, 1901.

57. *Anglo-American Times*, April 17, 1891.

58. *Scottish-American Journal*, August 5, 1880, April 17, 1884, April 8, 1896; *Fall River Weekly News*, March 26, 1885.

59. *Drych*, July 31, 1879; James J. Davis, *The Iron Puddler* (Indianapolis, 1922), p. 100.

60. *Dictionary of American Biography* (New York, 1928–1937), XX, 554.

61. *Scottish-American Journal*, November 24, 1881.

62. *Ibid.*, September 7, 1904; *Canadian American*, June 10, 1887.

63. *Scottish-American Journal*, November 20, 1884, September 24, 1890, August 17, 1892, June 30, 1897.

64. *Ibid.*, May 18, 1892; *Fall River Weekly News*, May 10, 1888, November 26, 1890.

65. *Scottish-American Journal*, 1881–1918, *passim*; *Fall River Weekly News*, 1884–1895, *passim*; *Canadian American*, 1885–1887, *passim*; *British Californian*, 1903–1904, *passim*; *Western British-American*, 1905–1918, *passim*.

66. *Fall River Weekly News*, November 26, 1890.

67. *Western British-American*, March 1, 1913, October 23, 1915, April 1, 1916.

68. *Emigrant and Old Countryman*, October 19, 1836.

69. *Scottish-American Journal*, September 1, 1866.

70. Thomas Wentworth Higginson, "A Day of Scottish Games," *Scribner's*, III (1872), 331–333; *Scottish-American Journal*, 1861–1919, *passim*.

71. *Ibid.*, November 21, 1868, December 5, 1872, June 26, 1873, June 25, 1874.

72. *Ibid.*, September 15, 1866, September 9, 1885, August 1, October 10, 1888, July 26, 1893; Samuel Crowther and Arthur Ruhl, *Rowing and Track Athletics* (New York, 1905), pp. 257–284.

73. *Drych*, August 5, 1880; *British-American*, June 29, July 13, 1889, November 2, 1895; *Druid*, August 15, 1907, July 23, 1908.

74. *Scottish-American Journal*, 1861–1918, *passim*.

75. Angus Murdoch, *Boom Copper* (New York, 1943), p. 216.

76. *Scottish-American*, December 5, 1894, November 30, 1910.

77. Maurice Farrar, *Five Years in Minnesota* (London, 1880), pp. 85–86; Illinois Bureau of Labor Statistics, *Third Biennial Report* (1883–1884), p. 433.

78. John Francis Campbell, *A Short American Tramp in the Fall of 1864* (Edinburgh, 1865), pp. 292–293.

79. *Scottish-American*, August 7, 1907.

80. *Ibid.*, January 16, 1901.

81. *Ibid.*, July 14, 1897, January 5, 1898, May 22, 1907; James B. Forgan, *Recollections of a Busy Life* (New York, 1924), pp. 117–119.

82. Jacob Van der Zee, *The British in Iowa* (Iowa City, 1922), p. 203.

83. *Labor Standard*, August 7, 1880; *Scottish-American*, August 31–October 19, 1887.

84. *Anglo-American Times*, September 11, 1869.

85. *Ibid.*, October 13, 1866, August 15, 1879.

86. Union Pacific Coal Company, *History of the Union Pacific Coal Mines* (Omaha, 1940), p. 32; Farrar, pp. 84–85; Van der Zee, pp. 193–194.

87. *Anglo-American Times*, September 12, 1868.

88. Viscount Knebworth, *Boxing* (London, 1931), pp. 20–55; *Dictionary of American Biography*, VI, 443.

89. *Canadian American*, October 22, December 3, 24, 1886; *Canadian*, January 1905, p. 25.

90. *Canadian American*, 1884–1888, *passim*; *Western British-American*, August 12, 1905.

91. James Naismith, *Basketball* (New York, 1941), pp. 39–49.

92. Rolvix Harlan, *John Alexander Dowie and the Christian Catholic Apostolic Church in Zion* (Evansville, Wisconsin, 1906), *passim*; *Scottish-American*, December 28, 1904.

93. Thomas F. G. Coates, *The Prophet of the Poor* (New York, 1906), pp. 121–128; Laurence L. Doggett, *History of the Young Men's Christian Association* (New York, 1922), pp. 110ff; *Scottish-American Journal*, March 18, 1880.

94. "Mormonism in Wales," *Spectator*, XXXVI (1863), 2142; W. G. Marshall, *Through America* (London, 1881), pp. 225–228; William D. Davies, *America a Gweledigaethau Bywyd* (Merthyr Tydfil, 1899), pp. 161–168; M. Hamlin Cannon, "Migration of English Mormons to America," "The English Mormons in America," *American Historical Review*, LII (1947), 436–455, LVII (1952), 893–908.

95. James Bryce, *The American Commonwealth* (London, 1888), III, 478.

96. Massachusetts Bureau of Statistics of Labor, *Second Annual Report* (1871), p. 486.

97. *Fall River Weekly News*, December 5, 1894, January 9, 1895.

98. *Church Militant*, February 1900, pp. 5–6; October 1904, pp. 98–101; Lincoln, p. 9.

99. "Reports of the Immigration Commission," *Senate Document*, 61 Cong., 2 sess., no. 633 (June 15, 1910), XVI, 376, 679; *Church Militant*, April 1898, p. 4, November 1901, p. 7, April 1904, p. 12, October 1904, pp. 49, 72, April 1905, p. 5, December 1905, p. 8; Van der Zee, pp. 243–244.

100. *Church Militant*, March 1908, p. 10, March 1912, p. 7.

101. *Ibid.*, November 1899, p. 5; *Fall River Churchman*, April 1894.

102. *Fall River Weekly News*, January 26, April 5, 1888.

103. Robert F. Wearmouth, *Methodism and the Working-Class Movements of England 1800–1850* (London, 1937), *passim*.

104. *Miners' Journal*, November 24, 1855.

105. Charles B. Spahr, "The Old Factory Towns of New England," *Outlook*, LXI (1899), 290–291; Elmer T. Clark, *The Small Sects in America* (Nashville, 1937), pp. 83–84; Wearmouth, pp. 14, 16, 192, 208–210, 227.

106. William Warren Sweet, *Religion in Colonial America* (New York, 1942), pp. 250–263.

107. Alexander Blaikie, *A History of Presbyterianism in New England* (Boston, 1881), pp. 336–471; Presbyterian Church in the United States of America, *Minutes of the General Assembly*, 1884, p. 182; 1889, p. 203; 1892, p. 303; 1896, p. 257; *Scottish-American Journal*, July 24, 1884, April 10, 1889, March 30, 1904; author's conversations and correspondence with Presbyterian ministers, 1949–1950.

108. *Scottish Journal*, February 6, 1841; *Scottish-American Journal*, June 20, 1861, February 17, 1866, August 15, 1872, November 27, 1895; *Western British-American*, February 22, 1913.

109. *Miners' Journal*, December 3, 1853.

110. New York *Evangelist*, May 5–June 2, 1887.

111. J. W. S. Lowry, *History and Church Directory of the Congregation of the Church of Scotland* (Cambridge, n.d.), *passim*.

112. Robert A. Woods, ed., *Americans in Process* (Boston, 1902), p. 262; private information.

113. *Scottish-American*, December 17, 1890.

114. Reformed Presbyterian Church of Boston, Session Book (MS), 1868–1877, *passim*; *Scottish-American Journal*, February 12, 1885, May 21, 1890.

115. John Buchan and George Adam Smith, *The Kirk in Scotland* (Edinburgh, 1930), pp. 88–106.

116. *Scottish-American Journal*, October 3, 1868.

117. *Boston Scotsman*, April 20, 1907; Blaikie, p. 445.

118. *British-American Citizen*, March 16, 1889.

119. *Scottish-American Journal*, March 27, 1884, February 14, October 17, 1894, December 5, 1900.

120. David Williams, *A History of Modern Wales* (London, 1950), pp. 123–124, 139–157, 246–251.

121. *Cambrian*, V (1885), 76.

122. Henry Rees and Moses Parry, *Y Genadaeth i'r America* (Caerleon, 1841), *passim*.

123. Jenkin T. Jenkins to Daniel Jenkins, March 5, 1851 (privately owned).

124. William Harvey Jones, "Welsh Settlements in Ohio," *Ohio Archaeological and Historical Quarterly*, XVI (1907), 213–215, 219–220; Daniel Jenkins Williams, *The Welsh Community of Waukesha County* (Columbus, 1926), pp. 146–162; David Jones, p. 114; *Miners' Journal*, June 27, 1846.

125. David Jones, pp. iii, v.

126. Benjamin W. Chidlaw, *Yr American* (Llanrwst, 1839), p. 35.

127. Robert D. Thomas, *Hanes Cymry America* (Utica, 1872), pt. III, pp. 20–23.

128. Davies, pp. 259–260; *Cambrian*, X (1890), 100, 156; XV (1895), 61.

129. Trefnyddion Calfinaidd, "Cofnodion o Weithrediadau y Gymanfa Gyffredinol," 1869–1920 (MS), I, 1; Daniel Jenkins Williams, *One Hundred Years of Welsh Calvinistic Methodism in America* (Philadelphia, 1937), pp. 56–281.

130. Benjamin W. Chidlaw, *The Story of My Life* (Philadelphia, 1890), pp. 79, 105–107; David Jones, *passim*.

131. *Cambrian*, XIV (1894), 58.

132. Erasmus Jones, "The Welsh in America," *Atlantic*, XXXVII (1876), 309–310.

133. *Cambrian*, XII (1892), 77; *Druid*, November 26, 1908; David Jones, pp. 115ff.

134. Daniel Jenkins Williams, *The Welsh of Columbus, Ohio* (Oshkosh, 1913), pp. 105–107.

135. Henry Blackwell, "A Bibliography of Welsh Americana," *National Library of Wales Journal*, Supplement 1942, *passim*; *Miners' Journal*, January 17, 1857.

136. *Cambrian*, XXVII (1907), 4.

137. Daniel Jenkins Williams, *The Welsh of Columbus*, p. 132.

138. Trefnyddion Calfinaidd, "Cofnodion," I, 120, 176, 235; Llewelyn Jones, *Moriah Presbyterian Church* (Utica, 1930), pp. 58–60; *Cambrian*, VII (1887), 88; XIII (1893), 25–27, 55–56; XVI (1896), 221.

139. Daniel Jenkins Williams, *The Welsh of Columbus*, pp. 124–129.

140. Paul DeMund Evans, "The Welsh in Oneida County" (unpublished master's thesis, Cornell University, 1914), pp. 61–72; U.S. Bureau of the Census, *Religious Bodies* (1906), II, 540–542; David Jones, *passim*; *Druid*, November 14, 1907, December 24, 1908, July 16, 1909.

141. Trefnyddion Calfinaidd, "Cofnodion," II, 34–35, 96; Daniel Jenkins Williams, *One Hundred Years of Welsh Calvinistic Methodism*, pp. 88, 125, 166, 205, 231, 238.

142. *Cambrian*, January 1, 1913.

143. Idwal Lewis, "Welsh Newspapers and Journals in the United States," *National Library of Wales Journal*, II (1942), 124–130; Bob Owen, "Welsh American Newspapers and Periodicals," *ibid.*, VI (1950), 373–384; Thomas, pt. III, pp. 47–51, 63–65; Evans, pp. 89–118. The author has examined files of most of these and other British-American periodicals mentioned below.

144. N. W. Ayer, *American Newspaper Annual*, 1881–1918, *passim.*

145. *Cambrian*, I (1880), 2.

146. Lewis, pp. 124–130; Owen, pp. 373–384; Ayer, 1914, pp. 681, 849.

147. Ayer, 1881–1920, *passim.* The paper was called *Scottish-American* after 1886.

148. *Idem*; *Anglo-American Times*, October 23, 1869; *Canadian American*, May 7, 1886; *Scottish-American*, May 14, 1913.

149. Order Sons of St. George, Massachusetts Grand Lodge, *Eleventh Annual Session* (1899), p. 61; Boston Victorian Club, "Minutes" (MS), March 8, 1906; *Anglo-American Times*, May 27, 1871.

150. Ayer, 1890–1918, *passim.*

151. *Idem.*

11. National Cultures and Immigrants' Societies

1. A nearly complete list of British-American societies, taken principally from the immigrant press and the existing societies' records, is in Appendix C of the dissertation copy of this book, in the Harvard University Library. Cf. D. MacDougall, ed., *The American Year Book-Directory of Scottish Societies and British Associations in the United States, Canada, and British Possessions* (New York, 1914), *passim*; A. Bain Irvine, ed., *The Scots Year Book* (London, 1927), *passim.*

2. Scots' Charitable Society of Boston, "Minutes" (MS), 1657–1950, *passim*; British Charitable Society of Boston, "Minutes" (MS), 1816–1950, *passim*; George Austin Morrison, *History of St. Andrew's Society of the State of New York* (New York, 1906), *passim*; *A History of St. George's Society of New York* (New York, 1913), *passim*; *History of the St. Andrew's Society of Charleston, South Carolina* (Charleston, 1929), *passim*; *Scottish-American Journal*, 1861–1919, *passim*; *Cambrian*, 1880–1920, *passim.*

3. British Charitable Society, "Minutes," 1882–1904, *passim.*

4. *Scottish-American Journal*, November 23, 1867.

5. Robert Louis Stevenson, *The Silverado Squatters* (New York, 1895), p. 337.

6. George A. Gordon, *My Education and Religion* (Boston, 1925), p. 34.

7. *Boston Scotsman*, April 7, 1906, February 16, 1907.

8. *Scottish-American Journal*, 1861–1919, *passim.*

9. *Ibid.*, August 4, October 6, 1886, March 7, 1894.

10. *Ibid.*, July 5, 1883; Thomas Wentworth Higginson, "A Day of Scottish Games," *Scribner's*, III (1872), 329–336.

11. Peter Ross, *The Scot in America* (New York, 1896), pp. 411–412.

12. *Ibid.*, p. 427; *Scottish-American*, March 2, 1887, September 5, 1894, October 11, 1899, February 7, 1906.

13. *Ibid.*, September 15, 1866, July 6, 1867, September 8, 1870, *et passim* to August 18, 1897, August 6, 1902.

14. *Ibid.*, January 9, 1873, November 28, 1878, April 17, 1895.

15. *Emigrant*, January 28, 1835; *Emigrant and Old Countryman*, January 13, 1836, January 18, 1837.

16. *Scottish-American Journal*, August 17–September 7, 1871, November 7, 1872.

17. *Boston Scotsman*, March 31, 1906.

18. Circular in records of Victorian Club of Boston.

19. *Emigrant and Old Countryman*, February 10, 1841; *Scottish-American Journal*, 1861–1919, *passim*.

20. *Ibid.*, February 5, 1859, July 22–August 5, 1896.

21. New York *Anglo-American*, January 30, 1847.

22. Walter Scott, *A Few Thoughts and Expressions* (New York, 1928), pp. 20–21, 28, 45.

23. *Scottish-American*, October 26, 1892, March 8, 1905, November 25, 1908; *Fiery Cross*, November 1904.

24. *Scottish-American*, May 27, 1903.

25. *Ibid.*, 1887–1914, *passim*.

26. *Ibid.*, April 30, 1885, March 9, 1892, March 1, 1893, April 11, 1894; *Western British-American*, January 6, 1917.

27. *Boston Scotsman*, March 31, 1906; *Scottish-American*, June 12, 1895.

28. *Western British-American*, February 7, 1914.

29. *Scottish-American*, June 21, July 26, October 4, 1893.

30. *Ibid.*, April 1, 1891, October 26, 1892, December 6, 1893, November 28, 1894, February 14, 1906.

31. *Ibid.*, August 18, 1881, April 29, 1896; *Western British-American*, May 1, 1915.

32. *Scottish-American*, August 5, 1891.

33. *Cambrian*, XII (1892), 41.

34. *Druid*, December 17, 1908.

35. *Cenhadwr Americanaidd*, IX (1848), pp. 243–244, 300–302, 370–371; *Drych*, 1851–1881, *passim*.

36. Anne E. Williams to Peter Williams, May 25, 1891, in National Library of Wales MS. 12290C.

37. John Owen, "Fy Nhaith i America," *Cymru*, XI (1896), 136; David E. Morgan, *Saga of the Edwards, Brynele* (Columbus, 1950), *passim*; *Cincinnati Daily Chronicle*, June 8, 1870.

38. Thomas Darlington, "The Welsh in America," *Wales*, I (1894), 350.

39. Daniel Jenkins Williams, *The Welsh of Columbus, Ohio* (Oshkosh, 1913), pp. 109–112.

40. Chester Lloyd Jones, *Youngest Son* (Madison, 1938), 39, 57, 80, 91; John Owen, VI (1894), 79.

41. William Davies Evans, *Dros Gyfanfor a Chyfandir* (Aberystwyth, 1883), p. 28; *Bulletin of the American Iron and Steel Association*, XXIX (1895), 217.

42. *Drych*, March 13, 1879.

43. Paul DeMund Evans, "The Welsh in Oneida County" (unpublished master's thesis, Cornell University, 1914), p. 66.

44. R. T. Jenkins, "The Development of Nationalism in Wales," *Sociological Review*, XXVII (1935), 175–182.

45. Jacob Potofsky, ed., *John E. Williams* (Chicago, 1930), p. 10.

46. *Drych*, December 23, 1880; *Druid*, June 10, 1909.

47. *Drych*, September 30, 1880.

48. *Druid*, July 24, 1907.

49. *Cincinnati Daily Chronicle*, May 31, 1870.

50. Wendell M. Jones, "The Gymanfa Ganu" (unpublished master's thesis, Ohio State University, 1946), p. 17.

51. *Cambrian*, VIII (1888), 208–210; XII (1892), 136–141; XIV (1894), 324–326; *Druid*, June 9, 1910.

52. *Cyfaill o'r Hen Wlad*, IV (1841), p. 346, XV (1852), pp. 151–152, XVII (1854), pp. 71, 198; *Cenhadwr Americanaidd*, XV (1854), pp. 72, 425, XVII (1856), p. 343; *Drych*, 1856–1857, *passim*.

53. *Druid*, October 21, 1909, January 27, 1910.

54. *Drych*, 1867–1920, *passim*; *Cambrian*, 1880–1919, *passim*; *Druid*, 1907–1918, *passim*; *The Royal Blue Book: Prize Productions of the Pittsburgh International Eisteddfod* (Pittsburgh, 1913), p. 10.

55. *Cambrian*, V (1885), 185.

56. Erasmus Jones, "The Welsh in America," *Atlantic*, XXXVII (1876), 310–311.

57. *Cambrian*, XII (1892), 29–30; XIII (1893), 257–263, 312–316; XXII (1902), 288; XXIII (1903), 281–285, 298–300; *Royal Blue Book*, p. 9.

58. Darlington, p. 351; *Druid*, February 24, 1910.

59. *Cambrian*, XIII (1893), 314–315.

60. Edith Brower, "The Meaning of an Eisteddfod," *Atlantic*, LXXV (1895), 59.

61. *Anglo-American Times*, November 30, 1883; *Cambrian*, XXII (1902), 331.

62. Robert D. Thomas, *Hanes Cymry America* (Utica, 1872), pt. III, pp. 57–60.

63. *Merthyr Express*, quoted in *Cambrian*, January 1, 1913. Cf. *Druid*, October 10, 1907, September 24, October 8, 1908, September 23, December 23, 1909.

64. Peter Crossley-Holland, ed., *Music in Wales* (London, 1948), pp. 54–55.

65. *Druid*, July 29, 1909.

66. *Cyfaill o'r Hen Wlad*, XIII (1850), p. 52; *Drych*, March 4–November 11, 1880; *Druid*, August 17, 1911; Wendell M. Jones, p. 43.

67. *Druid*, 1907–1918, *passim*.

68. *Idem*; *Drych*, 1851–1920, *passim*; *Cambrian*, 1880–1919, *passim*.

69. *Western British-American*, January 11, 1913, August 1, 1914; statement of Joseph B. Toy to author, August 23, 1949; Mrs. Henry G. Avis to author, November 1, 1949.

70. North American Manx Association, *Bulletin*, March 1945.

71. *Scottish-American*, September 16, 1908.

72. London *Times, A Visit to the States* (London, 1887), I, 124.

73. Victorian Club of Boston, "Minutes" (MS), May 12, 1903.

74. Massachusetts Bureau of Statistics of Labor, *Second Annual Report* (1871), p. 469.

75. "Study of a New England Factory Town," *Atlantic*, XLIII (1879), 697–698.

76. "History of the English Social and Mutual Improvement Club" (MS); Washington Club, *Opening Souvenir* (1906); statements of John S. Gardner and Emil Fortin, November 17–18, 1949.

77. Affiliated British-American Clubs of New England, *Directory* (1927).

78. Milo M. Quaife, ed., *An English Settler in Pioneer Wisconsin* (Madison, 1918), p. 39.

79. Jonathan Thayer Lincoln, *The City of the Dinner Pail* (Boston, 1909), p. 15; *Fall River Weekly News*, January 1, 1874.

80. *British-American*, March 2, 1889; *Church Militant*, January 1900, October 1904.

81. *Labor Standard*, August 28, 1880.

82. *Scottish-American Journal*, July 13, 1877, July 31, 1879; *British-American Citizen*, August 18, 1888, August 9, 1890, July 25, 1891; *Western British-American*, August 12, 1905, August 11, 1906.

83. Victorian Club of Boston, "Minutes" (MS), 1897–1918, *passim*; *Western British-American*, May 30, 1914; Spencer H. Over to author, August 12, 1949.

84. *Scottish-American*, December 14–21, 1887, January 27, 1909.

85. Scots' Charitable Society, "Minutes," 1865–1918, *passim*; *Canadian American*, March 5, August 13, 1886; *Fiery Cross*, April 1904.

86. *Ottawa Journal*, quoted in *Canadian American*, March 26, 1886.

87. Oscar Handlin, *Boston's Immigrants* (Cambridge, 1941), p. 160; *American Protestant*, January 20, 1872; *Scottish-American Journal*, July 28, 1881, May 13, 1891; *Boston Scotsman*, December 8, 1906; *Canadian American*, October 7, 1887; statement of James J. Wilcox, December 4, 1949.

88. J. Castell Hopkins, *Historical Sketch of the Canadian Club Movement* (n.p., 1907), pp. 2–8; *Canadian*, August 1904, p. 9.

89. *Christian Science Monitor*, January 2, 1910; statements of J. Ernest Kerr, November 24, 1949, and Asa R. Minard, December 10, 1949.

90. Benjamin Rand, ed., *The Canadian Club of Harvard University* (Cambridge, 1909), *passim*; Canadian Society of Philadelphia, *Yearbook*, 1919, p. 23; Victorian Club, "Minutes," March 28, 1907; *Canadian American*, June 19, 1884; *Canadian*, February 1904, p. 12.

91. British Schools and Universities Club of New York, *Yearbook*, 1912, *passim*; *Scottish-American*, February 27, June 12, 1901; *Canadian*, January

1905, p. 32; *Western British-American*, April 12, December 6, 1913; *New York Daily Tribune*, February 3, 1901.

92. *Western British-American*, November 14, 1903, January 25, August 9, 1913, June 13, 1914; *Canadian*, May 1904, p. 14.

93. *New York Daily Tribune*, January 23, 1901; *British Californian*, December 1904, p. 22; *Western British-American*, October 24, 1914.

94. *Boston Herald*, June 22, 1887; *British-American Citizen*, October 29, 1887, January 14, 1888.

95. William Todd, *The Seventy-Ninth Highlanders* (Albany, 1886), *passim*; *Scottish Journal*, June 11, 1842; *Scottish-American Journal*, May 16, 1861, March 17, 1870, March 7, 1872, December 22, 1897.

96. *Ibid.*, May 4, 1882, July 12, 1893, January 31, 1894, July 1, 1896.

97. *Ibid.*, December 9, 1875, June 22, 1898, August 23, 1899, April 1, 1908, January 21, June 3, 1914.

98. James A. Stark, *The Loyalists of Massachusetts* (Boston, 1910), pp. 473–475; *Scottish-American*, September 1, 1897, August 29, 1906; *Inter-Nation*, I (1905), 9–11.

99. *Scottish-American Journal*, March 16, April 13, 1867, May 5, 1881, December 17, 1890, January 30, 1901, April 5, 1911; *British-American Citizen*, December 1, 1888.

100. Order Sons of St. George, Grand Lodge, *Proceedings of the Semi-Annual Meeting*, 1876, p. 6; *Scottish-American Journal*, 1865–1919, *passim*.

101. *Scottish-American Journal*, June 22, 1867, January 5, 1887, January 12, September 14, 1898; *Western British-American*, February 20, 1915.

102. Albert C. Stevens, *Cyclopedia of Fraternities* (New York, 1899), p. 257; T. Rodgers, *History of Odd Fellowship* (Paterson, 1925), pp. 63–69; *Labor Standard*, January 17, 1880, April 16, 1881; *Fall River Weekly News*, January 17, 1889; *Druid*, December 17, 1908.

103. Stevens, pp. 223–229; *Scottish-American Journal*, November 11, 1875, November 13, 1884, July 22, 1891; *Fall River Weekly News*, December 25, 1880; *Druid*, December 5, 1907, January 30, 1908.

104. *American Protestant*, May 27, 1871; *Lawrence Journal and Citizen*, November 19, 1874, May 1, 1875; *Scottish-American*, April 3, 1889, July 29, 1891, July 5, 1893.

105. John O. Thomas, *Yr Urdd Iforaidd Americanaidd: Ei Hanes am Haner Can Mlynedd* (Utica, 1917), *passim*; Urdd y Gwir Iforiaid Americanaidd, *Cylchlythyrau Blynyddol*, 1898–1949, *passim*; *Drych*, 1870–1898, *passim*.

106. Order Sons of St. George, Grand Lodge, *Proceedings of the Annual Meetings*, 1876–1888, Supreme Lodge, *Journal of the Proceedings of the Sessions*, 1889–1925, *passim*; *American Silk Journal*, IX (1890), 52; Connecticut Bureau of Labor Statistics, *Seventh Annual Report* (1891), pp. 216–217, 1002.

107. *Boston Scotsman*, September 1, 1906.

108. *Scottish-American Journal*, 1879–1919, *passim*; *Fiery Cross*, 1900–1950, *passim*.

109. American Order of Scottish Clans, Royal Clan, "Minutes" (MS), 1899–1949, *passim*; *Scottish-American*, June 19, 1889.

110. *Ibid.*, November 27, 1895, July 15, October 21, 1896, January 13, August 25, 1897.

111. *Ibid.*, June 30, 1881, May 1, 1884.

112. *British-American Citizen*, June 11, 1892, November 25, 1893.

113. *Post*, pp. 190–191, 201.

114. *Scottish-American*, October 10, 1900, August 28, 1918; Ina R. Clarkin to author, April 18, 1950.

115. *British-American*, September 7, 1889, September 5–12, 1891, August 28, 1915; Order Sons of St. George, Supreme Lodge, *Journal of the Proceedings of the Tenth Session* (1913), pp. 114–115.

116. John O. Thomas, pp. 40ff.

117. *Western British-American*, March 8, 1913, January 15, 1916.

118. *Welsh-American* [*Druid*], August 1, 1915, June 1, 1918.

119. Owen Morgan, *A Souvenir: The Visit of the Iron and Steel Institutes of Great Britain and Germany to America* (Cardiff, 1890), pp. 66–67.

120. *Scottish-American*, September 10–17, 1913.

121. *British-American*, April 19–26, 1890; Order Sons of St. George, Supreme Lodge, *Journal of the Proceedings of the Twelfth Session* (1919), pp. 92–94; *Twentieth Session* (1946), p. 2.

12. Welding the British-American Community

1. *British-American Citizen*, March 10, 1888; *Scottish-American*, February 25, October 28, 1914.

2. *Scottish-American Journal*, March 19, 1885.

3. *Ibid.*, April 15, 1865.

4. *Drych*, April 4, 1878.

5. *Ante*, p. 140.

6. *Drych*, July 19–August 30, 1877, February 24, 1881; *Cambrian*, 1880–1919, *passim*; *Druid*, 1907–1918, *passim*.

7. Philip H. Bagenal, *The American Irish and Their Influence on Irish Politics* (London, 1882), *passim*.

8. *Scottish-American Journal*, June 9, 1866.

9. *English-American*, February 14, 1885; William Lane Booker to Earl Granville, April 7–9, 1885, in F.O. 5/1931.

10. Meyer Moses to Granville, March 4, 1884, in F.O. 5/1928; S. D. Shrewsbury to Granville, June 28, 1884, in F.O. 5/1929; W. Newton to Granville, July 1, 1884, in F.O. 5/1930; G. O. W. Corbett to Earl of Iddesleigh, September 7, 1886, in F.O. 5/1975.

11. John H. Stevenson to Marquis of Salisbury, May 10, 1878, in F.O. 5/1707.

12. Sir Lionel Sackville-West to Granville, May 16, 1882, in F.O. 5/1818.

13. Arthur Redford, *Labour Migration in England 1800–1850* (Manchester,

1926), pp. 114–142; James Edmund Handley, *The Irish in Scotland* (Cork, 1945) and *The Irish in Modern Scotland* (Cork, 1947), *passim*; David Williams, *A History of Modern Wales* (London, 1950), pp. 229–230; "Poor Inquiry (Ireland)," *Parliamentary Papers*, 1836, XXXIV, Appendix G, *passim.*

14. A. P. Swineford, *History and Review of the Mineral Resources of Lake Superior* (Marquette, 1876), pp. 70–71; James K. Jamison, "The Copper Rush of the '50's," *Michigan History Magazine*, XIX (1935), 384–388; *Drych*, May 2, 1878.

15. *Fall River Weekly News*, April 28, 1881.

16. William A. Itter, "Early Labor Troubles in the Schuylkill Anthracite District," *Pennsylvania History*, I (1934), 32.

17. *Druid*, July 24, 1907. Cf. *Miners' Journal*, June 13–19, 1846, May 1, 1852, March 31–May 19, 1855.

18. J. Walter Coleman, *Labor Disturbances in Pennsylvania 1850–1880* (Washington, 1936), pp. 19–69, 102–103.

19. *Scottish-American Journal*, January 2, 1869.

20. William J. Walsh, *The United Mine Workers of America as an Economic and Social Force in the Anthracite Territory* (Washington, 1931), p. 66; *Drych*, February 4, 1875.

21. David Jones, *Welsh Congregationalists in Pennsylvania* (Utica, 1934), p. 38.

22. *Miners' Journal*, May 20, 1871; *Drych*, May 25, 1871.

23. *Fall River Weekly News*, May 11, 1871.

24. *Miners' Journal*, April 27, 1877. Cf. Coleman, pp. 78, 100.

25. *Miners' Journal*, October 15, 1875.

26. *Ibid.*, June 4, 1875.

27. *British-American*, February 14, 1891.

28. *Canadian American*, June 10, 1887.

29. *British-American*, February 14, 1891.

30. Order Sons of St. George, Supreme Lodge, *Journal of the Proceedings of the Third Meeting* (1892), pp. 32–36, 99–100.

31. Order Sons of St. George, Grand Lodge, *Proceedings of the Annual Meeting*, 1885, p. 27.

32. Henry Jones Ford, *The Scotch-Irish in America* (Princeton, 1915), pp. 181ff.

33. *Dictionary of American Biography* (New York, 1928–1937), X, 274–275.

34. *Ibid.*, VII, 347–350; Rollo Ogden, ed., *Life and Letters of Edwin Lawrence Godkin* (New York, 1907), *passim.*

35. Albert C. Stevens, *Cyclopedia of Fraternities* (New York, 1899), pp. 306–307; Leslie H. Saunders, *The Story of Orangeism* (Toronto, 1941), *passim*; Handley, *Irish in Scotland*, pp. 305–313, and *Irish in Modern Scotland*, pp. 113–120; *American Protestant*, October 5, 1872.

36. Winston Spencer Churchill, *Lord Randolph Churchill* (New York, 1906), II, 65.

37. *New York Spectator*, July 16, 1824; *New York Times*, July 12, 1871.

38. *New York Tribune*, April 13–18, 1842; *New York Evening Post*, April 13–14, 1842; *New York Herald*, April 13, 1842; Allan Nevins, ed., *The Diary of Philip Hone* (New York, 1927), II, 596.

39. Louis Dow Scisco, *Political Nativism in New York State* (New York, 1901), p. 68; Stevens, p. 298.

40. *American Protestant*, July 18, 1874; American Protestant Association of the United States, R. Worthy Grand Lodge, *Proceedings*, 1889, pp. 66ff.

41. American Protestant Association, Pamphlet, 1888, pp. 3–4.

42. F.O. 5/1706, p. 33.

43. *American Protestant*, June 20, 1874.

44. *Ibid.*, October 21, 1871, October 18, 1873; Loyal Orange Institution, Massachusetts Grand Lodge, Fiftieth Anniversary pamphlet (1924), pp. 3–6.

45. *American Protestant*, August 22, 1874; Stevens, p. 308.

46. Cf. list of Orange lodges in dissertation copy, Appendix C.

47. *New York Daily Tribune*, July 13, 1883.

48. *American Protestant*, June 20, 1874.

49. *Purple Bell*, 1902–1904, *passim*.

50. *American Protestant*, October 21, 1871; *British-American Citizen*, August 4, 1900.

51. *New York Times*, July 11, 1871; *American Protestant*, March 23, 1872; *Protestant Standard*, June 23, 1892.

52. *Anglo-American Times*, July 31, 1869.

53. *Ibid.*, July 16–August 6, 1870; *New York Times*, July 13, 1870.

54. *New York Times*, July 8–14, 1871; *Anglo-American Times*, July 15–29, 1871; *Irish People*, July 8, 1871.

55. *New York Times*, July 11–13, 1871; *American Protestant*, July 15, 1871.

56. *New York Times*, July 12, 1873.

57. *Ibid.*, July 13, 1877.

58. *Ibid.*, July 13, 1872; *American Protestant*, July 20, 1872, March 8, 1873, July 18, 1874.

59. *New York Times*, July 13, 1875.

60. *Workingman's Advocate*, November 10, 1866.

61. *Fall River Weekly News*, December 15, 1887.

62. *British-American*, October 27, 1888, March 9, June 22, 1889.

63. *Anglo-American Times*, October 3, 1868; *ante*, p. 134.

64. James Ernest Nesmith, *The Life and Works of Frederick Thomas Greenhalge* (Boston, 1897), pp. 255–256; Michael E. Hennessy, *Twenty-Five Years of Massachusetts Politics* (Boston, 1917), pp. 45–48. Cf. *Dictionary of American Biography*, XII, 180–181; XIV, 548–549; *Druid*, November 26, 1908.

65. *British-American*, October 14, 1893.

66. *Ante*, pp. 102–104.

67. *Cenhadwr Americanaidd*, *Cyfaill o'r Hen Wlad*, 1844–1860, *passim*; *Drych*, 1856–1880, *passim*.

68. Jay Monaghan, "The Welsh People in Chicago," *Journal of the Illinois State Historical Society*, XXXII (1939), 502–503.

69. *Cymhelliadau i'r Cymry i Bleidleisio Dros Etholiad yr Enwog James S. Wadsworth, yn Llywydd ar Dalaeth New York* (Utica, 1862); *Cenadwri Flynyddol James T. Lewis, Llywodraethwr Talaeth Wisconsin* (Milwaukee, 1865); Henry Blackwell, "A Bibliography of Welsh Americana," *National Library of Wales Journal*, Supplement 1942, pp. 8, 35; Paul DeMund Evans, "The Welsh in Oneida County" (unpublished master's thesis, Cornell University, 1914), pp. 105, 116; *Miners' Journal*, October 9, 1852; *Druid*, 1907–1918, *passim;* statement of John Owen Jones to author, February 8, 1950.

70. *Cenadwri Ei Uchelder J. F. Hartranft i'r Cynulliad Cyffredinol Pennsylvania* (Hyde Park, 1875); *Cenadwri J. F. Hartranft i Ddeddfwrfa Pennsylvania* (Hyde Park, 1876).

71. *Drych*, October 16, 1879; *Druid*, January 14, 1909.

72. *Druid*, June 22, 1911.

73. Thomas E. Hughes *et al.*, *History of the Welsh in Minnesota* (Mankato, 1895), pp. 114–116; Howell D. Davies, ed., *History of the Oshkosh Welsh Settlement* (Amarillo, 1947), p. 74; *Miners' Journal*, October 14, 1871, November 3, 1876; *Cambrian*, I (1880), 87; *Druid*, May 4, 1911.

74. *Drych*, October 22, 1874, September 20, 1877, February 14, November 28, 1878, July 26, 1888.

75. Alvin Packer Stauffer, "Anti-Catholicism in American Politics 1865–1900" (unpublished doctoral thesis, Harvard University, 1933), pp. 89–113.

76. *Anglo-American Times*, November 14, 1874.

77. *Fall River Daily Evening News*, October 28, 1876.

78. *Labor Standard*, December 6, 1879.

79. *Fall River Weekly News*, December 11, 1880.

80. *Ibid.*, December 3–10, 1881.

81. British-American Society of Worcester, *Constitution, By-Laws and Rules of Order* (1884).

82. *Canadian American*, September 17, 1886.

83. *British-American Citizen*, November 19, 1887, April 4, 1888, October 8, 1892.

84. *Cleveland Penny Press*, quoted in *Canadian American*, July 3, 1884.

85. *Canadian American*, October 23–30, 1884.

86. British-American Association, *Faneuil Hall: Who Are its Conservators?* (Boston, 1887), *passim*.

87. *British-American Citizen*, October 29–November 12, 1887, January 21, 1888.

88. *Boston Herald*, July 26, 1887.

89. *Ibid.*, August 17–November 7, 1887.

90. *Anglo-American Times*, June 17, 1887; *Drych*, July 5, August 23–30, 1888.

91. *Canadian American*, June 17, September 30, October 21, November 18, 1887; *Scottish-American*, September 14, October 5–19, November 2, December 7, 1887; *British-American Citizen*, November 26, 1887; *British-American*, December 17, 1887.

92. *Western British-American*, March 9, 1918; *ante*, p. 163.

93. *Chicago Tribune*, January 10, February 2, October 23, 1888; *Anglo-American Times*, October 19–26, November 16, 1888; *Canadian American*, October 28–December 23, 1887. Cf. dissertation copy, Appendix C.

94. *British-American Citizen*, October 29, 1887, June 22–29, 1889, June 28, September 27, 1890.

95. *Boston Daily Advertiser*, June 9, 1884; *Protestant Standard*, November 20, 1884.

96. *Chicago Tribune*, November 3, 1888. Cf. *British-American*, March 9, 1889.

97. Sackville-Salisbury correspondence, October 26–November 15, 1888, in F.O. 5/2017, 2020.

98. *British-American*, November 10, 1888.

99. *British-American Citizen*, May 5, July 7–28, August 18, September 15, 1888.

100. D. O. Kellogg, "Alien Relations of the Democratic Party," *American*, XVI (1888), 343–344.

101. Thomas F. Byron, "The British-American Movement," *American*, XVI (1888), 394–395.

102. Allan Nevins, *Grover Cleveland* (New York, 1932), pp. 428–431; *Drych*, November 1, 1888.

103. *British-American Citizen*, 1887–1903, *passim*.

104. *Protestant Standard*, June 27, 1889, June 9, 23, 1892, June 15, 1893.

105. *British-American Citizen*, December 17, 1892, October 20, 1894.

106. *Ibid.*, May 27, 1893; Stevens, pp. 290–292; Stauffer, pp. 272–273, 284–291.

107. *British-American Citizen*, 1888–1890, *passim*; Stauffer, pp. 251–272.

108. *British-American Citizen*, December 7, 1889, August 2, 1890.

109. *Ibid.*, April 5, 1890, August 25, 1894, April 29, 1899; *British-American*, April 23, 1892.

110. *British-American*, October 6–13, 1888.

111. *Canadian American*, January 12, 1888; *Anglo-American Times*, November 2, 1888; *British-American Citizen*, February 20, 1892; *British Californian*, April 1897.

112. *British-American Citizen*, 1892–1913, *passim*.

113. J. J. Tighe, *The A.P.A.* (New York, 1894), p. 8.

114. *Fall River Weekly News*, June 8, 1892; Stevens, pp. 295–296; Stauffer, pp. 192, 355–356.

115. *Protestant Standard*, January 6, 1921.

116. D. MacDougall, ed., *The American Year Book-Directory of Scottish Societies and British Associations in the United States, Canada, and British Possessions* (New York, 1914), *passim*; *World Almanac* (New York, 1914), p. 532.

117. Loyal Orange Institution, Massachusetts Grand Lodge, *Reports of the Annual Sessions*, 1903–1940, *passim*, and Supreme Grand Lodge, *Report of*

the Thirty-Fifth Session (1914), *passim*; *British-American Citizen*, 1888–1903, *passim*; *Purple Bell*, July 25, 1903; *Western British-American*, June 13, 1914; statements of David Dawson, August 4, 1949, and William J. Kirkland, April 3, 1950.

118. Vyrnwy Morgan, *The Cambro-American Pulpit* (New York, 1898), p. 61; *Cambrian*, XV (1895), 286; XVII (1897), 51; *Drych*, June 10, 1897.

119. *Druid*, February 15, May 16, 1912, April 15, 1915.

120. *British-American Citizen*, October 31, 1896.

121. *Boston Herald*, August 14, 1900; *Scottish-American*, December 11, 1901; *Boston Scotsman*, June 16, 1906.

122. *British Californian*, November 1903, February 1904.

123. *British-American Citizen*, December 28, 1895.

124. *Scottish-American*, December 18, 1895–January 1, 1896.

125. *Drych*, December 26, 1895–January 1, 1896.

126. F. O. 5/2302, 80/364, 80/367.

127. George Burton Adams, *Why Americans Dislike England* (Philadelphia, 1896), pp. 28–30.

128. *Drych*, June 3–July 22, 1897.

129. Sir Julian Pauncefote to Salisbury, June 6, 1898, in F.O. 5/2362.

130. Lionel M. Gelber, *The Rise of Anglo-American Friendship* (Oxford, 1938), pp. 17–36; Anglo-American Committee, *An American Response to Expressions of English Sympathy* (New York, 1899), *passim*; Harry S. Foster to Salisbury, January 2, 1899, in F.O. 5/2410; Pauncefote to Salisbury, July 10, 1900, in F.O. 5/2428.

131. *Baltimore Sun*, September 13, October 28, 1898.

132. Reginald Tower to Salisbury, October 18, 1899, in F.O. 5/2392.

133. Edward Sudlow to A. G. Vansittart, April 14, 1902, in F.O. 5/2486.

134. *Boston Scotsman*, March 24, 1906.

135. *Scottish-American*, November 22, 1899–June 20, 1900; *British-American Citizen*, February 3, March 10, April 7, 1900; *Inter-Nation*, I (1905), 41; British Charitable Society of Boston, "Minutes" (MS), May 3, 1900.

136. London *Anglo-American*, June 9, 1900.

137. Victorian Club of Boston, "Minutes" (MS), May 15, 1900; Silas M. MacVane, *The South African Question* (Boston, 1900); James H. Stark, *The British and Dutch in South Africa* (Boston, 1900); Hugh Chisholm, *Anglo-American Relations vis-a-vis the Other Great Powers* (Boston, 1903); British-American Association, *In Memoriam* (Columbus, 1901), pp. 20–21.

138. *Drych*, December 7, 1899; *Druid*, September 23–December 2, 1909.

139. David Williams, pp. 280–282.

140. *Drych*, January 31, 1901.

141. James H. Stark, *The Loyalists of Massachusetts and the Other Side of the American Revolution* (Boston, 1910).

142. Thomas Stone to Salisbury, December 26, 1896, in F.O. 5/2303.

143. Republican Independent Association, *An Appeal to Men of British Birth on the Present Political Situation* (Boston, 1909); *Boston Herald*, October

26, 1909, October 20–November 9, 1910; statement of Asa R. Minard to author, December 10, 1949.

144. Victorian Club, *In Commemoration of the One Hundredth Anniversary of the Death of Nelson at the Battle of Trafalgar* (Boston, 1905); United British Societies of Boston, Banquet Program, May 24, 1905.

145. *Druid*, November 18, 1909.

146. *Scottish-American*, November 9, 1898, May 18, 1910, May 29, 1912; *Cambrian*, XXIII (1903), 543; British Empire Celebration Committee of Boston, Program, 1909.

147. *Scottish-American*, November 18, 1914, February 10, 1915.

148. *Ibid.*, 1914–1918, *passim*; *Western British-American*, 1914–1918, *passim*; *Druid*, 1914–1918, *passim*; *British Californian*, 1914–1918, *passim*.

149. *British Californian*, February 1915; *Scottish-American*, June 4, 1919; *English-Speaking World*, July 1919.

150. *Scottish-American*, May 3, June 21, December 6, 1916.

151. *Ibid.*, September 2, 1914; *Western British-American*, September 19, 1914.

152. *Western British-American*, 1914–1918, *passim*; *Scottish-American*, 1914–1918, *passim*.

153. *English-Speaking World*, October 1917–October 1918.

154. *Western British-American*, June 30, 1917; statement of J. Ernest Kerr, November 22, 1949.

155. *English-Speaking World*, March-October 1918; *Western British-American*, May 18, August 17, 1918.

156. *English-Speaking World*, August 1918.

157. *Scottish-American*, September 30, November 25, 1914; *Western British-American*, February 13, 1915.

158. *Druid*, July 1, 1915, March 1, 1916.

159. *British Californian*, February-April 1915.

160. "Philosophus," *What Is England Doing?* (London, 1916).

161. Amalgamated Society of Carpenters and Joiners, *Monthly Report*, September 1915, pp. 4–5.

162. Sir Frederick Smith, *My American Visit* (London, 1918), pp. 66–67; London *Times*, July 20, 1938.

163. Clifton James Child, *The German-Americans in Politics* (Madison, 1939), pp. 111–153; *Druid*, July–November 1916; *Western British-American*, November 4, 1916.

164. Order Sons of St. George, Supreme Lodge, *Journal of the Fourteenth Session* (1925), pp. 4–5.

165. Smith, p. 64.

166. *Anglo-American Times*, August 12, 1871.

167. "Fenian Brotherhood," in F.O. 5 series.

168. Reports of the Consul-General at New York, 1875–1883, in F.O. 282/21, 282/25; J. Pierrepont Edwards to Earl of Clarendon, July 13, 1870, in F.O. 115/513; Sackville-West to Salisbury, January 15, 1888, in F.O. 5/2018; draft

letter to Sackville-West, February 22, 1888, in F.O. 5/2017; J. Hayes Sadler to Salisbury, January 26, 1888, in F.O. 5/2044, and December 4, 1890, in F.O. 5/2359; Pauncefote to Salisbury, September 7, 1900, in F.O. 5/2428.

169. Sackville-West to Salisbury, May 2, 1887, in F.O. 5/1980; Salisbury to Sackville-West, May 14, 1887, in F.O. 5/1978.

170. Pauncefote to Marquess of Lansdowne, February 18, 1901, in F.O. 5/2456; draft letter to Thomas Townsend Stokes, March 9, 1901, in F.O. 5/2473.

171. *Anglo-Californian*, I (1897), 94–95; *Western British-American*, April 14, 1906; *British Californian*, March 1917.

172. "Report of the Foreign Office Committee on British Communities Abroad," *Parliamentary Papers*, 1920, LI (Cmd. 672), 3–4.

13. Epilogue

1. J. Hamilton Birrell, "Emigration with Special Reference to Scotland," *Scottish Geographical Magazine*, XLVI (1930), 163; London *Times*, September 14, December 13, 1923.

2. Roy L. Garis, *Immigration Restriction* (New York, 1927), pp. 154–160.

3. *Ibid.*, pp. 169–285; William S. Bernard, ed., *American Immigration Policy* (New York, 1950), pp. 27, 42.

4. U.S. Immigration and Naturalization Service, *Monthly Review*, VI (1949), 168.

5. Order Sons of St. George, Supreme Lodge, *Journal of the Proceedings of the Sixth Session* (1901), p. 118; John O. Thomas, *Yr Urdd Iforaidd Americanaidd: Ei Hanes am Haner Can Mlynedd* (Utica, 1917), p. 82.

6. Chester Lloyd Jones, *Youngest Son* (Madison, 1938), p. 94.

7. *Eleventh Census of the U.S.* (1890), II, 484–489, 508–513.

8. "Reports of the Immigration Commission," *Senate Document*, 61 Cong., 2 sess., no. 633 (June 15, 1910), VI, 50; X, 83, 669; XI, 37; XVI, 27–28, 230; XIX, 111–113.

9. London *Times*, December 21, 1895.

10. Charles W. Stubbs, "Some Impressions of America," *Outlook*, LXV (1900), 448.

11. Mrs. G. Cooke Adams to author, June 17, 1950; Mrs. J. L. Vopalecky to author, February 7, 1951.

12. National Gymanfa Ganu Association, Annual Programs, 1930–1950, *passim*.

Index